The Science of Interest

Paul A. O'Keefe • Judith M. Harackiewicz
Editors

The Science of Interest

 Springer

Editors
Paul A. O'Keefe
Department of Psychology
Yale-NUS College, Singapore

Management and Organisation
NUS Business School
National University of Singapore, Singapore

Judith M. Harackiewicz
Department of Psychology
University of Wisconsin
Madison, Wisconsin, USA

ISBN 978-3-319-55507-2   ISBN 978-3-319-55509-6   (eBook)
DOI 10.1007/978-3-319-55509-6

Library of Congress Control Number: 2017943862

Printed on acid-free paper

This Springer imprint is published by Springer Nature
The registered company is Springer International Publishing AG
The registered company address is: Gewerbestrasse 11, 6330 Cham, Switzerland

Foreword

In her book *Gifted Children*, Ellen Winner (1997) describes child prodigies. Michael was one of them. As a very young child, he played endless games involving letters, words, and numbers and asked his parents endless questions about them. Michael's mother reports that when he was 4 months old, he asked his parents, "Mom, Dad, what's for dinner?" At 3 years of age, his father tells us, Michael was discovering and proving algebraic rules. Every day, when his father came home from work, Michael would pull him toward the math books and say, "Dad, let's go do work."

Michael may well have started with a special ability, but, for me, his most remarkable characteristic is his relentless interest. His parents could not pry him away from the activities he craved. And this is true for every prodigy that Winner describes.

I have always been fascinated by the relationship between interest and ability. Which comes first and how do they feed each other? When you look at case studies of prodigies, such as the one above, and see the intense fascination they had for their area of expertise, you are left to ask: did these children come with an outsized ability or with an outsized interest that led them to develop extraordinary abilities?

When you look at the person who represents the ultimate genius, Albert Einstein, you are left with a similar question. Despite his extraordinary intellectual accomplishments, in a letter to Carl Seelig, a German-Swiss writer (11 March 1952, Einstein Archives 39-013), Einstein wrote, "I have no special talent. I am only passionately curious." Indeed, he repeatedly chalked his accomplishments up to his relentless curiosity.

Yet when it comes to the science and politics of achievement, so much of the emphasis has been on ability—on people's aptitudes and talents. Education, too, has understandably been focused on ability, but in considering how to build it, educators are often fixated on refining the curriculum or finding teaching techniques that convey the information more skillfully, rather than on the nurturing of students' interest or motivation for learning.

This is perplexing, since developmental psychologists continually observe that children are born with a powerful orientation toward novelty and toward mastering new skills. Novelty and optimally challenging problems are inherently interesting to them, and the processing of novelty and the mastery of new skills are intrinsically rewarding. In other words, we are prewired to find interest in our worlds and to explore and conquer that which interests us. How is it that only a few years later, as children pass through school, this interest is curtailed? And why do educators try to get around this with strategies aimed at more effectively communicating knowledge rather than with practices aimed at restoring students' interest?

What is this thing called interest and what are the forms it can take—curiosity, passing interest, passion, or obsession? Where does it come from? What are its benefits—for self-regulation, persistence, and learning? How does it create these benefits? And how can we actively promote and sustain it? In this outstanding volume, the top scientists in the field address these fascinating questions. The reader will discover the many faces and functions of interest, as revealed by the latest work in the area. Researchers already in the field will certainly have their work enriched by this book, and those in the neighboring fields of learning and motivation will be drawn to integrate the study of interest into their thinking.

Reference

Winner, E. (1997). *Gifted children: Myths and realities*. New York: Basic Books.

Stanford, CA, USA   Carol S. Dweck

Preface

Toward a New Science of Interest

Since the seminal volume, *The Role of Interest in Learning and Development* (Renninger, Hidi, & Krapp, 1992), there has been renewed attention to the construct of interest in psychology. One of the major contributions of this work was the simple, yet important, distinction between *situational interest* and *individual interest*. By making this distinction, the authors clarified that interest has different forms and developmental stages. Situational interest, they argued, involves a state of heightened attention plus positive affect sparked by something external to the individual, such as an exciting physics lecture or a challenging puzzle. By contrast, they argued that individual interest is a more internal process. It reflects an idiosyncratic and enduring relationship between an individual and particular content that is associated with increased attention, positive affect, accrued relevant knowledge, and personal value. This distinction has since inspired research to further understand the construct of interest.

In the 25 years following the publication of the seminal volume of Renninger et al. (1992), 10,544 academic papers have been published on the topic as it relates to motivation, whereas only 2,279 had been published between 1900 and 1991. The enthusiasm for this line of research is palpable. Perhaps more than anyone, social and educational psychologists have pioneered the recent academic work on interest. Researchers in those fields who study motivational processes—particularly achievement motivation—recognized a critical link between interest and intrinsic motivation; that people's desire to understand something new or to acquire interest-relevant knowledge motivates them to act and think for reasons of their own choosing. For social psychologists, interest is a variable that contributes to their understanding of self-regulation and why (at times) people do what they do (Sansone & Smith, 2000; Chap. 2). For educational psychologists, research on interest helps explain the motivation to learn, and how to best promote interest in educational contexts (Harackiewicz, Smith, & Priniski, 2016).

In years past, however, many researchers used the term "interest" and "intrinsic motivation" interchangeably (e.g., see Sansone & Harackiewicz, 2000). In other words, intrinsic motivation and interest both referred to doing something for the pure enjoyment of the activity itself. Contemporary researchers, however, stress the independence and interrelation of these separate constructs. Interest can initiate the motivation to understand particular content or engage in particular activities, as well as to maintain that motivation over time. Interest can also result from engagement in particular content and activities. Therefore, interest is not simply the same as enjoyment or intrinsic motivation, but instead reflects a relationship a person has with particular content or activities. At the level of situational interest, this relationship may be triggered and supported by environmental factors. With regard to individual interest, the relationship is more idiosyncratic and self-perpetuating. Both situational and individual interest can spark and sustain intrinsic motivation.

The recent uptick in research on interest by psychologists has also brought another change: a more scientific approach. Up until about 20 years ago, much of the published work on interest relied on a scant literature, conjecture, case studies, and the like, to inform theory. Recent psychological research, however, has applied rigorous scientific methods, enabling researchers to make more definitive, empirical, and often causal, conclusions. Furthermore, previous research and theory, largely conceived of by educational researchers, has been *applied research*. That is, it has primarily focused on understanding and promoting interests for particular topics in educational contexts. Psychological researchers have since taken a more *basic research* approach, conducting studies and developing theory to more broadly understand the role of interest in human functioning. In turn, this basic research has informed a new wave of intervention research (Harackiewicz & Knogler, 2017; Lazowski & Hulleman, 2016).

Purposes of This Volume

One purpose of this volume is to document the current state of research and theory on interest as it relates to motivational processes. In doing so, we highlight research, largely conducted by social psychologists, that implements rigorous scientific methods. This theoretically based experimental research is also intended as a reference to inspire and inform psychological interventions that increase interest, motivation, and achievement among multiple populations.

Another purpose of this volume is to help bring various traditions of relevant research and theorizing together under the umbrella of "interest." Interest scholars come from a diverse array of fields, such as psychology, education, and neuroscience. Meanwhile, there is little agreement on how different interest-related constructs are defined, how terms are used, or their taxonomy. For example, some scholars use the term "situational interest" to mean the same thing as "curiosity" (e.g., Chap. 4), whereas others draw a sharp distinction between the two constructs (e.g., Renninger & Hidi, 2016). As you read through this volume, you will see some disagreement with regard to conceptualizations of constructs among researchers, and this is to be expected in an active research community.

To this end, yet another purpose of this volume is to provide a more inclusive understanding of what we call the *interest spectrum*, acknowledging the various forms and developmental stages it comprises. The predominant model of interest development is the four-phase model (Hidi & Renninger, 2006). The model has been critical to understanding how interest can begin as an externally elicited situational response to an internalized interest, which is then integrated into the self--concept and can be pursued without external supports. That said, it is our goal to explicitly acknowledge other constructs that fall under the umbrella of "interest" as well as to extend the spectrum beyond four phases.

Organization and Content of This Volume

This volume is organized into four parts, covering the different theoretical perspectives of interest, its functions, spectrum, as well as its promotion and development.

Part I covers leading contemporary theoretical perspectives and conceptualizations of interest. In Chap. 1, Mary Ainley contributes an overview of these issues in which she describes how interest can be triggered by external events (situational interest), while other times remains largely internally supported (individual interest). Ainley then discusses two dominant theories explaining how interests arise and develop, in an attempt to better understand how a triggered situational interest can transform into a well-developed individual interest. She also highlights the lacuna in our understanding of this developmental process and its complex dynamics.

Part II focuses on several central functions of interest: its role in self-regulation, motivation, and learning. First, Dustin B. Thoman, Carol Sansone, and Danielle Geerling discuss the role of interest in self-regulation (Chap. 2). In attempting to understand why people maintain motivation over time, the authors argue that it is important to understand interest as an experiential aspect of their engagement in a task or activity. To this end, the authors argue that interest, whether anticipated or experienced, can influence the decision to engage in an activity, how engagement is experienced, and whether one chooses to reengage in the activity. Furthermore, the anticipation or experience of interest is affected by the degree of congruence between the purpose of the activity and the individual's goal.

In Chap. 3, Paul A. O'Keefe, E. J. Horberg, and Isabelle Plante discuss interest as a motivational variable and the qualities of engagement it manifests. Specifically, they discuss research on the psychological experience of interest, as well as how and when interest can increase performance and persistence. They further discuss research suggesting that implicit theories of interest can influence whether someone might acquire new interests and ultimately engage in related content or activities. Finally, the authors discuss research demonstrating how and when interest can result from engagement.

Finally, Jerome I. Rotgans and Henk G. Schmidt discuss the role of interest in knowledge acquisition (Chap. 4). They review research suggesting that situational interest—sparked by a gap in knowledge—leads to the acquisition of knowledge in order to increase understanding. They further argue that individual interest is a by-product of knowledge acquisition, which, in turn, causes situational interest.

Part III of the volume presents the spectrum of interest. Traditionally, interest has either been dichotomized into two categories (i.e., situational and individual interest), or thought of as a developmental continuum starting from triggered situational interest and ending with well-developed interest (Hidi & Renninger, 2006). Contemporary theory and research, however, suggests that interest may comprise a larger, more nuanced spectrum. In this volume, we present chapters from researchers who focus on different forms of interest that follow and expand upon the four-phase model (Hidi & Renninger, 2006). To this end, these chapters generally reflect interest as an externally supported construct to a mostly internally supported one, which, respectively, includes curiosity, situational interest, individual interest, passion, and obsession. Most notably, although curiosity, passion, and obsession share many central features of what most researchers refer to as "interest," they are seldom discussed as different instantiations of interest. Our motivation for including these constructs in the "interest spectrum" is to offer a more complete picture of interest and its various forms, which vary in internality and intensity. By doing so, we hope to contribute a more unified framework for studying interest and its different forms.

The first chapter of this section (Chap. 5) covers curiosity. Paul Silvia takes a functional approach to understanding curiosity and describes it as an emotion. As such, he makes an evolutionary argument that it serves three important functions. The first is that curiosity motivates people to learn for the sake of learning. Next, he argues that, although novelty can sometimes cause anxiety, curiosity counteracts our tendency to avoid the unknown. Finally, he argues that curiosity also counteracts our tendency to only seek enjoyment, causing us to approach stimuli that are not necessarily reliable sources of reward.

In Chap. 6, Maximilian Knogler discusses situational interest. He argues that researchers commonly and implicitly use the term "situational interest" to describe it as both a psychological state and as being a less developed, largely externally supported form of interest. This lack of definitional precision has caused some confusion in the field and Knogler argues for the need to clarify these distinctions.

Moving along the spectrum to more internalized and enduring forms of interest, Amanda M. Durik, Meghan Huntoon Lindeman, and Sarah L. Coley discuss individual interest (Chap. 7). They present a theoretical model to explain why people choose to engage in particular activities or content. Furthermore, they draw from research on various motivation constructs—for example, desired possible selves, mastery goals, goal schemas, and construal level—to explain what supports engagement, its experience, and competence valuation.

In the next chapter (Chap. 8), Robert J. Vallerand discusses passion, which can be considered a more internalized and self-defining form of well-developed interest. He outlines a program of research on the Dualistic Model of Passion that distinguishes two types of passion: harmonious and obsessive. *Harmonious passion* for an activity, he argues, is autonomously internalized. It exists in harmony with other aspects of one's life. By contrast, *obsessive passion* is experienced as more externally controlled, such that one feels they must engage in the activity, which can cause conflicts with other aspects of life, such as with one's obligations.

The last chapter in this section (Chap. 9) focuses exclusively on obsession and approaches it as an extreme form of well-developed interest. Here, Dean Keith Simonton discusses the role of interest and obsession in exceptional performance, and, to this end, highlights research on four types of people: creative geniuses, polymaths, child prodigies, and autistic savants. In doing so, he demonstrates that obsession plays different roles in exceptional performance among these populations.

It should be noted that, although we present various forms of interest along a continuum in Part III, there is some overlap among some of the constructs. For example, some researchers distinguish curiosity from triggered situational interest (e.g., Renninger & Hidi, 2016), whereas others do not make such a strong distinction (e.g., Chap. 4). Well-developed interest and passion also share many qualities, such as being largely internally supported. It is our hope that this volume motivates researchers to develop clearer distinctions among these constructs with the goal of better understanding the spectrum of interest.

Part IV addresses the development and promotion of interest. In Chap. 10, Chris S. Hulleman, Dustin B. Thoman, Anna-Lena Dicke, and Judith M. Harackiewicz discuss the role of values in the development of individual interest. Furthermore, they review intervention research demonstrating how interest can be promoted.

Finally, in Chap. 11, Allison Master, Lucas P. Butler, and Gregory M. Walton discuss the role of social processes in the promotion of interest. In particular, they argue that engagement in an activity with others, whether real or imagined, promotes interest in the task.

Considered together, these chapters provide a broad overview of the new science of interest. Together, we hope to have successfully (a) highlighted the contemporary scientific research on interest, (b) extend the four-phase model (Hidi & Renninger, 2006) by illuminating additional forms that interest can take, (c) present interest as a spectrum that varies in its degree of internality and intensity, and (d) enabled interest researchers to share a common vocabulary, as well as conceptualizations of the various forms of interest.

Singapore, Singapore   Paul A. O'Keefe
Madison, WI, USA   Judith M. Harackiewicz

References

Harackiewicz, J. M., & Knogler, M. (2017). Interest: Theory and application. In A. J. Elliot, C. S. Dweck, & D. S. Yeager, (Eds.). *Handbook of competence and motivation: Theory and application*. New York: Guilford Publications.

Harackiewicz, J. M., Smith, J. L., & Priniski, S. J. (2016). Interest matters: The importance of promoting interest in education, *3*, 220–227. *Policy Insights from the Behavioral and Brain Sciences*. doi:10.1177/2372732216655542

Hidi, S., & Renninger, K. A. (2006). The four-phase model of interest development. *Educational Psychologist, 41*(2), 111–127.

Lazowski, R. A., & Hulleman, C. S. (2016). Motivation interventions in education: A meta-analytic review. *Review of Educational Research, 86*(2), 602–640.

Renninger, K. A., & Hidi, S. (2016). *The power of interest for motivation and learning*. New York: Routledge.

Renninger, A., Hidi, S., & Krapp, A. (Eds.). (1992). *The role of interest in learning and development*. Psychology Press.

Sansone, C., & Harackiewicz, J. M. (2000). *Intrinsic and extrinsic motivation: The search for optimal motivation and performance*. San Diego: Academic.

Sansone, C., & Smith, J. L. (2000). Interest and self-regulation: The relation between having to and wanting to. In: C. Sansone, & J. M. Harackiewicz (Eds.), *Intrinsic and extrinsic motivation: The search for optimal motivation and performance*. San Diego, CA: Academic.

Sansone, C., Thoman, D. B., & Smith, J. L. (2000). Interest and self-regulation. In: C. Sansone, & J. M. Harackiewicz (Eds.), *Intrinsic and extrinsic motivation: The search for optimal motivation and performance* (pp. 343–374). San Diego, CA: Academic.

Contents

Contributors

Mary Ainley, PhD University of Melbourne, Melbourne, VIC, Australia

Lucas P. Butler, PhD University of Maryland, College Park, MD, USA

Sarah L. Coley Department of Psychology, Northern Illinois University, DeKalb, IL, USA

Anna-Lena Dicke, PhD University of California, Irvine, Irvine, CA, USA

Amanda M. Durik, PhD Department of Psychology, Northern Illinois University, DeKalb, IL, USA

Carol S. Dweck, PhD Department of Psychology, Stanford University, Stanford, CA, USA

Danielle Geerling Department of Psychology, University of Utah, Salt Lake City, UT, USA

Judith M. Harackiewicz, PhD Department of Psychology, University of Wisconsin, Madison, WI, USA

E.J. Horberg, PhD Department of Psychology, Yale-NUS College, Singapore, Singapore

Chris S. Hulleman, PhD University of Virginia, Charlottesville, VA, USA

Maximilian Knogler, PhD Technical University of Munich, TUM School of Education, Munich, Germany

Meghan Huntoon Lindeman Department of Psychology, Northern Illinois University, DeKalb, IL, USA

Allison Master, PhD University of Washington, Seattle, WA, USA

Paul A. O'Keefe, PhD Department of Psychology, Yale-NUS College, Singapore

Management and Organisation, NUS Business School, National University of Singapore, Singapore

Isabelle Plante, PhD University of Quebec, Montréal, Quebec, Canada

Jerome I. Rotgans, PhD Nanyang Technological University, Singapore, Singapore

Carol Sansone, PhD Department of Psychology, University of Utah, Salt Lake City, UT, USA

Henk G. Schmidt, PhD Erasmus University Rotterdam, Rotterdam, The Netherlands

Paul J. Silvia, PhD Department of Psychology, University of North Carolina, Greensboro, Greensboro, NC, USA

Dean Keith Simonton, PhD Department of Psychology, University of California, Davis, Davis, CA, USA

Dustin B. Thoman, PhD Department of Psychology, San Diego State University, San Diego, CA, USA

Robert J. Vallerand, PhD Laboratoire de Recherche sur le Comportement Social, Département de Psychologie, Université du Québec à Montréal, Montreal, QC, Canada

Institute for Positive Psychology and Education, Australian Catholic University, Banyo, QLD, Australia

Gregory M. Walton, PhD Department of Psychology, Stanford University, Stanford, CA, USA

Part I
Theories and Perspectives

Chapter 1
Interest: Knowns, Unknowns, and Basic Processes

Mary Ainley

> It appears self-evident, therefore, that to the primal inspiration for the uplifting of human-
> ity, we must now add the intelligent direction of psychological science. (De Garmo, 1894,
> p. viii)

Why is *interest* a phenomenon of interest for psychological science? There is something intriguing about a term that means different things in different contexts. Interest can refer to deep and passionate engagement with specific content. It is also a term used to politely avoid giving a negative assessment such as when a debater asks a friend "What did you think of my speech?" and the friend hesitantly replies "It was … interesting". There are myriad shades of meaning between these two extremes. In addition, there is the point and counterpoint between defining what interest is and analysis of the psychological processes that operate when interest is observed in behavior. For example, is attention a function of interest or a defining attribute of interest?

Throughout history educational theorists and philosophers have invoked interest both as a motivation for learning and as an outcome of learning, positing interest as both cause and effect, initiating condition and outcome (e.g., Dewey, 1913; Piaget, 1981; see Krapp & Prentzel, 2011, for a review). Psychological science has long been recognized as providing appropriate ways to address these issues. At the turn of the century, Sansone and Harackiewicz (2000) focused attention on the accession of "intrinsic motivation" as a way of understanding the motivation of behaviors characterized by "positive feelings of interest, enjoyment, satisfaction" (Sansone & Harackiewicz, 2000, p. 2). Prominent in the debates of the time was the possibility that intrinsic motivation for a task could be undermined by introduction of extrinsic rewards for the same task. Lepper and Henderlong (2000) suggested that tighter conceptualization of the potential relations between intrinsic and extrinsic motivations was required to adequately interpret this literature. In particular they

M. Ainley (✉)
University of Melbourne, Melbourne, VIC, Australia
e-mail: maryda@unimelb.edu.au

© Springer International Publishing AG 2017
P.A. O'Keefe, J.M. Harackiewicz (eds.), *The Science of Interest*,
DOI 10.1007/978-3-319-55509-6_1

3

distinguished three ways that intrinsic and extrinsic motivations might be related to behavior: in competition, coexisting, or as complementary motives. Identification of these different ways that intrinsic and extrinsic factors function served to direct emphasis to processes related to features of both task and context. In addition, Ryan and Deci (2000) drew attention to personal or individual difference factors that might impact on the ways intrinsic and extrinsic motivations influence behavior. Building on de Charms' (1968) concept of personal causation, Ryan and Deci pointed to ways intrinsic and extrinsic motivations were expressed through self-regulatory mechanisms of personal causality orientations. Externally controlled behavior was contrasted with autonomous or self-determined behavior. Contemporary approaches to understanding the interest construct owe a lot to these debates on intrinsic motivation.

At the end of their volume, Sansone and Harackiewicz (2000) argued that the future direction for this field was to focus "more closely on process" (p. 453). Currently, contributions to understanding the "how" of interest, both how it arises and how it impacts behavior, can be found in a range of literatures, including social psychology, social and personality psychology, developmental psychology, and educational psychology.

Theories on interest purport to both describe and account for what is happening when attention is ensnared by a specific feature of the context, when person and object are connected in-the-moment. For example:

> Intermittent flashes of bright light explode in a darkening night sky. A young child notices. She stops in her tracks and stares intently. She continues to stare upward as if her staring will bring about further exploding lights.

Equally the term can apply to consistent personal preferences that extend across time, and the individual's impulse to action is a relatively stable response directed to a valued aspect of the environment. For example:

> A 16-year-old consults the internet to locate secondhand music shops. He visits a number of them spending hours rummaging through stacks of old vinyl records to add to his collection of original Beatles' music. He buys a couple and makes notes on several others intending to return the following week.

In this chapter, I explore how some prominent contemporary theories conceptualize interest. I will examine how differences in usage add to the richness of our understanding of *interest* and its influences on behavior and simultaneously I will raise questions that are open for investigation using the tools of psychological science.

Interest: A Dynamic Relational Construct

One important feature of current perspectives on interest is that the construct identifies a quality of relation between a person and some content of their environment. As has been emphasized by a number of writers, interest cannot be defined simply as a characteristic of an individual (Hidi & Renninger, 2006; Krapp, 2007; Renninger

& Hidi, 2011; Schiefele, 2009; Valsiner, 1992). Any reference to a person being interested or expressing interest needs to be qualified by naming the object of interest; for example, *the young child's interest is caught by the colored lights in the sky*; *the teenager has an interest in Beatles' music*. It simply does not make sense to label the child or the teenager as "interested"; they are interested in something. Hence, awareness of the object or content of interest is an essential part of what it means to be interested. In this way it is recognized that by definition, interest refers to a quality of relation between a person and an object. This relation, or quality of awareness, generally includes positive feelings, a desire to explore and engage with the object, and a sense that it has personal meaning and value. However, the balance among these components may vary with the temporal extension of this relation in the individual's personal history. When interest is activated by something encountered for the first time, something novel, as in the example above when a young child's gaze is caught by colorful lights in the sky, affective components are likely to dominate. The child feels caught-up, excited, and absorbed; their facial expression shows eyes open wide and eyebrows raised conveying openness to take in the new experience. The teenager who has spent many hours interacting with Beatles' music and who readily identifies as a Beatles fan also feels excitement and anticipation. Facial expressions conveying pleasure and openness to what might be encountered are likely to be combined with a sense that they are engaging with something personally important and that they are about to find something excitingly different about Beatles' music. That is, importance or value components, and expansion of knowledge co-occur with affective processes to define the interest experience.

Essentially the changing balance among the components of interest and the increasing complexity of the schema being activated point to the dynamic character of interest. Here I borrow from dynamic systems theory (see, e.g., Lewis & Granic, 2000; Thelen & Smith, 2006) with its central proposition that the individual is inherently a self-organizing system: "pattern and order emerge from the interactions of the components of a complex system without explicit instructions, either in the organism itself or from the environment" (Thelen & Smith, 2006, p. 259). When interest is described as a quality of the relation between a person and an object, event, activity, or idea, from the perspective of the individual, the quality of the relation is internally represented in a mental unit or schema. This means that at any particular point in time, interest as a state will reflect the unique organization of an individual's immediate experiences and their past experiences with the interest object or content. Further interactions with the interest object or content brings about change. A new and more complex organization or schema emerges as an existing personal schema is modified through new experience with the object of interest. Hence, in relation to interest, we would expect to see differences in both the components and the relations between components, as an individual's experience with an object or domain increases (Ainley, 2006, 2007). This formulation is consistent with theories such as Izard's differential emotions theory (see Izard, 1977) emphasizing behavior as a dynamic system. In his early work on infant emotions, Izard described the basic features of interest as an emotion in terms of facial expression and consequent exploratory behavior (see Izard & Malatesta, 1987). These early writings referred to affective-cognitive structures and organizations that developed from the co-occurrence of emotions and cognitions in early experience. Combinations of emotions and cognitions persist as organized units and are activated in new encounters with similar objects and events in the environment. With expanding experience such affective-cognitive structures become a complex network for processing experience. More recently, Izard (2007, 2009) has recast this perspective and refers to *emotion schema* rather than *affective-cognitive structures*.

Hence, with respect to interest, the content and structure of interest schema have accrued from the individual's personal history of interaction with the object, event, activity, or idea and so the balance between affective, cognitive, value, and intention to explore will vary in relation to the extent of past interactions and expectations for future interaction opportunities (Ainley, 2010; Ainley & Hidi, 2014). Therefore, one challenge for the psychological science of interest is to identify combinations of cognitions and affect, the functional components of interest schema at different levels of interest development.

The Dynamics of Situational and Individual Interest: Interest and Interests

A fundamental distinction in contemporary perspectives on interest is between interest as an in-the-moment experience and as a more-enduring personal characteristic influencing choices and behavior. This section will describe a number of perspectives that distinguish two forms of interest and will explore the bases of these distinctions.

Interest and Situational Interest

Interest as in-the-moment experience has widely been described as *situational interest* (see, e.g., Alexander, 2003; Hidi, 1990; Hidi & Renninger, 2006; Krapp, 2007; Schiefele, 2009). Others use the unqualified term *interest* (e.g., Silvia, 2006). Interest triggered in-the-moment motivates exploration. Some object or aspect of the environment catches the individual's attention. The person orients themselves toward the "interesting" event and engages in activities that explore features of that event. Typically, through this activity, information and knowledge of the event are acquired. What are the issues and research questions associated with the in-the-moment triggering of interest or situational interest?

There is substantial agreement among writers who adopt the term situational interest that it is a form of interest occurring at a relatively limited or defined point in time. It is variously referred to as "temporary", "fleeting", in the "here and now", and "bound to the immediate situation" (Alexander, 2003, 2004); "triggered in the moment ... which may or may not last over time" (Hidi & Renninger, 2006); "current engagements" (Krapp, 2007); and "spontaneous and context specific" (Schraw & Lehman, 2001). A substantial portion of the research on situational interest has been generated from an educational-psychological perspective in order to identify conditions that will trigger situational interest. While most of the earliest endeavors related to students' responsiveness to reading and text-based materials (Hidi, 1990; Kintsch, 1980), more recently identification of triggers of situational interest can be found in research across a variety of domains, including mathematics and science (see e.g., Durik & Harackiewcz, 2007; Maltese & Harsh, 2015; Nieswandt & Horowitz, 2015; Palmer, 2009), writing (Boscolo, Ariasi, Del Favero, & Ballarin, 2011), physical education (Chen & Ennis, 2004; Krapp, 2007), psychology (Harackiewicz, Durik, Barron, Linnenbrink-Garcia, & Tauer, 2008), problem-based learning (Rotgans & Schmidt, 2011), aesthetics (Silvia, 2010), and vocational studies (Krapp, 2007). It is well-documented that interest is associated with learning and achievement, but there are ongoing concerns over the difficulties educational practitioners face in their efforts to motivate students who are aptly described as academically unmotivated (Hidi & Harackiewicz, 2000). The assumption is that knowing how to trigger situational interest offers a way to engage students in curriculum and classroom activities.

Triggering Situational Interest

So what do we know about the triggers for in-the-moment or situational interest? Berlyne's (1957, 1960) classic research on interest and curiosity has influenced current perspectives on environmental triggers. Berlyne proposed that a set of environmental conditions, referred to collectively as collative variability, activate attention, curiosity, and interest. Novelty, uncertainty, ambiguity, and complexity are some of the stimulus features subsumed by the term collative variability. These are conditions that involve some conflict or uncertainty. In addition, these terms are relational terms and depend for their effects on certain knowledge or experience that can be assumed. Berlyne (1957), for example, used a stimulus which consisted of the head of an elephant on the body of a lion as an example of incongruity-conflict within the broader category of collative variability. According to Berlyne, this type of stimulus pattern had "characteristics which S has been trained to regard as incompatible" (p. 400).

A large volume of research on situational interest has taken place in the educational domains of reading, literacy, and developing expertise. This subset of interest phenomena has been researched as text-based interest, and specific text characteristics that activate interest responses have been documented in a number of reviews (Hidi, 1990, 2001; Schraw & Lehman, 2001; Wade, 2001). Hidi distinguished between triggers associated with text structure including dimensions such as novelty, surprisingness, unexpected events, or ideas and triggers associated with text content which included "universally interesting concepts, human activity, intensity factors, and life themes" (Hidi, 1990, p. 559). Similar text characteristics are reiter- ated by Alexander (2003). Schraw and Lehman (2001) summarized the critical trig- gers in text as "a variety of factors such as prior knowledge, unexpected text content, text structure, and reader goals" (p. 27). After reviewing the existing body of litera- ture, these factors were grouped into three categories: "variables that affect seduc- tiveness (i.e., the importance and relevance of information), vividness (i.e., imagery, suspense, unexpectedness) and coherence (i.e., ease of comprehension, relevance, poor organization) are related to interest" (p. 37). While this research has provided considerable guidance to educational practitioners a caveat is required. While "seductive details" trigger situational interest, by definition these triggers are not the important text features for learning and so are distracting students from the primary purpose of the text (Garner, Brown, Sanders, & Menke, 1992). This has stimulated investigations identifying differences in processing of *interesting* and *important* information.

Another strand in the burgeoning research on interest refers to interest as "state interest" or "momentary feelings of interest" (Silvia, 2006). In recent years, interest has been described by a number of emotion theorists as belonging to a group of knowledge emotions that includes emotions such as surprise, awe and confusion (Ellsworth, 2003), and curiosity (Silvia, 2010). This perspective focusing on interest as an emotional state is linked with the wider study of emotions and has a primary focus of understanding the dynamics of interest as an emotion and its role in com- plex human behavior (see e.g., Izard, 2007, 2009; Silvia, 2006). While a large part of situational interest research has been concerned with identification of the triggers of situational interest, the perspective represented by Silvia (see 2005, 2006, 2008) focuses on understanding the specific processes operating when interest is experi- enced, in particular, appraisal processes that trigger interest.

The Experience of Interest

What are the psychological processes that constitute interest, and how do they oper- ate? According to Hidi and Renninger (Hidi, 2006; Hidi & Renninger, 2006), the in-the-moment experience of interest is characterized by "… increased attention, concentration and affect" (Hidi, 2006, p. 70). One of the unresolved questions con- cerns the measurement of attention processes in relation to situational interest. On the one hand, it has been asserted that interest is likely to be associated with faster processing, that is, shorter reaction times. On the other hand, it has been pointed out that when the task requires "less automated cognitive activity", sustained and per- sistent attention, or longer reaction times, are likely to indicate interest (Hidi, 1990)

I will consider some of this argument as it highlights how further investigations of underlying processes will extend understanding of the role of interest in learning and achievement. Both contemporary emotion theory (e.g., Jarymowicz & Imbir, 2015) and cognitive psychology (e.g., Stanovich & Toplak, 2012) distinguish auto- matic and controlled processing, although this is not without some challenge (e.g.,

Kruglanski & Gigerenzer, 2011). Basing her argument on text-based research on situational interest, Hidi (1995) suggested that differentiating between automatic and reflective attention processes is critical for interpreting behavioral indicators of attention such as reading time measures. For example, different levels of processing may be in play for appraising whether text segments are *interesting* than for appraising whether text segments are *important* (see also Wade, Schraw, Buxton, & Hayes, 1993). Overall reading time measures do not distinguish these two processing levels: the time for immediate evaluation of salience in terms of interest and the time for reflective judgments concerning the importance of a particular segment for the meaning of the whole text. Using a distraction measure of attention, McDaniel, Waddill, Finstad, and Bourg (2000) tested Hidi's proposition by examining attentional intensity when reading texts of different interest levels. Their findings indicated lower reaction times to the secondary task for the high interest texts supporting the proposal that higher interest texts are associated with more automatic allocation of attention. In addition, their findings suggested that text-based interest may have qualitatively different processing effects contingent on the type of text processing required by specific types of tasks. While these findings apply to the processing underpinning situational interest when reading text, they suggest the need for further investigation of the attention and concentration processes operating when situational interest is triggered in a variety of other task contexts.

As indicated earlier, theory and research on situational interest has predominantly been located within education and educational psychology and has addressed issues of how to activate interest in educational contexts, and how to develop longer lasting interest in particular educational domains. On the other hand, researchers from psychology and social psychology have focused on interest as it functions in wider examples of human behavior and in particular exploring interest as affect. Berlyne extended his research on curiosity and interest into experimental aesthetics (e.g., Berlyne, 1974). Izard's perspectives on interest come from his broader developmental studies of human emotion (e.g., Izard & Malatesta, 1987), and most recently his research into children's emotional regulation (Izard, 2007). Drawing on general psychological and social psychological perspectives, Silvia (2006, 2008) links curiosity with interest as a state emotion and explores how interest functions through examination of appraisal processes.

The in-the-moment experiences which educational and educational psychology researchers have come to refer to as situational interest, Silvia (2006) designates simply as *interest*. Interest is distinguished from *interests* which are the analog of what other writers refer to as personal interest or individual interest. To describe the onset and development of experiences of interest, Silvia draws on Arnold's (1960) analysis of primary and secondary appraisals. Crucial to this position is the distinction between perception and apperception, between simple physical registration of an event and awareness of the event's personal significance. Silvia argues against what he refers to as a behavioristic emphasis in theories explaining the source of interest in characteristics of the stimulus: "the perception argument attributes interest to events." He proposes that appraisal or cognitive processing of events provides the basis for interest. Primary appraisal is a judgment of whether an object is worthy of further attention, whereas secondary and further appraisals involve assessment of the importance and significance of the object or event. Each level of appraisal is part of the processing system. With respect to interest, Silvia's laboratory studies using a variety of stimulus events such as complex and abstract art, random polygons, and complex poems (e.g., Silvia, 2005) have shown that appraisals of novelty and comprehensibility lead to higher judgments of interest. Hence, Silvia concluded that appraisals of novelty and comprehensibility can explain both between-person and within-person variations in reported interest.

Like the earlier theories, Silvia's emphasis on secondary appraisal processes also implies that interest does not reside in either person or object but in the relation between them, more specifically appraisals of novelty and comprehensibility. The character of the appraisal processes underlying experiences of interest in different environments and from different personal histories and backgrounds is open for further investigation.

Contemporary neuroscience research is an important source of evidence concerning processes operating when interest is triggered. From a neuroscience perspective, Immordino-Yang (2011; Immordino-Yang & Christodoulou, 2014) suggests that affective neuroscience research and psychological and educational research be viewed as mutually constraining. The findings from predominantly laboratory research in neuroscience with its expertise in mapping brain functioning can be tested alongside the complementary insights generated across the wider range of settings and measurement tools used in psychological and educational research. Simultaneously, the latter perspectives will inform specific research questions amenable to neuroscientific study. "Learning theories and neurological theories must be compatible, and cross-disciplinary grappling with inconsistencies or contradictions could improve thinking in both domains" (Immordino-Yang & Christodoulou, 2014, p. 621).

It is clear from this discussion across a range of perspectives on interest that understanding the processes through which interest functions requires further knowledge of how processes such as attention, emotion appraisals, both intuitive and reflective, and the intertwining of emotion and cognition operate. As Immordino-Yang suggests, "While skills like reading and math certainly have cognitive aspects, the reason why we engage in them, the importance we assign to them, the anxiety we feel around them, and the learning that we do about them, are driven by the neurological systems for emotion, social processing and self" (Immordino-Yang, 2011, p. 101). Hence, questions concerning many of the processes operating in-the-moment when interest is experienced across a wide range of phenomena are still wide open for investigation.

Interests and Individual Interest

The language of interests and individual interest is distinguished by a focus on the person rather than the situation and highlights the relative stability of the patterns of thoughts, feelings, and actions labeled as interests or individual interest. Like interest and situational interest, the constructs of interests and individual interest are content specific; they identify a relation between person and particular objects, class of objects, ideas, or content domains. By virtue of this temporal extension the focus in theories of interests and individual interest is the individual's personal organization, the self or personality as expressed in recurring states of in-the-moment interest experience.

Whether the language is individual interest or interests, it is clear that these terms refer to the relatively stable personal organizations that underlie an individual's engagement and re-engagement with particular objects and activities. For Hidi and Renninger such organizations are characterized by positive affect, value, and knowledge components and are conceptualized as predispositions (Renninger, 2000; Renninger & Hidi, 2011). The term *predisposition* is intended to sharply demarcate individual interest from stable personality dispositions represented in theories of vocational interest as personal preferences for types of work and work environments (see Holland, 1985). It should be noted that other individual interest theorists such as Krapp and colleagues (Krapp, 2005; Krapp & Prenzel, 2011; Schiefele, 2009) use the terminology of dispositions and define individual interest as components of a person's habitual motivational structure or part of the self, that is, "a relatively stable tendency to occupy oneself with an object of interest" (Krapp, 2007, p. 9). In addition to the specificity of content, individual interest is characterized by values or personal significance and associated positive affect. Activities that arise from individual interest are marked by self-intentionality in that they reflect a person's preferred goals and values and are distinguished by "readiness to acquire new domain-specific knowledge" (Krapp & Prenzel, 2011, p. 31).

With respect to the content of individual interests, it is possible to conceptualize content on a continuum from very specific contents such as the earlier example of the teenage collector of Beatles' music through to interest in broad content domains such as science, mathematics, literature, or aesthetics. While this is seen as separate from vocational interests, the boundaries between these levels of personal organization have not been the central focus of interest theories. However, as shown in an earlier paper by Ellsworth, Harvey-Beavis, Ainley, and Fabris (1999), individual interest measured at the level of key schooling domains is closely associated with students' location using Holland's (1985) vocational interests RIASEC hexagon.

Theories of individual interest propose that individual interest represents the individual's propensity to experience interest in specific situations, that is, to engage and re-engage with interest contents. However, there is only brief reference to processes that might underpin engagement and re-engagement episodes. Hidi and Renninger (2006) use the example of a person finding a magazine article related to an individual interest. The process consists of recognition that the article is of personal significance, associated feelings of excitement, and activity to engage with the content of the article, thereby adding to their knowledge. Krapp (2005) goes further and describes a dual regulation system that underpins both the operation of actions motivated by individual interest and the development of individual interest. In regard to current behavior, the dual regulation system includes the operation of a predominantly biological system whereby emotional experience provides the system with information about current circumstances. Positive feedback from this system combines with the output from the second system, a conscious-rational regulatory system, generating intentions and control over actions. In this way positive feelings and value or personal significance are the key processes directing actions.

On the other hand, interests as defined and described by Silvia (2006) are conceptualized as emotion dispositions that bridge emotion and personality. Built on the appraisal theory of emotion represented in his model of interest, Silvia describes the operation of dispositional interests in terms of emotional knowledge and meta-emotional experience. Together, these allow a person to make attributions concerning the causes of emotional experience and concomitant expectations regarding likely emotional consequences of future actions. Applying this to the magazine article example, the processing might look something like the following. The person is flipping through the magazine and happens to notice the title of an article. This event triggers appraisals of novelty and comprehensibility together with meta-emotional attributions locating the source of these feelings to the title of the article. Such attributions generate expectations that as in past encounters with this topic, the article will be exciting and stimulating and will extend their knowledge of the topic. The action following this processing sequence will most likely involve picking up the magazine and reading the article: appraisal – attribution – expectations – action. As with Krapp's (2005, 2007) dual processing model, this theory is also a model of the development of individual interests.

A number of researchers have considered the self and identity development in adolescence from a perspective related to constructs of interests and individual interest. For example, Hunter and Csikszentmihalyi (2003) refer to an individual differences factor of *chronic interest* which represents an orientation to experience, or disposition, involving approach to what are perceived to be enjoyable and challenging experiences. Their research with high school students identified a dimension of chronic interest which was associated with other self-factors of global self-esteem, internal locus of control, and a sense of hope in their future. "At one end are youth who experience stimulation, enthusiasm and pleasure, and on the other, adolescents in a disconnected state of apathy" (p. 30). A similar dimension was identified by Flum and Kaplan (2006), who refer to an exploratory orientation whereby adolescents seek self-knowledge in their interactions with the environment. While this is seen by Flum and Kaplan as an expression of intrinsic motivation, they suggest that this orientation generally can be observed in action in situations that involve conditions of subjective uncertainty, ambiguity, and incoherence. In such situations adolescents with an exploratory orientation are likely to show flexibility, tolerance of ambiguity and to perceive the situation as challenging.

At the empirical level, results from research using structural equation modeling techniques (Cribbs, Hazari, Sonnert, & Sadler, 2015) point to a mediation role for interest in relation to students' identity in mathematics. Focusing on the content of identity, Cribbs et al. modeled relations between perceived competence in math, recognition (perception of how teachers and parents perceive their math competence), individual interest in math, and personal identity as a "math person". The best fitting model indicated perceived competence as a direct predictor of both recognition and individual interest, and both recognition and interest directly predicted identity. Within this complex of self-perceptions there was evidence of interest in mathematics as a significant mediator of the relation between perception of competence and identity in mathematics.

While suggestive of an important mediation process, there are a number of factors that restrict interpretation of these findings. Although based on data from a large stratified random sample of colleges and universities across the United States, this research is correlational and depends exclusively on students' self-reports recorded at one point in time. A broader range of research designs, both longitudinal and experimental, is required to more conclusively identify causal relations and patterns of individual differences. The nature of the basic processes linking individual interest, whether conceptualized as predisposition, disposition or emotional disposition, to the broader structure of personality and self, is a question open to further investigation.

Thus far our discussion of, first, interest and situational interest, and, second, interests and individual interest has been directed to identifying meaning and processes associated with these terminological distinctions. At certain points it has been impossible to exclude reference to interest development. I now turn to look at some developmental perspectives on interest to highlight some of the questions and issues ripe for investigation using the tools of psychological science.

Interest Development: From Interest to Interests

The Four-Phase Model of Interest Development (Hidi & Renninger, 2006) was primarily developed to address issues concerned with exploring the contribution of interest to learning and achievement. More particularly, two of the basic characteristics for each of the phases of the four-phase model are defined in terms of, first, the level of external support required for interest to continue to develop at each phase and, second, the type of instructional or learning conditions required for expression and continuing development in each phase of interest development. These phases of interest development directly concern the development of the specified interest and are not necessarily tied to particular human developmental stages. The dynamics of development through the phases from triggered situational interest through maintained situational interest, emerging individual interest, and well-developed individual interest as described by Renninger and Hidi assert that interest develops "through the interaction of the person and his or her environment" (2011, p. 170). It is the history of engagements and re-engagements under external conditions that include supports from significant others and instructional facilitation that takes the initial in-the-moment experience of triggered situational interest and allows it to develop to the self-initiating, autonomous re-engagements that characterize the phase of well-developed individual interest.

The developmental process proposed by Krapp (2003) in his person-object theory of interest (POI), also identifies environmental supports and conditions that promote the development of interest from a triggered situational interest (catch facet), through a stabilized situational interest (hold facet) to an individual interest. In addition, Krapp proposes a dual-regulatory system to describe how actions arising out of an individual interest also underpin interest development.

In his writings on the development of interests, Silvia (2006) emphasizes that "the mere iteration of experience is less important than the inferences and expectations related to the experience" (p. 150). From his review of a range of theories of motivation development, Silvia argues there is an underlying theme: "a general source of motivation interacts with a mechanism that connects the motivation to a specific activity" (p. 130). It is through the accrual of emotional and meta-emotional knowledge that interests develop. People make attributions concerning the cause of their emotional experience and form expectations as to what will be the outcome of the different actions they consequently pursue. Silvia refers to this as an emotion-attribution theory of interest development that can generate testable hypotheses because each of the components – emotions, emotional knowledge, attributions and expectations – can be subject to experimental manipulation or changed through appropriate intervention.

From the perspective elaborated by Silvia (2006), interests are categories of emotional knowledge. "To have an enduring interest in something is to know that certain things have created interest in the past, to expect that they can create interest in the future, and to know how to bring about feelings of interest" (p. 147). The Beatles' music collector knows and anticipates that if he returns to the secondhand music shop he will have the same feelings of excitement and pleasure as he rummages through the old vinyls. As with the theories of interest development that focus on motivation of learning and achievement, experience is key. However, Silvia's model with its articulation of underlying process makes explicit relations at the process level that can generate further investigation and understanding of interest development. Simple repetition of the experience is not sufficient. It is the underlying network of attributions and expectations that are generated from the meta-emotional knowledge associated with emotions experienced in the situation that lead to interest development.

Consideration of the different emphases in these theories of interest development indicate that there is more to do before we understand clearly the processes involved and the factors that can be manipulated to support interest development.

Interest: State Interest, Actualized Interest, and Psychological State of Interest

In what has been covered so far in this chapter, I have treated the points of difference in terminology interest/situational interest and interests/individual interest as secondary to the features of the models. In this section, I consider something of the tension between terminological differences – interest and interests, or, situational and individual interest.

At one level the terminology of situational and individual interest distinguishes two sources of interest experiences or interest states. Krapp, Hidi, and Renninger (1992) referred to three types of interest – situational, individual, and actualized interest – to distinguish general classes of the source of interest from in-the-moment experience. A number of other writers, for example, Schraw and Lehman (2001) and O'Keefe and Linnenbrink-Garcia (2014), also refer to "actualized interest" to designate in-the-moment experience. Preferring to simply distinguish interest and interests, Silvia suggests the differences are "technical and subtle but important nevertheless" (Silvia, 2006, p. 184) and argues that the complications generated by the term *actualized interest* are unnecessary.

The crux of this issue is whether the experiential state that arises from situational interest sources has the same characteristic features as the experiential state that arises from individual interest sources. Krapp et al. (1992) suggest it is an empirical question: "although the state of interest, in the sense of actualized individual interest, seems closely related to the experiential state of situational interest, it *has not been demonstrated* (my italics) that the psychological processes and the effects of the two states are identical, or even comparable" (p. 10). In a later paper, Hidi (2006) describes the relation between both individual and situational interest and the experiential state in a way that suggests the states may be very similar: "The best way that I can think of clarifying the relationship between individual interest, situational interest and the psychological state of interest, is to consider individual interest as a sufficient but not necessary condition to elicit the psychological state of interest and to acknowledge that situational interest *can also trigger this state* (my italics)" (p. 73). A number of our studies using real-time measures of individual interest and on-task measures of successive interest states (see Ainley, Corrigan & Richardson, 2005; Ainley, Hidi & Berndorff, 2002; Ainley, Hillman, & Hidi, 2002) have demonstrated a predictive relation between individual interest in a domain and the experiential state reported when working on a task in that domain.

At its core, this issue relates to the perceived need to distinguish the two general classes (individual and situational interest) with their separate temporal extension implications, from in-the-moment experiences. It is of interest to note that Silvia's volume was published in the same year as Hidi and Renninger's Four-Phase Model of Interest Development (Hidi & Renninger, 2006). Situational and individual interest are presented as phases in the development of an interest and further distinctions are made within each of these phases to capture temporal distinctions within the course of interest development. Other researchers distinguish catch and hold facets within situational interest. For example, Krapp (2003, 2005) published a similar model with two stages of situational interest – emerging situational interest or a "catch" stage, and stabilized situational interest or a "hold" stage. It is worth re-iterating that these situational-individual interest models are firmly located in a context of enquiry into how situational and individual interest contribute to the relation between interest and learning in educational contexts, and to understanding how interest can be developed to the point where it is a self-sustaining part of the way the individual interacts with experience. Hence, the purposes guiding Silvia's model with its central focus on understanding the appraisal structure diverge from those of the situational-individual interest proponents.

So, with respect to the character of the state that pertains to the in-the-moment experience of interest related to different sources and at different phases or stages in the development of interests, it becomes an empirical question whether these are similar states or whether they are markedly different states. The four-phase model proposes that the balance between affect, value, and knowledge will vary across the course of development with value and knowledge components having a stronger presence in later rather than earlier phases. Earlier it was suggested that one of the important questions that needed to be addressed concerns the relative balance of these components at different phases of interest development. The additional questions that arise from Silvia's critique suggest that research into the similarities and differences between in-the-moment interest states at different phases or stages of interest development is also crucial.

Interest Experience: Emerging Evidence

Some evidence in relation to these questions is starting to accumulate. A number of our own studies have shown that individual interest in the relevant domain impacts on the level of interest in a specific topic reported early in a learning experience. Later reports of the experience are more closely related to the level of interest in the specific experience than to individual interest in the domain (see, e.g., Ainley, Hidi, & Berndorff, 2002; Holstermann, Ainley, Grube, Roick, & Bögeholz, 2012). However, these studies have not specifically included all of the measures that would be required to determine unequivocally the character of the in-the-moment experience under different combinations of individual interest and situational interest triggers.

A novel exploratory measure of interest for adolescent students (Ely, Ainley, & Pearce, 2012) has shown that the profile of affect reported is similar across interests that vary in their temporal extension. The profile of affect ratings for interest triggered in-the-moment while exploring a pool of potential interests was not significantly different to profiles for interests held over an extended period of time. Irrespective of temporal extension, interests selected by the adolescent participants indicated high ratings for positive affects—*happy, excited,* and *proud*—and very low ratings for the negative affects—*frustrated, anxious,* and *sad.* Again these findings need to be investigated further, but they do suggest strong similarity in the affective content of interest experience whether just triggered or related to longer term individual interest.

Recently, Knogler, Harackiewicz, Gegenfurter, and Lewalter (2015) have shed further light on this issue by asking "How situational is situational interest?" and examining "the relative influence of situational factors on SI and whether the label 'situational interest' is warranted" (p. 39). In this study high school students reported their individual interest in the topic prior to the commencement of a problem-based learning project which consisted of six standardized modules implemented in 15 classes over 3 weeks. Situational interest was measured at the end of each module and the measure included items to distinguish four components of situational interest: catch, hold (defined as value), affect, and epistemic orientation (defined as intention to re-engage). Latent state-trait analysis was used to separate situation-specific and cross-situation variance for two of these components: catch and hold. Knogler et al. (2015) were able to show both situation-specific variance and cross-situational consistency with their longitudinal measures of catch and hold components of situational interest. While there was evidence of consistency across the situational measures, more of the variance in situational interest measures was situation-specific than due to cross-situational consistency. In addition, the situation-specific components of catch and hold were not predicted by individual interest, but a substantial amount of the cross-situational consistency was significantly associated with individual interest in the topic.

These findings indicate that what is reported as interest at specific points in time carries the imprint of individual interest factors, factors that are common across a set of situations and factors that are specific to each situation. Knogler et al. (2015) only included catch and hold measures in their analysis. Further analysis of the relative importance of all four situation components—catch, hold, affect, and epistemic orientation—would also allow comment on the changing balance of components in the momentary experience as well as their dependence on students' individual interest in the broader topic or domain. This type of research has considerable potential for answering basic questions concerning the character of both individual and situational interest as well as giving further definition to the character of in-the-moment experiences of interest and addressing the technical, subtle, and important differences underpinning current terminological distinctions.

Interest and Self-Regulation

In-the-moment interest experiences are part of larger units of behavior and so investigations of how interest functions within the framework of the self-regulatory processes that define extended sequences of behavior are also appearing in recent interest research and theory. An early pointer to ways that interest operates to regulate ongoing behavior suggested that when constrained in a boring or tedious environment a person may generate their own idiosyncratic ways of making the situation interesting, for example, by changing their view of what the task is about (Sansone, Weir, Harpster, & Morgan, 1992). In addition, when a person's cognitive resources have been depleted through engaging with a task, introducing a novel element can trigger interest sustaining further task engagement (Thoman, Smith, & Silvia, 2011). A fresh way of looking at a task can facilitate persistence with what has become an unappealing circumstance. How does this happen?

Perception of task value appears to be a critical factor. Harackiewicz and Hulleman (2010) proposed that individuals' goals and interests when entering a situation influence the value they perceive when pursuing tasks in that setting. Perceived value predicts further task interest and is likely to extend to future task encounters (Hulleman, Durik, Schweigert, & Harackiewicz, 2008). Sansone and colleagues (Sansone & Thoman, 2005; Sansone, Thoman, & Fraughton, 2015) have developed a model of self-regulation that describes the dynamics of motivation and regulation of an activity episode. This analysis is embedded within a framework that includes goals (e.g., achievement goals), values, and expectancies similar to those described in expectancy-value theory (Wigfield & Eccles, 2000). The research underpinning these models has been conducted in a range of educational settings and includes laboratory as well as field studies (see, e.g., Canning & Harackiewicz, 2015; Hulleman, Godes, Hendricks, & Harackiewicz, 2010).

Sansone et al. (2015) describe the dynamics of an activity episode in the following way. An activity occurs in a specific context whose features can be defined. The person comes to the activity with their own personal characteristics and the specific goals they wish to achieve in that context. The actual values and expectations activated in the specific activity context are then "updated" through initial interaction with the activity. Simultaneously, interest in the activity is constantly being updated in relation to perceived value and expectancies. Hence, the interest experience ("the phenomenological experience of interest", Sansone et al., 2015, p. 113) draws on broader personal characteristics, including individual interests and goals in combination with specific activity goals, values, and expectations. The motivation for any activity is derived from individuals' goals-defined motivation (goals, values and expectancies) and experience-defined motivation as generated in the interaction of goals-based motivation and features of the activity. Hence, the ongoing direction of a person's participation in the activity is a transactional process linking "individuals' goals, task characteristics, and the context in which the person performs the activity at a particular point in time" (p. 115). A central process in this transactional sequence is the interest experience; that is, interest is embedded in the ongoing self-regulatory processes that direct behavior.

Hence, as Harackiewicz and Hulleman (2010) point out, goals affect interest through their facilitation of specific value perceptions. Or, applying Silvia's (2006) appraisal theory of interest, the interest appraisal involves perception that participating in the activity, whether it be the programming assignments investigated by Sansone and colleagues (Sansone et al., 2015), or the learning of new mathematics procedures reported by Harackiewicz and Hulleman (2010), will provide an experience of personal significance and also that mastery is within their competence.

One feature of these self-regulation models is that the individual's perception of task value and expectancy is not necessarily the same as intended by the instructor or the curriculum designer. Sansone et al. (2015) highlight the possibility that in educational settings, as students commence an activity the perceived value of the task may take them in a direction which is not optimal for their learning but which involves activities they appraise as interesting, that is, personally significant and worthy of investment of time and energy. Interest is an important process in the network of processes contributing to self-regulation.

Interest as Self-Regulation: Emerging Evidence

Substantial support for these theories concerning the role of interest in the self-regulation of achievement behavior is emerging. For example, Fulmer, and Frijters (2011) have shown that under conditions of difficult and challenging reading tasks, high school students' rated interest in and enjoyment of texts was predictive of their persistence with reading tasks. They suggest that interest "buffered" students against potential negative feelings and attributions associated with task difficulty and complexity.

Importantly, these theories locating interest within a network of self-regulatory processes also identify new avenues for investigation of how interest operates. In a recent paper, O'Keefe and Linnenbrink-Garcia (2014) focused on affect and value as primary components of individual interest and explored them as separate processes (affect-related and value-related interest) contributing to individuals' management of self-regulatory resources as they performed laboratory tasks. Their findings indicated that conditions for both optimizing performance and optimizing resource management consisted of high affect-related interest combined with high value-related interest. Hence, one way individual interest functions is by making it possible for individuals to sustain high levels of performance in concert with strong self-regulation of mental resource usage. "If people experience these goals as both exciting and personally significant, their chance of success increases. The pursuit of personally interesting goals not only improves performance, but also creates an energized experience that allows people to persist when persisting would otherwise be too depleting" (O'Keefe & Linnenbrink-Garcia, 2014, p. 77). As O'Keefe and Linnenbrink-Garcia indicate, there are many more questions and issues to do with the operation of interest processes that are ripe for investigation.

Conclusions

The two and a half decades since Hidi published her review (Hidi, 1990) on interest as a resource for learning have seen the growth of an extensive research literature on interest and interest development. In this chapter I have presented some of the most widely cited perspectives to consider questions and issues for future psychological science researchers. Existing models highlight some of the important dimensions that contribute to our understanding of interest and how it impacts learning and a range of complex human behaviors. There are important differences in the emphases of the theories and perspectives discussed in this chapter. It is the contention of this writer that only through careful consideration of the substance of these differences and similarities, new research directions and new understandings will emerge. Consideration of the details of these perspectives shows that there are issues and questions as yet unresolved, opportunities to find answers to the present unknowns and to shape the direction of future empirical research on interest.

References

Ainley, M. (2006). Connecting with learning: Motivation, affect and cognition in interest processes. *Educational Psychology Review, 18*(4), 391–405. doi:10.1007/s10648-006-9033-0.

Ainley, M. (2007). Being and feeling interested: Transient state, mood, and disposition. In P. Schutz & R. Pekrun (Eds.), *Emotions and education* (pp. 147–163). Burlington, MA: Academic Press.

Ainley, M. (2010). Interest in the dynamics of task behavior: Processes that link person and task in effective learning. In T. Urdan & S. A. Karabenick (Eds.), *Advances in motivation and achievement. The decade ahead: Theoretical perspectives on motivation and achievement* (Vol. 16A, pp. 235–264). Bingley, UK: Emerald Group.

Ainley, M., Corrigan, M., & Richardson, N. (2005). Students, tasks and emotions: Identifying the contribution of emotions to students' reading of popular culture and popular science texts. *Learning and Instruction, 15*(5), 433–447. doi:10.1016/j.learninstruc.2005.07.011.

Ainley, M., & Hidi, S. (2014). Interest and enjoyment. In R. Pekrun & L. Linnenbrink-Garcia (Eds.), *International handbook of emotions in education* (pp. 205–227). New York: Routledge.

Ainley, M., Hidi, S., & Berndorff, D. (2002). Interest, learning and the psychological processes that mediate their relationship. *Journal of Educational Psychology, 94*(3), 545–561. doi:10.1037//0022-0663.94.3545.

Ainley, M., Hillman, K., & Hidi, S. (2002). Gender and interest processes in response to literary texts: Situational and individual interest. *Learning and Instruction, 12*(4), 411–428.

Alexander, P. A. (2003). The development of expertise: The journey from acclimation to proficiency. *Educational Researcher, 32*(8), 10–14.

Alexander, P. A. (2004). A model of domain learning: Reinterpreting expertise as a multidimensional, multistage process. In D. Y. Dai & R. J. Sternberg (Eds.), *Motivation, emotion and cognition: Integrative perspectives on intellectual functioning and development* (pp. 273–298). Mahwah, NJ: Lawrence Erlbaum Associates.

Arnold, M.B. (1960). *Emotion and personality* (Vol. 1: Psychological aspects). New York: Columbia University Press.

Berlyne, D. E. (1957). Conflict and information-theory variables as determinants of human perceptual curiosity. *Journal of Experimental Psychology, 53*(6), 399–404.

Berlyne, D. E. (1960). *Conflict, arousal and curiosity*. New York: McGraw-hill.

Berlyne, D. E. (1974). *Studies in the new experimental aesthetics: Steps toward an objective psychology of aesthetic appreciation*. Washington, DC: Hemisphere.

Boscolo, P., Ariasi, N., Del Favero, L., & Ballarin, C. (2011). Interest in an expository text: How does it flow from reading to writing? *Learning and Instruction, 21*, 467–480. doi:10.1016/j.learninstruc.2010.07.009.

Canning, E. A., & Harackiewicz, J. M. (2015). Teach it, don't preach it: The differential effects of directly-communicated and self-generated utility value information. *Motivation Science, 1*, 47–71. doi:10.1037/mot0000015.

Chen, A., & Ennis, C. D. (2004). Goal, interest, and learning in physical education. *The Journal of Educational Research, 97*, 329–338. doi:10.1080/0304430290000.753.

Cribbs, J. D., Hazari, Z., Sonnert, G., & Sadler, P. M. (2015). Establishing an explanatory model for methematics identity. *Child Development, 86*(4), 1048–1062. doi:10.1111/cdev.12363.

De Garmo, C. (1894). Introduction to: Apperception. A monograph on psychology and pedagogy. In C. De Gamo (Ed.), *Apperception. On psychology and pedagogy* (p. viii). Boston: D.C. Heath & Co.

deCharms, R. (1968). *Personal causation: The internal affective determinants of behavior*. New York: Academic Press.

Dewey, J. (1913). *Interest and effort in education*. Boston: Houghton Miffler.

Durik, A., & Harackiewicz, J. M. (2007). Different strokes for different folks: How individual interest moderates the effects of situational factors on task interest. *Journal of Educational Psychology, 99*(3), 597–610. doi:10.1037/0022-0663.99.3.597.

Ellsworth, P. C. (2003). Confusion, concentration, and other emotions of interest: Commentary on Rozin and Cohen (2003). *Emotion, 3*(1), 81–85. doi:10.1037/1528-3542.3.1.81.

Elsworth, G. R., Harvey-Beavis, A., Ainley, J., & Fabris, S. (1999). Generic interests and school subject choice. *Educational Research and Evaluation, 5*(3), 290–318. doi:10.1076/edre.5.3.290.3882.

Ely, R. B. W., Ainley, M., & Pearce, J. M. (2012). *Establishing the interests of young people, a new exploratory approach: The My Interest Now for Engagement (MINE) project*. Paper presented at the International Conference for the Learning Sciences, Sydney, Australia.

Flum, H., & Kaplan, A. (2006). Exploratory orientation as an educational goal. *Educational Psychologist, 41*(2), 99–110. doi:10.1207/s15326985ep4102_3.

Fulmer, S. M., & Frijters, J. C. (2011). Motivation during an excessively challenging reading task: The buffering role of relative topic interest. *The Journal of Experimental Education, 79*(2), 185–208. doi:10.1080/00220973.2010.481503.

Garner, R., Brown, R., Sanders, S., & Menke, D. J. (1992). "Seductive details" and learning from text. In K. A. Renninger, S. Hidi, & A. Krapp (Eds.), *The role of interest in learning and development* (pp. 239–254). Hillsdale, NJ: Lawrence Erlbaum Associates.

Harackiewicz, J. M., Durik, A. M., Barron, K. E., Linnenbrink-Garcia, L., & Tauer, J. (2008). The role of achievement goals in the development of interest: Reciprocal relations between achievement goals, interest, and performance. *Journal of Educational Psychology, 100*(1), 105–122. doi:10.1037/0022-0663.100.1.105.

Harackiewicz, J. M., & Hulleman, C. S. (2010). The importance of interest: The role of achievement goals and task values in promoting the development of interest. *Social and Personality Psychology Compass, 4*(1), 42–52. doi:10.1111/j.1751-9004.2009.00207.x.

Hidi, S. (1990). Interest and its contribution as a mental resource for learning. *Review of Educational Research, 60*(3), 549–571.

Hidi, S. (1995). A reexamination of the role of attention in learning from text. *Educational Psychology Review, 7*(4), 323–350.

Hidi, S. (2001). Interest, reading, and learning: Theoretical and practical considerations. *Educational Psychology Review, 13*(3), 191–209.

Hidi, S. (2006). Interest: A unique motivational variable. *Educational Research Review, 1*(2), 69–82.

Hidi, S., & Harackiewicz, J. M. (2000). Motivating the academically unmotivated: A critical issue for the 21st century. *Review of Educational Research, 70*, 151–179.

Hidi, S., & Renninger, K. A. (2006). The four-phase model of interest development. *Educational Psychologist, 41*(2), 111–127.

Holland, J. L. (1985). *Making vocational choices: A theory of vocational personalities and work environments* (2nd ed.). Odessa, FL: Psychological Assessment Resources.

Holstermann, N., Ainley, M., Grube, D., Roick, T., & Bögeholz, S. (2012). The specific relation-ship between disgust and interest: Relevance during biology class dissections and gender dif-ferences. *Learning and Instruction, 22*, 185–192. doi:10.1016/j.learninstruc.2011.10.005.

Hulleman, C. S., Durik, A. M., Schweigert, S. A., & Harackiewicz, J. M. (2008). Task values, achievement goals, and interest: An integrative analysis. *Journal of Educational Psychology, 100*, 398–416. doi:10.1037/0022-0663.100.2.398.

Hulleman, C. S., Godes, O., Hendricks, B. L., & Harackiewicz, J. M. (2010). Enhancing interest and performance with a utility value intervention. *Journal of Educational Psychology, 102*(4), 880–895. doi:10.1037/a0019506.

Hunter, J. P., & Csikszentmihalyi, M. (2003). The positive psychology of interested adolescents. *Journal of Youth and Adolescence, 32*, 27–35.

Immordino-Yang, M. H. (2011). Implications of affective and social neuroscience for educational the-ory. *Educational Philosophy and Theory, 43*(1), 98–103. doi:10.1111/j.1469-5812.2010.00713.x.

Immordino-Yang, M. H., & Christodoulou, J. A. (2014). Neuroscientific contributions to under-standing and measuring emotions in educational contexts. In R. Pekrun & L. Linnenbrink-Garcia (Eds.), *International handbook of emotions in education* (pp. 607–624). New York: Routledge.

Izard, C. E. (1977). *Human emotions.* New York: Plenum Press.

Izard, C. E. (2007). Basic emotions, natural kinds, emotion schemas, and a new paradigm. *Perspectives on Psychological Science, 2*(3), 260–280. doi:10.1111/j.1745-6916.2007.00044.x.

Izard, C. E. (2009). Emotion theory and research: Highlights, unanswered questions, and emerging issues. *Annual Review of Psychology, 60*, 1–25. doi:10.1146/annurev.psych.60.110707.163539.

Izard, C. E., & Malatesta, C. E. (1987). Perspectives on emotional development I: Differential emotions theory of early emotional development. In M. Lewis & J. M. Haviland-Jones (Eds.), *Handbook of infant development* (second ed., pp. 494–510). New York: John Wiley & Sons.

Jarymowicz, M. T., & Imbir, K. (2015). Toward a human emotions taxonomy (based on their auto-matic vs. reflective origin). *Emotion Review, 7*(2), 183–188. doi:10.1177/1754073914555923.

Kintsch, W. (1980). Learning from text, levels of comprehension, or: Why anyone would read a story anyway. *Poetics, 9*, 87–98.

Knogler, M., Harackiewicz, J. M., Gegenfurtner, A., & Lewalter, D. (2015). How situational is situational interest? Investigating the longitudinal structure of situational interest. *Contemporary Educational Psychology, 43*, 39–50. doi:10.1016/j.cedpsych.2015.08.004.

Krapp, A. (2003). Interest and human development: An educational-psychological perspective. *Development and Motivation, BJEP Monograph Series, Series II*(2), 57–84.

Krapp, A. (2005). Basic needs and the development of interest and intrinsic motivational orienta-tions. *Learning and Instruction, 15*(5), 381–395. doi:10.1016/j.learninstruc.2005.07.007.

Krapp, A. (2007). An educational-psychological conceptualisation of interest. *International Journal of Educational Vocational Guidance, 7*, 5–21. doi:10.10007/s10775-0007-9113-9.

Krapp, A., Hidi, S., & Renninger, K. A. (1992). Interest, learning and development. In K. A. Renninger, S. Hidi, & A. Krapp (Eds.), *The role of interest in learning and development* (pp. 3–25). Hillsdale, NJ: Lawrence Erlbaum Associates.

Krapp, A., & Prenzel, M. (2011). Research on interest in science: Theories, methods and findings. *International Journal of Science Education, 33*(1), 27–50. doi:10.1080/09500693.2011.518645.

Kruglanski, A. W., & Gigerenzer, G. (2011). Intuitive and deliberate judgments are based on com-mon principles. *Psychological Review, 118*(1), 97–109. doi:10.1037/a0020762.

Lepper, M. R., & Henderlong, J. (2000). Turning "play" into "work" and "work" into "play": 25 years of research on intrinsic versus extrinsic motivation. In C. Sansone & J. M. Harackiewicz (Eds.), *Intrinsic and extrinsic motivation: The search for optimal motivation and performance* (pp. 257–307). New York: Academic Press.

Lewis, M. D., & Granic, I. (Eds.). (2000). *Emotion, development, and self-organization: Dynamic systems approaches to emotional development.* Cambridge, UK: Cambridge University Press.

Maltese, A. V., & Harsh, J. A. (2015). Students' pathways of entry into STEM. In K. A. Renninger, M. Nieswandt, & S. Hidi (Eds.), *Interest in mathematics and science learning* (pp. 203–223). Washington, DC: American Educational Research Association (AERA).

McDaniel, M. A., Waddill, P. J., Finstad, K., & Bourg, T. (2000). The effects of text-based interest on attention and recall. *Journal of Educational Psychology, 92*(3), 492–502. doi:10.1037//0022-0663.92.3.492.

Nieswandt, M., & Horowitz, G. (2015). Undergraduate students' interest in chemistry: The roles of task and choice. In K. A. Renninger, M. Nieswandt, & S. Hidi (Eds.), *Interest in mathematics and science learning* (pp. 225–242). Washington, DC: American Educational Research Association (AERA).

O'Keefe, P. A., & Linnenbrink-Garcia, L. (2014). The role of interest in optimizing performance and self-regulation. *Journal of Experimental Social Psychology, 53*, 70–78. doi:10.1016/j.jesp.2014.02.004.

Palmer, D. H. (2009). Student interest generated during an inquiry skills task. *Journal of Research in Science Teaching, 47*, 147–165. doi:10.1002/tea.20263.

Piaget, J. (1981). Intelligence and affectivity:Their relationship during child development. In T. A. Brown & M. R. Kaegi (Eds.), *Annual review monographs*. Palo Alto, CA: Annual Reviews.

Renninger, K. A. (2000). How might the development of individual interest contribute to the conceptualization of intrinsic motivation. In C. Sansone & J. M. Harackiewicz (Eds.), *Intrinsic and extrinsic motivation: The search for optimal motivation and performance*. New York: Academic Press.

Renninger, K. A., & Hidi, S. (2011). Revisiting the conceptualization, measurement, and generation of interest. *Educational Psychologist, 46*(3), 168–184. doi:10.1080/00461520.2011.587723.

Rotgans, J. I., & Schmidt, H. G. (2011). Situational interest and academic achievement in the active-learning classroom. *Learning and Instruction, 21*(1), 58–67. doi:10.1016/j.learninstruc.2009.11.001.

Ryan, R. M., & Deci, E. L. (2000). When rewards compete with nature: The undermining of intrinsic motivation and self-regulation. In C. Sansone & J. M. Harackiewicz (Eds.), *Intrinsic and extrinsic motivation: The search for optimal motivation and performance* (pp. 13–54). New York: Academic Press.

Sansone, C., & Harackiewicz, J. M. (Eds.). (2000). *Intrinsic and extrinsic motivation: The search for optimal motivation and performance*. New York: Academic Press.

Sansone, C., & Thoman, D. B. (2005). Interest as the missing motivator in self-regulation. *European Psychologist, 10*, 175–186. doi:10.1027/1016-9040.10.3.175.

Sansone, C., Thoman, D. B., & Fraughton, T. (2015). The relation between interest and self-regulation in mathematics and science. In K. A. Renninger, M. Nieswandt, & S. Hidi (Eds.), *Interest in mathematics and science learning* (pp. 111–131). Washington, DC: American Educational Research Association (AERA).

Sansone, C., Weir, C., Harpster, L., & Morgan, C. (1992). Once a boring task always a boring task? Interest as a self-regulatory mechanism. *Journal of Personality and Social Psychology, 63*(3), 379–309.

Schiefele, U. (2009). Situational and individual interest. In K. Wentzel & A. Wigfield (Eds.), *Handbook of motivation at school* (pp. 196–222). New York: Routledge.

Schraw, G., & Lehman, S. (2001). Situational interest: A review of the literature and directions for future research. *Educational Psychology Review, 13*(1), 23–52.

Silvia, P. J. (2005). What is interesting? Exploring the appraisal structure of interest. *Emotion, 5*(1), 89–102. doi:10.1037/1528-3542.5.1.89.

Silvia, P. J. (2006). *Exploring the psychology of interest*. New York: Oxford University Press.

Silvia, P. J. (2008). Interest – The curious emotion. *Current Directions in Psychological Science, 17*(1), 57–60.

Silvia, P. J. (2010). Confusion and interest: The role of knowledge emotions in aesthetic experience. *Psychology of Aesthetics, Creativity, and the Arts, 4*(2), 75–80. doi:10.1037/a0017081.

Stanovich, K. E., & Toplak, M. E. (2012). Defining features versus identical correlates of type 1 and type 2 processing. *Mind and Society, 11*, 3–13. doi:10.1007/s11299-011-0093-6.

Thelen, E., & Smith, L. B. (2006). Dynamic systems theories. In W. Damon & R. M. Lerner (Eds.), *Handbook of child psychology* (Vol. 1, 6th ed., pp. 258–312). Hoboken, NJ: John Wiley & Sons.

Thoman, D. B., Smith, L. B., & Silvia, P. J. (2011). The resource replenishment function of interest. *Social Psychological and Personality Science, 2*, 592–599. doi:10.1177/19485506114025.

Valsiner, J. (1992). Interest: A metatheoretical perspective. In K. A. Renninger, S. Hidi, & A. Krapp
(Eds.), *The role of interest in learning and development* (pp. 27–41). Hillsdale, NJ: Lawrence
Erlbaum.

Wade, S. E. (2001). Research on importance and interest: Implications for curriculum development
and future research. *Educational Psychology Review, 13*, 243–261.

Wade, S. E., Schraw, G., Buxton, W. M., & Hayes, M. T. (1993). Effects of importance and interest
on recall of biographical text. *Reading Research Quarterly, 28*, 93–114. doi:10.2307/747885.

Wigfield, A., & Eccles, J. S. (2000). Expectancy-value theory of achievement motivation.
Contemporary Educational Psychology, 25, 68–81.

Part II
Functions of Interest

Chapter 2
The Dynamic Nature of Interest: Embedding Interest Within Self-Regulation

Dustin B. Thoman, Carol Sansone, and Danielle Geerling

We began our study of interest by thinking about why and how people maintain motivation over longer periods of time—and what is missing when they do not. To maintain motivation in the short term, extrinsic rewards or other valued outcomes (e.g., winning, getting a positive evaluation) are often sufficient. But when thinking about how people sustain motivation over the longer term, even for an important activity, their experience *during* the activity (not just why they started doing it) matters. That is, sustaining motivation over weeks or months to keep up an exercise routine or stay engaged with a weeks-long class project, for example, seems much easier when the person regularly experiences some level of interest. Persisting and maintaining engagement with these kinds of activities is more difficult when the experience of interest is missing, requiring more psychological resources and often resulting in quitting the activity when possible (O'Keefe & Linnenbrink-Garcia, 2014; Sansone & Harackiewicz, 1996; Thoman, Smith, & Silvia, 2011).

This experience of interest can be thought of as the source of *intrinsic motivation*. Traditionally, the term intrinsic motivation has been used to refer to when individuals engage in an activity for its own sake because it is interesting and

Author Note:
Preparation of and research reported in this chapter was supported in part by grants from the National Science Foundation (DRL 1420271/1644344; DRL 0735264) and National Institutes of Health (1R01GM098462). Any opinions, findings, and conclusions or recommendations expressed in this material are our own and do not necessarily reflect the views of the NSF or NIH.

D.B. Thoman (✉)
Department of Psychology, San Diego State University, San Diego, CA, USA
e-mail: dthoman@mail.sdsu.edu

C. Sansone • D. Geerling
Department of Psychology, University of Utah, Salt Lake City, UT, USA

© Springer International Publishing AG 2017
P.A. O'Keefe, J.M. Harackiewicz (eds.), *The Science of Interest*,
DOI 10.1007/978-3-319-55509-6_2

enjoyable (Deci & Ryan, 2000; Sansone & Harackiewicz, 2000). However, people start many activities for reasons unrelated to interest. For example, a student might start a class project because it was assigned and he or she wants to earn a good grade. Because the student is not engaging in the project for its own sake, he or she would be exhibiting extrinsic motivation. This traditional distinction between extrinsic and intrinsic motivation thus restricts intrinsic motivation to only those activities that do not (knowingly) lead to other desired outcomes. Even when interest does not drive the choice to start an activity, however, individuals could still experience interest during engagement, and this experience can motivate persistence and progress toward the goal of completing the project. We thus suggest that people are intrinsically motivated when their behavior is motivated by the *anticipated, actual,* or *sought experience of "interest"* (Sansone & Harackiewicz, 1996; Sansone & Smith, 2000; Sansone & Thoman, 2005), whether or not that was their initial or only reason for engaging in an activity. From this perspective, distinguishing between intrinsically and extrinsically motivated activities becomes less useful when considering engagement over a longer time period.

As described in other papers (Renninger & Hidi, 2011; Sansone & Morgan, 1992; Sansone & Smith, 2000; Sansone & Thoman, 2005), we focus on interest as a phenomenological experience involving both cognitive and affective components. Attention is directed and focused and the general affective tone is positive. At its extreme, this may be experienced as "flow" (Csikszentmihalyi, 1975). We have also noted (e.g., Sansone, Thoman, & Fraughton, 2015) that the experience of interest has important motivational implications at all phases of interest development (Hidi & Renninger, 2006) because it reflects what individuals feel in the moment while engaged with an activity (whether the activity is novel or relevant to well-developed individual interests). Thus, our focus on the interest experience is similar to what Knogler (see Chap. 6) refers to as the "interest state." We consider this experience as a dynamic state that arises through an ongoing transaction among individuals' goals, activity characteristics, and the surrounding context. That is, interest arises during the pursuit of goals, as a function of both what a person brings to the activity and the activity parameters. Importantly, this experience is not necessarily stable over time. One's experience may vary as the activity itself changes or the activity context changes. These changes might be influenced by the nature of the activity itself, those who structure the task (e.g., teachers, parents, or peers), or even by the individual doing the activity.

We place our study of interest within a framework of self-regulation for two main reasons. First, it opens up potential sources of interest to include a variety of goals that might motivate individuals to engage with an activity, and suggests that the entire process of goal-striving can be important for interest. Second, it allows us to capture the possibility that individuals may actively regulate their experiences during the pursuit of important goals to make them more interesting and thus more motivating.

Specifying the Source of Interest and Accounting for Changes in Interest Over Time

How a model conceptualizes the source of interest has important implications for whether and how interest might change over time. For example, Silvia's (2006) appraisal model conceptualizes interest as a "knowledge" emotion and places the source of interest primarily within the person. Like all emotions, the experience is preceded by a cognitive appraisal. Silvia's work has mapped out appraisal structures of interest (Silvia, 2005) and demonstrates that individual differences in appraisal structures can explain variability of interest across people and situations (Silvia, Henson, & Templin, 2009). This model suggests that, as people learn more about an activity or topic, their appraisal structures can change and these cognitive changes explain fluctuations in interest over time.

Other models, most notably Hidi and Renninger's model of interest development (Hidi & Renninger, 2006; Renninger & Hidi, 2016), view the role of time and changes in interest through a developmental lens. This model attempts to explain the processes through which an individual's interest in a topic sparks, deepens, and ultimately becomes part of that person's identity. This model suggests that the source of interest begins with external triggers (e.g., interesting text). Interest can subsequently grow if initial interest leads individuals to seek out and gain more knowledge about the topic or domain and comes to value it more. When supported, over time and experiences, this initial interest potentially can continue to grow into well-developed individual interests that become a part of the person's identity. In this approach, interest begins as surface-level reactions to stimuli and becomes "interests" integrated and embedded within the person's knowledge structures and their predispositions toward the world.

Our model focuses on the motivational properties of the experience of interest and integrates interest within a self-regulatory framework. This framework recognizes that interest can be actively created and controlled both for its own sake and as a means to sustain motivation for valued activities. Our definition of the interest experience locates the source of interest primarily in the person, but we emphasize that the person is not the same over time. Interest fluctuates once the person is placed into time and setting because the experience arises from ongoing engagement in goal-directed activity. In our model, interest is neither a passive experience nor a stable individual predisposition toward task features or topics. The experience of interest can change over time, as a function of what the person brings to the activity (e.g., goals, individual differences), the activity context (including activity parameters and the social context), and how the person works on the activity (behaviors), all of which can change over time. Shifts in interest often occur unintentionally (as the activity context changes, for example), but individuals can also take advantage of this point by actively doing something to change their experience, even if not always done consciously. Identifying the location of interest in a person who is both actively and reactively engaging with the environment/task is what

Time	Prior to engagement	During engagement	After engagement

Interest Stage	Expected interest	Interest experience	Evaluation of interest
Additional impact of self-regulatory process	Anticipated match with goals and values Anticipated identity fit	Degree of match with goals/values, identity, regulatory mode Can actively work to • create greater match • create greater interest	Access to own experience Salience of other reasons to engage/disengage Social feedback
Consequences/Outcomes	When have choice, whether choose to engage; if do, expectations shape initial approach	How engage (allocation of time/attention; strategies; inclusion of others; persistence; effort) Potential performance tradeoffs	Whether persevere, return and/or re-engage if have choice

Fig. 2.1 Identification of determinants of interest that emerge from embedding interest within the dynamics of self-regulation as well as the consequences for choices and actions. *Dashed arrows* indicate that the outcomes of self-regulation processes at each stage have implications for interest at the next point of activity engagement

gives rise to our self-regulation model and differentiates our dynamic approach to the psychological science of interest.

To illustrate the dynamic nature of the interest experience as an ongoing transaction between the person and activity, we describe studies from our program of research that highlight this dynamic aspect of interest experience across time, relative to activity engagement. As outlined in Fig. 2.1, for the purpose of the present chapter we focus on the determinants of interest that emerge when considering interest as embedded within the process of goal-striving over time. The overarching self-regulation framework integrates previous research that identifies certain factors as impacting interest in negative (e.g., deadlines) or positive (e.g., personal relevance) directions, but also helps to understand why there might be circumstances under which they do not have those effects. Moreover, this framework allows the identification of additional determinants of interest that are tied specifically to the dynamics of self-regulation.

The figure illustrates two central points. The first is that rather than certain factors always being associated with greater or lesser interest, it is important to know whether those factors match or are congruent with the person's goals. For example, two students could both decide to learn Hypertext Markup Language (HTML) but with different goals. The first student might be learning in order to make his or her blog more eye-catching; the second student might be learning in order to be able to update product information on his or her company's website. Our approach suggests that the same factor (e.g., instruction on how to make animated cartoon characters appear on the web page) might lead to different interest experiences for the two students.

The second point is that individuals actively monitor and react to their experiences, and take these anticipated or actual experiences into account when deciding whether to start, persist, or re-engage with an activity or related activities. This active role includes engaging with activities in ways that make them more congruent with goals (e.g., the student learning HTML to enrich his or her blog might skip over instructions about how to create forms to collect information from viewers, and instead spend more time exploring different kinds of cartoon characters that could be added). This active role could also mean engaging with the activity in ways that makes the experience more interesting whether or not it advances progress toward the goal (e.g., the same student could spend time texting cartoon characters to friends). This active role in how they engage with the activity has implications for performance behaviors as well as subsequent evaluations of performance by self and by others upon completion.

As noted elsewhere (e.g., Sansone, Wiebe & Morgan, 1999; Sansone & Thoman, 2006), we are not suggesting that interest is the only source of motivation to persist, nor that it is always necessary for persistence. Rather, we are suggesting that the experience of interest (or its lack) is integral to the self-regulatory process, and thus its presence or absence has consequences on our choices and actions at each stage of engagement. In the following sections, we review research that illustrates the implication of these points when individuals are deciding whether to engage with an activity or domain (prior to engagement), when individuals are engaged (during engagement), and when individuals are evaluating their experience (after engagement).

A Dynamic Basis of Expected Interest

As noted by Bandura (1991), one of the important things we regulate is whether we enter a context or begin an activity in the first place. For our present purpose, we focus on how anticipating that an activity or domain will be interesting shapes these choices. We have examined these questions in the context of understanding why individuals from different groups (e.g., as defined by gender, SES, etc.) might differentially select STEM (Science, Technology, Engineering, and Mathematics)-related careers. Individuals often have multiple goals for engaging in an activity. For example, in academic achievement contexts, students often want to learn and to demonstrate competence to others (Barron & Harackiewicz, 2001), or have interpersonal goals as well as competence goals (e.g., Sansone & Morgan, 1992). If individuals from different backgrounds systematically differ in some of these goals, then the goal-matching concepts outlined previously would suggest that they might anticipate different levels of interest if the activity and surrounding context are not perceived as congruent with those goals.

Morgan, Isaac, and Sansone (2001) examined whether women and men undergraduates expected that STEM careers might be differentially interesting as a function of match with goals. They asked one group of students what their work plans were, and why, and then coded the reasons provided for these career preferences. They found that overall, both men and women cited the anticipated interestingness of the work most frequently, and this was cited equally frequently by both men and women. The second most cited reason overall was "people-oriented," framed in terms of wanting to work with or to help other people. However, this was also cited by more women than men. Pay and status were cited least frequently overall, but also were cited significantly more by men than by women. Morgan et al. then asked a second group of students to rate a variety of potential careers in terms of their perceived affordances for different kinds of goals, including the "people-oriented" goals and pay and status goals identified by the first group of students. They also asked them to rate how interesting they thought careers in the different fields might be. In support of the matching hypothesis, both men and women perceived that mathematical and physical science careers were less likely to afford interpersonal goals and more likely to afford extrinsic reward goals, and perceptions of these affordances predicted how interesting individuals expected careers in these fields to be. A similar effect was later found by Diekman, Brown, Johnson, and Clark (2010), who examined gender differences in anticipated interest in STEM fields as a function of anticipated match with "communal goals" (defined as wanting to work with or help other people).

Recent research has focused on match with culturally connected values, demonstrating that underrepresented minority (URM) and first-generation (FG) college students (for whom neither parent graduated with a four-year degree) tend to more strongly value prosocial goals of helping society and giving back to one's community through work than white students and continuing generation students (Harackiewicz, Canning, Tibbetts, Priniski, & Hyde, 2016; Thoman, Brown, Mason, Harmsen, & Smith, 2015). URM students who see science as providing opportunities to fulfill these goals expressed greater interest in science careers, but these perceptions did not influence career interest for non-URMs or continuing generation students (Allen, Muragishi, Smith, Thoman, & Brown, 2015; Jackson, Galvez, Landa, Buonora, & Thoman, 2016; Thoman et al., 2015).

Together, these studies suggest that perceived mismatch with goals creates the perception of an activity or domain that it would be less interesting to do compared to other options. A consequence is that individuals are less likely to select these kinds of activities initially when given a choice.

The Dynamic Basis of Interest Once Engaged

Once engaged with an activity, individuals' goals can again influence whether the same activity performed in a given context is experienced as interesting. For example, in Sansone, Sachau, and Weir (1989), individuals performed a fantasy-based computer game that prompted adoption of goals to become involved in the fantasy adventure. Some students were randomly assigned to conditions which instead prompted adoption of competence-related goals (e.g., they received performance feedback relative to other students (Study 1); they read task descriptions that described the game as a test of skill (Study 2)). Students then received feedback that provided suggestions for how to increase their scores. When contextual cues had first prompted the adoption of skill-related goals, this instructional feedback was associated with *greater* subsequent interest and with participants being more likely to take a company brochure when they left. However, the same feedback was associated with *decreases* in interest and participants being less likely to take the game brochure when individuals' goals were focused on the fantasy adventure. A mediation analysis indicated that individuals in the mismatch condition (i.e., those with fantasy adventure goals who received instructions about scoring) experienced a lower degree of positive affect (including interest) while engaged. Although performing ostensibly the same activity, individuals experienced different levels of interest depending on whether or not the instruction was congruent with their initial goals.

A similar matching effect has been found for achievement goals (e.g., Harackiewicz & Elliott, 1993) and interpersonal goals (e.g., Isaac, Sansone, & Smith, 1999; Morf, Weir, & Davidov, 2000; Smith & Ruiz, 2007). Although the presence of others might make an activity more interesting to do for most people (e.g., Plass, O'Keefe et al., 2013; Sansone, Weir, Harpster, & Morgan, 1992; Tauer & Harackiewicz, 2004), the presence of others can be especially impactful for those for whom interpersonal goals are especially important. For example, in Isaac et al. (1999), individuals higher in characteristic interpersonal orientation (who characteristically approach activities with interpersonal goals) experienced greater interest in a math-related activity and were more likely to request further information about the topic when they worked with or even just alongside another person (a confederate), as opposed to when they worked alone.

Isaac et al. also videotaped the work sessions to explore *how* the presence of others might have resulted in a more interesting experience. They found that individuals higher in interpersonal orientation reached out and engaged with the other person, displaying a more interpersonally involving interaction style (e.g., expressing thoughts and information to a greater degree). These actions drew more off-task conversation out of the other person, and this in turn predicted greater interest in the activity (and more interest in getting further information about the topic in the future). These results demonstrate that the goals that individuals bring to the activity not only influence how they engage with the task but also how they engage with the surrounding context. If they can, individuals will actively create experiences that are congruent with their goals, resulting in greater interest. In other words, when goals are matched with context, either because they match initially or are made to match through individuals' actions while engaged (Smith & Ruiz, 2007), individuals will experience greater interest.

This research suggests that interest can be a by-product of regulation that brings the activity in line with initial goals. However, our approach also suggests that interest itself can be the target of regulation. Even if individuals are sufficiently motivated to begin an activity, motivation can wane as time passes. Because interest is an important source of motivation for persistence and effort, whether the experience is interesting can be critical for whether individuals persist or re-engage. Moreover, when the experience is not interesting, individuals can actively change how they engage with the activity, with the purpose of enhancing interest. In this case, interest is not a by-product of self-regulation—it is the thing being regulated.

Initial work on this hypothesis was reported in Sansone et al. (1992), who outlined the conditions under which individuals should be most likely to actively engage in strategic actions to enhance interest: (1) when the activity is currently not interesting (i.e., there is a need to regulate), (2) there is a good reason to persist anyway, and (3) the actions that would make the experience more interesting (e.g., varying how the activity is performed) are possible in that situation. They created an experimental paradigm to test these hypotheses using identical materials across conditions, comparing an initially boring task (copying letters matrices) and an initially interesting task (finding words hidden in those same matrices). A subset of those doing the copying task were also provided a reason to value the task (i.e., health benefits). Those who performed the copying task with knowledge of health benefits were most likely to engage in interest-enhancing actions (e.g., varying the procedure) while engaged with the copying task. For example, they attempted to copy the particular type font displayed in each matrix (although that was not necessary for the task), varied the pattern with which they copied the letters (e.g., did all the diagonals first), and so on. Individuals who performed the hidden words task were least likely to vary how they performed the task, and individuals who performed the copying task without the health benefit information fell between the two. Moreover, varying the procedure predicted greater likelihood of doing the activity in the future (i.e., requests for matrices to take away with them). Importantly, the health benefit information by itself did not predict greater likelihood of doing the activity again. Rather, the health benefit information made it more likely that individuals would do the interest-enhancing actions, and it was these actions that predicted greater likelihood of future engagement.

The purposeful regulation of the interest experience also raises the question of how these actions might work with (or against) performance. In Sansone et al. (1992), for example, although individuals who varied the procedure were more likely to do the activity again, they also copied fewer letters in the time allowed. In a later study, Sansone et al. (1999) found that when individuals were free to choose how long they worked on the copying task, those who varied the procedure persisted longer, and thus copied more letters, than individuals who did not engage in these strategies. These results suggest that there can be trade-offs, at least in the short term, between regulating the interest experience and performance. However, these results were also limited to a laboratory paradigm with no consequences for poor performance, and so it was possible that these trade-offs do not occur in other situations, such as in academic situations.

Later research suggested that trade-offs can occur within academic domains as well. For example, Sansone, Smith, Thoman, and MacNamara (2012) found that undergraduates in an online section of an upper division psychology course were more likely than students in the on-campus section to report trying to make studying for an exam more enjoyable by exploring material on the class web page (which was available to students in both class sections). Although overall students in the online section reported lower interest than students in the on-campus section, online students who reported exploring material on the class web page had interest levels equivalent to students in the on-campus section. The more that students in the online section reported using the strategy, however, the greater their interest but the poorer their exam performance.

In a series of follow-up laboratory studies using an online learning paradigm, a similar possibility for trade-offs emerged. Undergraduates were provided a good reason to value learning HTML (Hypertext Markup Language) through a utility value manipulation (Eccles & Wigfield, 2002). Specifically, students in utility value conditions were provided information about how learning HTML could be useful in personal or organizational applications. Students who received the utility value information were more likely to engage with the examples and exercises in the online lesson in ways that predicted greater interest and likelihood of continuing to learn about HTML on their own. For example, they were more likely to experiment with sample HTML commands displayed in the examples. However, for some students, the higher degree of engagement was associated with running out of time to submit the assignment (Sansone, Butner, Fraughton, & Zachary, 2011). Taken together, these studies suggest that once engaged in an activity, individuals can actively monitor and regulate the degree of interest they experience. They can do so purposely, in order to maintain motivation for a valued or necessary activity. However, in some circumstances the time and effort directed toward regulating interest might come at a cost to efforts more directly related to external requirements and evaluated outcomes, at least in the short term.

A Dynamic Basis of Interest after Engagement

One implication of our self-regulation model is that individuals can continue to think about and evaluate their interest even *after* activity engagement. That is, individuals not only evaluate progress toward goals (Carver & Scheier, 1990), they also evaluate their experience. Of course, one important source of information for this evaluation is the person's own immediate perception of their experience, as well as their attributions about what led to that experience (Silvia, 2006). However, people's perceptions of how they felt after an event or experience is over can be colored by initial expectations (e.g., Klaaren, Hodges & Wilson, 1994), and by how they think others feel about the same event (e.g., Gilbert, Killingsworth, Eyre, & Wilson, 2009). After behavioral engagement stops, people think about past events and this process of recalling events and activities has implications for reconstructing our memories and experiences (Pasupathi, 2001), including attributions for and appraisals of experiences of interest (Silvia, 2006). Just as was found at other points in the engagement process, other people may play an important role in this reconstruction of our experience.

For example, in a study by Pasupathi and Rich (2005), pairs of friends (college students) came into the lab, and one person was randomly assigned to play a novel computer game and subsequently describe the game to his or her friend. Participants who were assigned to play the game rated their interest in the game both before and after the conversation. These participants were unaware that experimenters had manipulated their friends' pattern of responsiveness as they listened to the description of the game. Pasupathi and Rich randomly assigned listeners to one of three conditions. In the unresponsive listener condition, listeners were instructed to count the number of 'th' words that the speaker said while describing the activity (i.e., which created the appearance of inattentive listening). This was compared to the condition where the listener was responsive but disagreed with the speakers' statements, and the condition where the listener was responsive and agreeable (as they would normally be with the friend). In the condition where listeners were instructed to count the "th" words, speakers' interest in the activity dropped from pre- to post-conversation. When listeners instead were instructed to listen to their friends as they normally would, interest levels were maintained. Importantly, when listeners had been instructed to disagree with the speaker's description, interest was also maintained. Thus, interest dropped after the conversation period only when the listener appeared unresponsive, suggesting that (un)responsiveness (conveying lack of interest or value) may be more important for evaluation of interest than whether one's descriptions of the activity are explicitly verified by the listener. Subsequent research replicated these findings, and also showed that listener responsiveness when individuals discussed their experience outside of the lab predicted subsequent interest over and above interest levels at the end of the lab session (Thoman, Sansone, & Pasupathi, 2007).

Two subsequent studies extended this research into the classroom (Thoman, Sansone, Fraughton, & Pasupathi, 2012). In Study 1, Thoman et al. examined conversations about class topics that took place as a structured part of an online psychology class (i.e., discussion board). They found that how often students posted on the discussion board did not predict their subsequent ratings of interest in the class. Rather, the important factor was how often other students had responded to their posts. In Study 2, college students in an introductory physics course completed diaries throughout the semester that included students' reports of everyday conversations about class topics and about class exams. Students' reports of perceived listener responsiveness in conversations about class topics predicted students' class interest, even when controlling for anticipated interest at the beginning of the semester. Importantly, this effect occurred only for conversations about class topics, and not for conversations about exams. This pattern suggests that subtle feedback conveying that listeners are interested (or disinterested) in the topic has implications for evaluations of interest in a way that feedback about issues of competence assessment or class difficulty do not.

This work suggests that interest in an activity is not only affected by the individual's experience during the activity but also by talking with others after the activity has occurred. The reactions of others—and particularly, whether they appear to be interested in what we are saying—can be an important determinant of our own evaluations of our experiences.

Moreover, this may be another point in the process that helps to explain why individuals from different backgrounds might differentially select into STEM careers. For those who are underrepresented in STEM (e.g., women and underrepresented minorities), the concern about being judged negatively based on their identity (i.e., social identity threat) can lead them to be vigilant for situational cues related to whether they are being socially accepted (Cohen & Garcia, 2008). Consistent with the idea that women in STEM experience social identity threat, a study on workplace interactions among STEM faculty members found that discussing research with male colleagues was associated with greater disengagement for women, whereas socializing with male colleagues was associated with less disengagement (Holleran, Whitehead, Schamder, & Mehl, 2011). When talking with someone about their STEM interest, therefore, women may be particularly sensitive to signs of (un)responsiveness (Thoman, Smith, Brown, Chase, & Lee, 2013). Recent findings from a larger longitudinal survey study of freshmen and sophomore college science majors support this prediction (Curti, Zambrano, Lee, Jackson, & Thoman, 2016). The part of the data from Curti et al. directly relevant to group-based differences indicated that for women, but not for men, feeling that one's interest in science had been encouraged and understood by others (i.e., listeners were responsive and encouraging) predicted greater end-of-semester science career interest. This was particularly true for women with low or average science identity at the beginning of the semester. Thus, these results suggest that underrepresented students might be most affected by responsive listeners. Even when they do engage with a STEM-related activity, their subsequent evaluations may be more vulnerable to the appraisals conveyed (sometimes subtly) by others.

In addition to regulating the evaluation of interest to align with the presumed appraisals by others, individuals may also regulate their evaluations of the experience in service of other goals—and in particular, to protect or promote the self. For example, in Festinger and Carlsmith's (1959) classic study on cognitive dissonance, participants who were given insufficient external justification ($1) to tell another participant that a boring task (e.g., repeatedly turning pegs a quarter turn) was interesting subsequently rated the task as more interesting. This and later studies (e.g., Fazio, Zanna, & Cooper, 1977; Stone & Cooper, 2001) have been considered evidence of how individuals will change attitudes in order to protect against negative evaluations of self (e.g., in Festinger and Carlsmith's study, to protect against having lied to another person). For our present purposes, these studies provide evidence that individuals can purposely change interest appraisals after engagement as a way to protect or promote the self.

Thoman and Sansone (2016) examined whether this possibility can help to explain how women and men can come to have different interest appraisals of a STEM-related activity after engagement even when their engagement experiences were similar. Research has shown that women and men can receive different feedback for similar performance (Moss-Racusin, Dovidio, Brescoll, Graham, & Handelsman, 2012), and Thoman and Sansone examined whether the experience of receiving different feedback for similar work could lead men and women to differentially evaluate how interesting the experience was. When participants arrived at the lab, they were assigned to work on a forensic activity independently from but in the same room as an opposite-sex participant. However, in Study 1, women were the real participants and the men were actually confederates; in Study 2, this was reversed. In both studies, after the activity was completed, the experimenter skimmed both sets of materials and commented that the woman and a man had performed about the same. Next, they "accidently" overheard the male researcher in charge of the study select the man as the outstanding group member (Major, Quinton, & Schmader, 2003). Some of the women in Study 1 and men in Study 2 also "accidently" overheard the head researcher saying that the reason he had selected the man was because men were better at science. Following the feedback, participants reported their interest in the activity and were also given the opportunity to request information on related careers. Compared to control conditions, when the feedback was perceived as due to pro-male bias, women (Study 1) reported lower interest and men (Study 2) reported greater interest in the science activity. Higher levels of interest, in turn, positively predicted whether participants subsequently requested career information. These findings suggest that individuals can purposely change their evaluations of activity interest after engagement as a way to protect or promote the self. For women, lowered interest would make them less likely to select similar activities in the future, thus allowing them to avoid future experiences of bias. For men, in contrast, greater interest would lead them to be more likely to select similar activities in the future (where they may also experience bias in their favor).

Together, the studies in this section suggest that the evaluation of interest after engagement is not a passive reaction to activity characteristics. Although the actual experience while engaged is an important source of information for the evaluation (Silvia, 2006), evaluations are an active process, influenced by others, and in service of potentially multiple goals (e.g., to have a good experience, to avoid rejection).

Implications of a Dynamic Model of Interest

The sections above highlight how approaching interest from a dynamic, self-regulatory framework can answer questions about the nature of interest and the role of interest in helping us to maintain motivation over time. In sum, the key points from this approach are:

- Interest can be actively monitored, evaluated, and regulated.
- Monitoring, evaluation, and regulation happen in context—which critically shapes, supports, and/or constrains the interest regulation process.
- It is important to examine not just *whether* someone engages with an activity, and *why*, but also *how* he/she chooses to engage.
- The *process* of interest regulation results in both between- and within-person differences in interest over time

These key points have important implications for research. In the next sections, we focus on two areas that seem especially fruitful areas of continued investigation.

Expanding the Examination of Meta-motivational Variables

Researchers have recently started to emphasize the need for expanding the examination of meta-motivational variables beyond inferences about reasons or perceptions about autonomy or control (e.g., Miele & Scholer, 2016). For example, how do theories about the nature of motivation affect whether and how individuals regulate their motivation? Furthermore, how do theories about the nature of interest affect whether and how individuals attempt to regulate interest?

Our framework also suggests that, in addition to the importance of considering people's beliefs, or implicit theories, about why they performed an activity (e.g., Lepper, Sagotsky, Dafoe, & Greene, 1982) or why they struggle or succeed (Blackwell, Trzesniewski, & Dweck, 2007), it is important to consider beliefs about one's experience during engagement. For example, across three studies, implicit theories about interest regulation (i.e., beliefs about whether it is possible to make the task interesting) predicted actual interest regulation (Thoman, Sansone, & Robinson, 2016). In two experimental studies using the copying task from Sansone et al. (1992), participants were asked to complete either the boring copy version of the task or the interesting hidden words version. All participants were told that doing this activity would help others and were asked to complete several activity sheets. Prior to the copy task having been introduced, however, participants' implicit theories of interest regulation were either measured (Study 1) or manipulated (Study 2). In both studies, for those who completed the boring copy task, those who believed that interest in an activity can change were more likely to regulate their interest than those who believed that interest experiences are stable. As expected, no such difference was found for those who completed the interesting task because there was no need to regulate interest. In a third study, Thoman et al. (2016) replicated these findings in a correlational survey study. College students were asked if they could recall any recent boring assignments from their actual classes, and if so, whether they used any interest-enhancing strategies. Across a range of academic domains, students who believed that interest in an activity could change were more likely to report having used interest-enhancing strategies than students who believed that experiences of interest were stable. Related research on implicit theories of interest by O'Keefe and colleagues has examined implications of whether people think their interests are inherent and relatively stable or developed. Their work suggests that believing that interests are developed leads to higher interest in a greater variety of topics and greater maintained interest in the face of difficulty (O'Keefe, Dweck, & Walton, 2016; Chap. 3).

Determining What Is "Effective" Regulation

Effective self-regulation of motivational and emotional states, in general, requires flexibility across time and situations (Bonanno & Burton, 2013). One important feature of our model is that the monitoring, evaluation, and regulation of interest happen in coordination with features of the activity, including what (and who) defines successful engagement. Thus, the context in which interest regulation is occurring critically shapes, supports, and/or constrains the process itself. By extension, whether regulation of motivation and interest is deemed "effective" thus depends on the activity context, the timeline of engagement, and on what grounds the evaluation is based (e.g., performance vs. persistence or retention).

When individuals choose to regulate their motivation by making a task more interesting, there are sometimes long-term benefits but short-term costs. For example, as noted previously, students who attempted to make a letter-copying task more interesting actually copied fewer letters in the limited time allowed than students who did not attempt to regulate their interest (Sansone et al., 1992). However, when the time frame was left open-ended, those who regulated their interest persisted longer and therefore copied more letters (Sansone et al., 1999). Moreover, the more that online students reported exploring the class webpage as a way to make studying more enjoyable, the lower were their exam grades (Sansone et al., 2012).

Thus, one barrier to effective interest regulation is the presence of competing goals (Sansone, 2009). Individuals may have competing goals themselves (Barron & Harackieweicz, 2001), but those who create or structure the activity (e.g., teachers) can also define activity goals that compete with an individual's other goals. For example, when externally set deadlines do not allow time for exploration or variety, individuals who engage in such interest-enhancing behaviors might be penalized with lower performance scores. Of course, individuals could avoid this penalty if they did not try to engage with the materials in ways that create or maintain interest, but rather focused narrowly on performance-related aspects of their work. However, this also means that these individuals may be less likely to persist or re-engage in the future. In situations when regulating interest and maximizing evaluated performance are incompatible, what type of engagement is more "effective"?

When an important goal is to promote sustained engagement (e.g., retention in a field of study), it may be possible to construct environments in ways that minimize incompatibilities. For instance, to encourage persistence in STEM fields, it would be important for educators to emphasize students' subjective experiences in STEM (e.g., by promoting exploration of novel and interest-enhancing portions of the course website) in addition to providing means for academic achievement within the field. Our framework thus suggests that it is important to consider the possibility of promoting both performance and interest goals when creating learning and working environments for ourselves and for others.

Although we have mostly emphasized the need to allow for the regulation of interest in order to promote long-term positive outcomes, it is possible that the focus on the interest experience at the expense of other considerations can also be problematic. For example, work by Vallerand and colleagues on "passions" suggests that some passions can be detrimental to well-being (see Chap. 8, this volume). Vallerand's description of passions is similar to Hidi and Renninger's (2006) description of well-developed individual interests, including the integration with a person's identity. However, Vallerand differentiates between "harmonious" and "obsessive" passions. Harmonious passions are positive; they are associated with autonomous activity choices and healthy adaptations. Obsessive passions are problematic; they can take over or control one's life, create conflicts within relationships and with work or school requirements, and so on. With obsessive passions, regulation is focused on maximizing engagement with these intensely interesting activities, but with serious costs to other aspects of well-being. In this case, the rewarding aspects of the interest experience can become addictive. "Effective" regulation thus needs to be judged within the overall context of the person's life, and the person might make different judgments than the people with whom he or she interacts at home, work, or play.

Unanswered Questions and Future Directions

Building upon the work described above and the implications of our dynamic self-regulation model of the interest experience, we identify key unanswered questions and directions for further research.

Can we teach effective self-regulation of interest? Our research has studied spontaneous interest regulation behaviors in laboratory paradigms and measured regulation strategies through surveys. Across these studies we have observed variability in whether and when individuals will regulate interest. In many instances the choice to regulate interest or not is likely rational (even if not always conscious). At other times, however, people might not change how they do the activity even though they could benefit from making it more interesting. The questions that follow are: Can we teach self-regulation of interest? And what is the best target, the individual or the situation (e.g., teachers, managers)?

Our self-regulatory framework highlights multiple potential areas for intervention. For example, encouraging individuals to find what is meaningful, useful, and of personal relevance in what they are doing can directly enhance interest (e.g., Hulleman & Harackiewicz, 2009), or indirectly enhance interest if it provides a "good reason" to exert the effort to make how they engage with the work more interesting. However, recent work suggests that utility value interventions can also lead to decreased interest, as a function of whether the value is externally provided by an experimenter (or teacher) or self-generated in a personal essay, as well as individuals' levels of perceived competence (e.g., Canning & Harackiewicz, 2015; Durik, Shechter, Noh, Rozek, & Harackiewicz, 2014). Thus, our perspective on interest regulation suggests that it is important for researchers to better understand whether and how increases in value might affect patterns of engagement and interest regulation over time.

Another potential area for intervention is to teach individuals to recognize when and how they might change how they work on uninteresting school- or work-related tasks when they have a good reason to persist. Helping individuals become aware of the benefits of interest regulation and teaching simple strategies for how they can change different types of activities seem relatively easy. But the implications of teaching self-regulation of interest become much more complicated when considering the findings above on trade-offs (e.g., performance costs). Rather than asking whether we can teach self-regulation of interest, therefore, it is far more important to ask whether we can teach *effective* self-regulation of interest within the complete dynamic context of activity engagement over time (Sansone et al., 2015).

Focusing on interest regulation for students, this more complex question becomes: Is it possible to design interventions to teach students how to engage with courses in order to maximize *all* of their performance- and experience-related goals, including the mastery of material, achievement of good grades, *and* an enhanced interest experience? This question is far more difficult to answer than the simpler version and may need to consider intervention not at the level of the student, but of the student within a learning context. For example, effectively creating such an intervention might mean developing a coordinated intervention program for both students and teachers. In this type of model, students would need to learn how to regulate their interest and teachers would need to learn how to recognize when students were pursuing goals to learning or goals to create interest, how to design activities that create the flexibility needed for each student to pursue interest regulation options, and how to create a scaffolding that would help students effectively manage trade-offs between multiple goals. At the minimum, our perspective suggests that instructors should be aware that interest regulation can be essential to maintaining motivation over the longer term. Our model clearly suggests that developing educational interventions must take into account the dynamic basis of interest to be effective.

Dynamic Analysis By emphasizing that there are differences in interest regulation processes both between and within individuals over time, our model opens up a host of complicated questions about how interest changes. For instance, our framework raises questions not only about *mean-level* group differences in interest, but also about group differences in interest *trajectories over time* (i.e., differences in the stability of interests). Further, our model allows us to ask more nuanced questions about how mechanisms involved in interest development might play into the interest regulation process. For example, we can ask how changes in perceived competence over the span of a semester might be coupled with changes in interest in order to determine if changes in one necessarily entail changes in the other.

Using traditional analytic approaches, we are unable to answer these complex, temporal questions. Along with other interest researchers (e.g., Goetz, Sticca, Pekrun, Murayama, & Elliot, 2016; Knogler, Harackiewicz, Gegenfurtner, & Lewalter, 2015; Tanaka & Murayama, 2014) we recognize the importance of new statistical approaches to test these questions. We believe that integrating a dynamic systems analysis can be very effective, because it allows modeling of multicomponent systems that interact to form complex temporal patterns (Butner, Gagnon, Geuss, Lessard, & Story, 2014). A variety of statistical techniques commonly used in systems modeling (e.g., multilevel modeling, structural equation modeling) can help us to describe and predict both between-groups and within-groups change in interest over time. Thus, dynamic systems approaches are key to helping us answer some of the more complicated, unresolved questions that follow from a dynamic model of interest.

Conclusions

Interest is often described as a static binary variable: you have it or you do not. At any one snapshot in time, this depiction might accurately describe a person's experience. Our approach to the psychological study of interest underscores that interest is far more complex and dynamic, particularly when considering how the experience of interest functions within a broader self-regulatory system in which motivation drives behavior and emerges during ongoing engagement. One's experience of interest necessarily fluctuates over time, but our model suggests that these changes are not capricious and that interest can in fact be purposely monitored and regulated. When we investigate experiences of people situated within activity contexts over time, we can better understand the causes and consequences of interest and the role of the interest experience in maintaining motivation over time.

References

Allen, J., Muragishi, G. A., Smith, J. L., Thoman, D. B., & Brown, E. R. (2015). To grab and to hold: Cultivating communal goals to overcome cultural and structural barriers in first generation college students' science interest. *Translational Issues in Psychological Science, 1*, 331–341. doi:10.1037/tps0000046.

Bandura, A. (1991). Social cognitive theory of self-regulation. *Organizational Behavior and Human Decision Processes, 50*(2), 248–287.

Barron, K. E., & Harackiewicz, J. M. (2001). Achievement goals and optimal motivation: Testing multiple goals models. *Journal of Personality and Social Psychology, 80*, 706–722. doi:10.1037/0022-3514.80.5.706.

Blackwell, L. S., Trzesniewski, K. H., & Dweck, C. S. (2007). Implicit theories of intelligence predict achievement across an adolescent transition: A longitudinal study and an intervention. *Child Development, 78*, 246–263. doi:10.1111/j.1467-8624.2007.00995.x.

Bonanno, G. A., & Burton, C. L. (2013). Regulatory flexibility: An individual differences perspective on coping and emotion regulation. *Perspectives on Psychological Science, 8*, 591–612. doi:10.1177/1745691613504116.

Butner, J. E., Gagnon, K. T., Geuss, M. N., Lessard, D. A., & Story, T. N. (2014). Utilizing topology to generate and test theories of change. *Psychological Methods*, 1–25. doi:10.1037/a0037802.

Canning, E. A., & Harackiewicz, J. M. (2015). Teach it, don't preach it: The differential effects of directly-communicated and self-generated utility value information. *Motivational Science, 1*, 47–71. doi:10.1037/mot0000015.

Carver, C. S., & Scheier, M. (1990). Principles of self-regulation: Action and emotion. In E. T. Higgins & R. M. Sorrentino (Eds.), *Handbook of motivation and cognition: Foundations of social behavior* (Vol. 2, pp. 3–52). New York: Guilford Press.

Cohen, G. L., & Garcia, J. (2008). Identity, belonging, and achievement: A model, interventions, implications. *Current Directions in Psychological Science, 17*, 365–369. doi:10.1111/j.1467-8721.2008.00607.x.

Csikszentmihalyi, M. (1975). Play and intrinsic rewards. *Journal of Humanistic Psychology, 15*(3), 41–63. doi:10.1177/002216787501500306.

Curti, C., Zambrano, J., Lee, G., Jackson, M. C., & Thoman, D. B. (2016). The importance of feedback appraisals when women share interests in STEM. Poster presented at the annual meeting for the Society for Personality and Social Psychology, San Diego, CA.

Deci, E. L., & Ryan, R. M. (2000). The "what" and "why" of goal pursuits: Human needs and the self-determination of behavior. *Psychological Inquiry, 11*, 227–268.

Diekman, A. B., Brown, E. R., Johnston, A. M., & Clark, E. K. (2010). Seeking congruity between goals and roles: A new look at why women opt out of science, technology, engineering, and mathematics careers. *Psychological Science, 21*(8), 1051–1057. doi:10.1177/0956797610377342.

Durik, A. M., Shechter, O. G., Noh, M., Rozek, C. S., & Harackiewicz, J. M. (2014). What if I can't? Success expectancies moderate the effects of utility value information on situational interest and performance. *Motivation and Emotion, 39*, 104–118.

Eccles, J. S., & Wigfield, A. (2002). Motivational beliefs, values, and goals. *Annual Review of Psychology, 53*, 109–132.

Fazio, R. H., Zanna, M. P., & Cooper, J. (1977). Dissonance and self-perception: An integrative view of each theory's proper domain of application. *Journal of Experimental Social Psychology, 13*, 464–479.

Festinger, L., & Carlsmith, J. M. (1959). Cognitive consequences of forced compliance. *Journal of Abnormal and Social Psychology, 56*, 276–278.

Gilbert, D. T., Killingsworth, M. A., Eyre, R. N., & Wilson, T. D. (2009). The surprising power of neighborly advice. *Science, 323*, 1617–1619. doi:10.1126/science.1166632.

Goetz, T., Sticca, F., Pekrun, R., Murayama, K., & Elliot, A. J. (2016). Intraindividual relations between achievement goals and discrete achievement emotions: An experience sampling approach. *Learning and Instruction, 41*, 115–125. doi:10.1016/j.learninstruc.2015.10.007.

Harackiewicz, J. M., Canning, E. A., Tibbetts, Y., Priniski, S. J., & Hyde, J. S. (2016). Closing achievement gaps with a utility-value intervention: Disentangling race and social class. *Journal of Personality and Social Psychology, 111*, 745–765. http://dx.doi.org/10.1037/pspp0000075.

Harackiewicz, J. M., & Elliot, A. J. (1993). Achievement goals and intrinsic motivation. *Journal of Personality and Social Psychology, 65*(5), 904–915. doi:10.1037/0022-3514.65.5.904.

Hidi, S., & Renninger, K. A. (2006). The four-phase model of interest development. *Educational Psychologist, 41*(2), 111–127. doi:10.1207/s15326985ep4102_4.

Holleran, S. E., Whitehead, J., Schamder, T., & Mehl, M. R. (2011). Talking shop and shooting the breeze: A study of workplace conversations and job disengagement among STEM faculty. *Social Psychological and Personality Science, 2*, 65–71. doi:10.1177/1948550610379921.

Hulleman, C. S., & Harackiewicz, J. M. (2009). Promoting interest and performance in high school science classes. *Science, 326*, 1410–1412. doi:10.1126/science.1177067.

Isaac, J. D., Sansone, C., & Smith, J. L. (1999). Other people as a source of interest in an activity. *Journal of Experimental Social Psychology, 35*(3), 239–265. doi:10.1006/jesp.1999.1385.

Jackson, M. C., Galvez, G., Landa, I., Buonora, P., & Thoman, D. B. (2016). Science that matters: The importance of a cultural connection in underrepresented students' science pursuit. *CBE Life Sciences Education, 15*(3), ar42.

Klaaren, K. J., Hodges, S. D., & Wilson, T. D. (1994). The role of affective expectations in subjective experience and decision-making. *Social Cognition, 12*, 77–101.

Knogler, M., Harackiewicz, J. M., Gegenfurtner, A., & Lewalter, D. (2015). How situational is situational interest? Investigating the longitudinal structure of situational interest. *Contemporary Educational Psychology, 43*, 39–50. doi:10.1016/j.cedpsych.2015.08.004.

Lepper, M., Sagotsky, G., Dafoe, J. L., & Greene, D. (1982). Consequences of superfluous social constraints: Effects on young children's social influences and subsequent intrinsic interest. *Journal of Personality and Social Psychology, 42*(1), 51–65. doi:10.1037/0022-3514.42.1.51.

Major, B., Quinton, W. J., & Schmader, T. (2003). Attributions to discrimination and self-esteem: Impact of group identification and situational ambiguity. *Journal of Experimental Social Psychology, 39*(3), 220–231. doi:10.1016/S0022-1031(02)00547-4.

Miele, D. B., & Scholer, A. A. (2016). Self-regulation of motivation. In K. R. Wentzel & D. B. Miele (Eds.), *Handbook of motivation at school*. New York: Routledge.

Morf, C. C., Weir, C., & Davidov, M. (2000). Narcissism and intrinsic motivation: The role of goal congruence. *Journal of Experimental Social Psychology, 36*(4), 424–438. doi:10.1006/jesp.1999.1421.

Morgan, C., Isaac, J. D., & Sansone, C. (2001). The role of interest in understanding the career choices of female and male college students. *Sex Roles, 44*(5–6), 295–320. doi:10.1023/A:1010929600004.

Moss-Racusin, C. A., Dovidio, J. F., Brescoll, V. L., Graham, M. J., & Handelsman, J. (2012). Science faculty's subtle gender biases favor male students. *Proceedings of the National Academy of the Sciences, 109*, 16474–16479. doi:10.1073/pnas.1211286109.

O'Keefe, P. A., Dweck, C. S., & Walton, G. M. (2016, in preparation). Implicit theories of interest: Finding your passion or developing it? *Unpublished manuscript.*

O'Keefe, P. A., & Linnenbrink-Garcia, L. (2014). The role of interest in optimizing performance and self-regulation. *Journal of Experimental Social Psychology, 53*, 70–78. doi:10.1016/j.jesp.2014.02.004.

Pasupathi, M. (2001). The social construction of the personal past and its implications for adult development. *Psychological Bulletin, 127*(5), 651–672. doi:10.1037/0033-2909.127.5.651.

Pasupathi, M., & Rich, B. (2005). Inattentive listening undermines self-verification in personal storytelling. *Journal of Personality, 73*, 1051–1086. doi:10.1111/j.1467-6494.2005.00338.x.

Plass, J., O'Keefe, P. A., Homer, B. D., Case, J., Hayward, E., Stein, M., & Perlin, K. (2013). The impact of individual, competitive, and collaborative mathematics game play on learning, performance, and motivation. *Journal of Educational Psychology, 105*, 1050–1066. doi:10.1037/a0032688.

Renninger, K. A., & Hidi, S. (2011). Revisiting the conceptualization, measurement, and generation of interest. *Educational Psychologist, 46*, 168–184. doi:10.1080/00461520.2011.587723.

Renninger, K. A., & Hidi, S. (2016). *The power of interest for motivation and learning*. New York: Routledge.

Sansone, C. (2009). What's interest got to do with it?: Potential trade-offs in the self-regulation of motivation. In J. P. Forgas, R. Baumiester, & D. Tice (Eds.), *Psychology of self-regulation: Cognitive, affective, and motivational processes* (pp. 35–51). New York: Psychology Press.

Sansone, C., Butner, J., Fraughton, T. B., & Zachary, J. L. (2011, April) Self-regulatory trade-offs when learning online: Interested engagement can hurt AND help. In P. O'Keefe & I. Plante (chairs), *Developments in Interest Theory and Research*. Symposium presented at the annual meeting of the American Educational Research Association, New Orleans, LA.

Sansone, C., & Harackiewicz, J. M. (1996). "I don't feel like it": The function of interest in self-regulation. In L. L. Martin & A. Tesser (Eds.), *Striving and feeling: Interactions among goals, affect, and self-regulation* (pp. 203–228). Hillsdale, NJ, England: Lawrence Erlbaum Associates, Inc.

Sansone, C., & Harackiewicz, J. M. (2000). Controversies and new directions—Is it déjà vu all over again? In *Intrinsic and extrinsic motivation: The search for optimal motivation and performance* (pp. 443–453). San Diego, CA: Academic Press.

Sansone, C., & Morgan, C. (1992). Intrinsic motivation and education: Competence in context. *Motivation and Emotion, 16*, 249–270. doi:10.1007/BF00991654.

Sansone, C., Sachau, D. A., & Weir, C. (1989). Effects of instruction on intrinsic interest: The importance of context. *Journal of Personality and Social Psychology, 57*(5), 819–829. doi:10.1037/0022-3514.57.5.819.

Sansone, C., & Smith, J. L. (2000). The "how" of goal pursuit: Interest and self-regulation. *Psychological Inquiry, 11*(4), 306–309.

Sansone, C., Smith, J. L., Thoman, D. B., & MacNamara, A. (2012). Regulating interest when learning online: Potential motivation and performance trade-offs. *The Internet and Higher Education, 15*, 141–149. doi:10.1016/j.iheduc.2011.10.004.

Sansone, C., & Thoman, D. B. (2006). Maintaining activity engagement: Individual differences in the process of self-regulating motivation. *Journal of Personality, 74*, 1697–1720. doi:10.1111/j.1467-6494.2006.00425.x.

Sansone, C., Thoman, D., & Fraughton, T. (2015). The relation between interest and self-regulation in mathematics and science. *Interest in K-16 mathematics and science learning in and out of school*, 111–131.

Sansone, C., & Thoman, D. B. (2005). Interest as the missing motivator in self-regulation. *European Psychologist, 10*(3), 175–186. doi:10.1027/1016-9040.10.3.175.

Sansone, C., Weir, C., Harpster, L., & Morgan, C. (1992). Once a boring task always a boring task? Interest as a self-regulatory mechanism. *Journal of Personality and Social Psychology, 63*, 379–390. doi:10.1037/0022-3514.63.3.379.

Sansone, C., Wiebe, D. J., & Morgan, C. L. (1999). Self-regulating motivation: The moderating role of hardiness and conscientiousness. *Journal of Personality, 67*, 701–733. doi:10.1111/1467-6494.00070.

Silvia, P. J. (2005). What is interesting? Exploring the appraisal structure of interest. *Emotion, 5*(1), 89–102. doi:10.1037/1528-3542.5.1.89.

Silvia, P. J. (2006). *Exploring the psychology of interest*. New York: Oxford.

Silvia, P. J., Henson, R. A., & Templin, J. L. (2009). Are the sources of interest the same for everyone? Using multilevel mixture models to explore individual differences in appraisal structures. *Cognition and Emotion, 23*(7), 1389–1406. doi:10.1080/02699930902850528.

Smith, J. L., & Ruiz, J. M. (2007). Interpersonal orientation in context: Correlates and effects of interpersonal complementarity on subjective and cardiovascular experiences. *Journal of Personality, 75*(4), 679–708. doi:10.1111/j.1467-6494.2007.00453.x.

Stone, J., & Cooper, J. (2001). A self-standards model of cognitive dissonance. *Journal of Experimental Social Psychology, 37*, 228–243.

Tanaka, A., & Murayama, K. (2014). Within-person analyses of situational interest and boredom: Interactions between task-specific perceptions and achievement goals. *Journal of Educational Psychology, 106*(4), 1122–1134. doi:10.1037/a0036659.

Tauer, J. M., & Harackiewicz, J. M. (2004). The effects of cooperation and competition on intrinsic motivation and performance. *Journal of Personality and Social Psychology, 86*, 849–861. doi:10.1037/h0087892.

Thoman, D. B., Brown, E. R., Mason, A. Z., Harmsen, A. G., & Smith, J. L. (2015). The role of altruistic values in motivating underrepresented minority students for biomedicine. *BioScience, 65*(2), 183–188. doi:10.1093/biosci/biu199.

Thoman, D. B., & Sansone, C. (2016). Gender bias triggers diverging science interests between women and men: The role of activity interest appraisals. *Motivation and Emotion*. Advanced online publication. doi: 10.1007/s11031-016-9550-1.

Thoman, D. B., Sansone, C., Fraughton, T., & Pasupathi, M. (2012). How students socially evaluate interest: Peer responsiveness influences evaluation and maintenance of interest. *Contemporary Educational Psychology, 37*, 254–265. doi:10.1016/j.cedpsych.2012.04.001.

Thoman, D. B., Sansone, C., & Pasupathi, M. (2007). Talking about interest: Exploring the role of social interaction for regulating motivation and the interest experience. *Journal of Happiness Studies, 8*(3), 335–370. doi:10.1007/s10902-006-9016-3.

Thoman, D. B., Sansone, C., & Robinson, J. (2016). Implicit theories of interest regulation. *Unpublished manuscript*.

Thoman, D. B., Smith, J. L., Brown, E. R., Chase, J., & Lee, J. Y. K. (2013). Beyond performance: A motivational experiences model of stereotype threat. *Educational Psychology Review, 25*(2), 211–243. doi:10.1007/s10648-013-9219-1.
Thoman, D. B., Smith, J. L., & Silvia, P. J. (2011). The resource replenishment function of interest. *Social Psychological and Personality Science, 2*(6), 592–599. doi:10.1177/1948550611402521.

Chapter 3
The Multifaceted Role of Interest in Motivation and Engagement

Paul A. O'Keefe, E.J. Horberg, and Isabelle Plante

Why does interest matter? *Wanting* to engage in an activity is a powerful motivator for initiating and maintaining engagement, as well as re-engagement, over time (Sansone & Smith, 2000; Chap. 2, this volume). Whether people want to understand something unexpected or novel, or whether they have a deep personal connection with a topic, interest elicits intrinsic motivation to engage in particular content or activities. That is, interest can spark and maintain intrinsic motivation—interest "motivates exploration and learning, and guarantees the person's engagement in the environment" (Izard & Ackerman, 2000, p. 257). As a motivational variable, interest plays key roles in organizing attention (e.g., Ainley, Hidi, & Berndorff, 2002; McDaniel, Waddill, Finstad, & Bourg, 2000), enhancing self-regulation (e.g., O'Keefe & Linnenbrink-Garcia, 2014; Sansone, Weir, Harpster, & Morgan, 1992), and facilitating achievement (e.g., Hulleman & Harackiewicz, 2009; O'Keefe & Linnenbrink-Garcia, 2014). In this fashion, interest plays a fundamental and multifaceted role in goal pursuit.

Author Note:
Paul A. O'Keefe, Division of Social Sciences, Yale-NUS College and Department of Management and Organisation, NUS Business School, National University of Singapore (by courtesy); E. J. Horberg, Division of Social Sciences, Yale-NUS College; Isabelle Plante, Département d'éducation et formation spécialisées, University of Quebec, Montreal.

P.A. O'Keefe (✉)
Department of Psychology,
Yale-NUS College, Singapore

Management and Organisation, NUS Business School,
National University of Singapore, Singapore
e-mail: paul.okeefe@yale-nus.edu.sg

E.J. Horberg
Department of Psychology, Yale-NUS College, Singapore, Singapore

I. Plante
University of Quebec, Montreal, Quebec, Canada

© Springer International Publishing AG 2017
P.A. O'Keefe, J.M. Harackiewicz (eds.), *The Science of Interest*,
DOI 10.1007/978-3-319-55509-6_3

49

Interest can be elicited both externally and internally, and broadly speaking, researchers classify these two types as *situational interest* and *individual interest*, respectively. Situational interest is elicited by a source external to the individual. A physics professor, for example, might pique students' situational interest by conducting an exciting class demonstration that grabs their attention. By contrast, individual interest refers to the personal interests we hold over time and across situations. They are idiosyncratic, valued, enduring, and part of our identity. Therefore, individual interest is dispositional; although it can be sparked by situational factors, it is not necessary. The same physics professor pursued a career in the field because of her deep, abiding interest in the topic. Once her interest in physics became internalized, she did not need external supports to maintain her motivation. Instead, she was motivated to engage in those interests by her own volition over time.

Furthermore, interest is content specific and has a learning function. Situational interest has a relation to content such that it might be unexpected, novel, complex, or mysterious, which makes salient a gap in one's knowledge—a gap that motivates people to engage with the content. Individual interest, on the other hand, can spark motivation and engagement because of its relation to particular content or activities one personally values. Someone with an individual interest in basketball would be motivated to play and engage in the sport. In other words, individual interest relates to content meaningful to the person. Furthermore, engagement may reinforce the positive feelings they have for the domain and increase understanding and stored knowledge.

Because interest, motivation, and engagement are highly related constructs, and the terms are often used interchangeably, they are worth distinguishing. A first distinction pertains to interest versus intrinsic motivation. Despite the fact that the constructs may correlate, they are conceptually separable. Intrinsic motivation refers to the desire to do something for its own sake, which occurs when engagement satisfies the need for competence and control (Deci & Ryan, 2000; Sansone & Harackiewicz, 2000). Notice that this is void of content—it refers only to a process. By contrast, interest has a relation with particular content and is a psychological state associated with increased attention, effort, concentration, and changes in affect while engaging with that content (Renninger & Hidi, 2016). Second, a distinction should also be made between motivation and engagement. Generally speaking, motivation refers to one's will or desire to do something, whereas engagement refers to one's actual involvement in an activity (Renninger & Hidi, 2016). Like motivation, engagement is theoretically void of content, and both constructs may or may not be influenced by interest.

The purpose of this chapter is to highlight several important roles interest plays in motivation and engagement. We begin by discussing how interest is experienced psychologically, with a focus on its relation to attention, affect, and one's mode of engagement. Next, we discuss implicit theories of interest—whether interests are believed to be inherent and fixed, or developed and subject to growth—and how implicit theories of interest can thwart or facilitate engagement. We then turn to a discussion of research on the relation of interest to task performance and persistence, and how different modes of interested engagement can affect these outcomes.

Finally, we discuss how interest can be an outcome, rather than an antecedent, of engagement. This chapter is not meant to be an exhaustive review but instead highlights important themes and findings in scientific examinations of interest as a motivational variable.

Psychological Engagement: The Experience of Interest

One of the factors that make interest an important motivational process is how it is experienced. Our experience of an activity can influence whether we are intrinsically motivated to maintain engagement or to re-engage in it in the future. How interest influences our attention and affect are two particularly important aspects of the experience. Furthermore, our attention and affect can vary widely, and different patterns of engagement tend to emerge depending on qualities of the situation or the activity. This section will explore these issues in more detail.

Interest and Attention

> Millions of items of the outward order are present to my senses which never properly enter into my experience. Why? Because they have no interest for me. My experience is what I agree to attend to. Only those items which I notice shape my mind—without selective interest, experience is an utter chaos. Interest alone gives accent and emphasis, light and shade, background and foreground—intelligible perspective, in a word. (James, 1890/1950, p. 402)

As William James suggested, interest has tremendous influence on our attention. More recently, research has shown that the relation between interest and attention is fascinatingly paradoxical, as interest can heighten attention yet reduce the need for attentional resources. When interest is aroused by external contextual features—whether it is because of something novel or complex, or whether it elicits uncertainty or conflict—our attention is piqued so that we can appraise and understand what we are experiencing (Berlyne, 1960; Silvia, 2005). To this end, interest can initiate intrinsically motivated learning and exploration (Silvia, 2008), such that the attention triggered by interest leads to learning about the world, others, and oneself.

Paradoxically, although we intuitively experience heightened attention while working on an interesting task, interest tends to reduce the need for attentional resources. Research shows that attention allocated during interesting tasks minimizes the self-regulatory resources needed (McDaniel et al., 2000; O'Keefe & Linnenbrink-Garcia, 2014). That is, interest can elicit spontaneous, rather than controlled, allocation of attention (Hidi, 1990, 1995). If a task is interesting, then it requires little-to-no effort to attend to it. In contrast, a boring task requires more attentional resources because people must self-regulate in order to maintain focus.

In a study by Shirey and Reynolds (1988), undergraduates read a set of individual sentences, one by one. After reading each sentence, students rated how interesting they thought it was. On half of the trials, a tone would sound and they were asked to indicate when they heard it. The researchers found that the greater the students' interest, the faster they were to recognize and respond to the tones. In other words, interesting sentences freed up attentional resources, allowing students to more quickly detect the tone. Similar results have been obtained in other research (e.g., Anderson, 1982; McDaniel et al., 2000).

Shirey and Reynolds (1988) also found that students' interest predicted recall of the sentences and shorter reading durations. Thus, although interest decreased the use of their attentional resources, it appeared to have increased the efficiency of engagement. Students spent less time reading while also recalling more content. How? Interest is also associated with a deep level of processing. For example, Schiefele and Krapp (1996) asked students to read a psychology essay and to then recall as much of it as they could. Their responses were later coded for various levels of processing. As predicted, the higher students' interest in the text, the more likely they were to recall individual ideas from the text and its main ideas. Furthermore, students were more likely to report new ideas—which demonstrated they had elaborated on the information in the essay—and to more accurately recall the sequence in which the ideas were presented. Similar findings have been found in longitudinal studies conducted in more naturalistic settings, such as classrooms (e.g., Krapp, 1999).

Interest and Affect

Although we tend to think of interest as a generally positive experience, interest—particularly situational interest—can feel either positive or negative. For example, when viewing the Milky Way on a clear night, people might experience it positively, accompanied by feelings of enjoyment, awe, or fascination. On the other hand, people could have their interest likewise piqued while driving passed a horrific traffic accident, causing them to examine the wreckage for something tragic. Horror and thriller films have a similar effect—we might be drawn to watch something that we know will fill us with fear, anxiety, or disgust, demonstrating that we can be both powerfully allured and attracted even as we are repelled (Miller, 1998).

Particular positive and negative experiences can also elicit interest. Silvia (2006; Chap. 5, this volume) argues that interest, in part, functions to counteract enjoyment and anxiety. If we continue to re-engage in something that we know will be enjoyable, we might never try anything new and forgo important learning opportunities. Similarly, if we avoid anything novel—possibly evoking uncertainty or conflict—we would not learn anything new. Interest, whether it is motivated by a positive or negative experience, motivates engagement.

Although situational interest can be associated with both positive and negative affect, people's more enduring and dispositional interests (i.e., individual interests), however, are typically associated with positive affect. We tend to engage with content and activities that make us feel good or contribute to the possibility of positive affect in the future, such as making progress toward our long-term goals. The four-phase model of interest development, proposed by Hidi and Renninger (2006), suggests that, although interest can be experienced positively or negatively when situational interest is triggered, it becomes experienced more positively as interest develops. As people begin to find relevance or personal value in particular content or activities, interest becomes more internalized and enduring. In turn, people develop positive feelings for the content or activity and freely choose to re-engage in them over time.

The Scope of Attention and Modes of Engagement

As discussed earlier, we often experience interest as something that *narrows* and focuses the scope of attention, such as when we try to solve a fascinating puzzle or when learning a challenging song on guitar. Narrowed attention can seemingly shut out competing stimuli, and the world appears to fade into the background. Other times we find ourselves in a more exploratory mindset where attention is *broad* in scope and our curiosity guides our engagement, such as when we explore different strategies for solving a puzzle. Both modes are important and lead to different modes of engagement.

One instantiation of extreme interest where attention feels narrowed and focused is *flow* (Csíkszentmihályi, 1990). Flow is a relatively rare psychological state during which one experiences several things. First, one's full attention is on the activity at hand. There is a loss of self-awareness, and objects outside of one's immediate interaction are not noticed. This seemingly contradicts prior work showing that interest reduces the need for controlled attentional resources (e.g., Anderson, 1982; McDaniel et al., 2000; Shirey & Reynolds, 1988); however, it could be argued that interest in particular sentences—as examined by Shirey and Reynolds (1988)—is qualitatively different than being enraptured by an activity. Furthermore, in a flow state, people feel a complete sense of control. Perhaps more importantly, they lack anxiety about losing control, such as a baseball pitcher experiencing flow in the middle of a no-hitter. Finally, a flow state alters one's sense of time. One is so invested in his or her moment-to-moment experiences that they lose track of the duration of their engagement. Although this is often the case during flow states, it is not exclusively so. Activities that are time sensitive, such as many competitive sports, require people to be conscious of time.

How do flow states come about? Csíkszentmihályi, Abuhamdeh, and Nakamura (2005) outline three primary conditions. First, flow requires a clearly set goal. The goal provides purpose and direction during engagement. Second, there must be a balance between the perceived required skill level for the task and one's perception of their actual skill level. In other words, they must be working at the edge of their abilities. For example, it would be difficult for professional musicians to experience flow if they were merely practicing scales. If they were in the middle of a challenging improvisation, however, it would require their full attention. Finally, the activity must provide clear and immediate feedback. Such feedback allows people to make online evaluations of their performance and progress.

While engaged, however, we are not always so narrow in focus. Flow is a relatively rare occurrence, after all. Instead, sometimes our interest causes us to be more broadly attentive. As previously noted, with some exceptions, interest is typically experienced positively. Fredrickson (1998; also see Izard, 1977) argued that positive emotions have a "broaden-and-build" effect, such that they broaden people's momentary thought-action repertoire, which in turn builds physical, intellectual, and social resources. Interest, she argues, is one of these emotions and has the function of exploration.

Carver and Scheier (2004) posited a somewhat similar thesis. They argued that affect operates as a self-regulatory feedback loop to inform people about their progress toward goals—it signals what action is needed. Negative affect signals that goal progress is deficient. Positive affect, on the other hand, signals that one is on track or has done better than needed. In this case, positive affect would last a relatively short period of time and ease on back to a neutral state. During that time, however, people are free to explore more broadly because their current needs are met. This process is called "coasting" (Carver, 2003).

What causes interest to broaden versus narrow the scope of one's attention? Often the goals in an exploratory state are not well defined, thus leading to a broader scope of attention. Working on a novel puzzle, for example, might motivate us to explore strategies for solving it, but without much familiarity with a particular type of puzzle, clear goals for solving it cannot be articulated. Furthermore, the perceived required skill level is too discrepant from one's perception of their current skill level. Without familiarity of a particular type of puzzle, our skill level does not match the skill needed to solve the puzzle. Consequently, obtaining immediate performance feedback would not be possible. Finally, the purpose of engagement might specifically be to explore, such that one searches for novel strategies for solving the puzzle without being concerned about performance. By contrast, a narrow scope of attention is likely to result from a focused state in which one seeks to perform well on a familiar activity for which one's skill level is appropriate to the demands of the task. Thus, interest can broaden or narrow attention for various reasons.

To sum, the psychological and experiential effects of interest are complex and varied. Interest can increase attention without increasing the allocation of attentional resources, it can instigate and cause both positive and negative affect, and it can cause us to narrow or broaden our attention. Together, interest, along with its attendant effects on affect and attention, serves to fill gaps in our knowledge and to aid the pursuit of goals. Additional empirical research will be needed to further understand how interest can influence the narrow and broad scope of attention.

The Role of Implicit Theories of Interest in Triggering Engagement

What prompts interest-based engagement in the first place? As discussed above, there are a number of reasons interest is elicited by an external source—novelty, complexity, conflict, or something unexpected. Another reason that has received less attention in the literature, however, concerns people's beliefs about the nature of interests—that is, the role of *implicit theories of interest*. Before engaging in particular activities or content areas, people approach the situation armed with different beliefs about the malleability of interest. They might believe that interests are fixed, inherent, and "revealed" at some point, or they might instead believe interests are developed and able to change and grow. These distinct beliefs about the nature of interest create meaning systems that influence the way people interpret their involvement with certain activities and content areas, as well as how to manage their engagement. Consequently, these two implicit theories have important implications for motivation and engagement, which have been examined by O'Keefe, Dweck, and Walton (2015).

First, if interests are believed to be inherent (a "fixed" theory) and one's interests have already been discovered, then it should preclude the adoption of other interests. In other words, if one's "true" interests have already been found, why keep looking for others? By contrast, engagement has a different meaning for someone who believes interests are developed (a "growth" theory). If interests are believed to be developed, then new interests can be fostered despite having already established core interests.

To examine these hypotheses, O'Keefe and colleagues (2015) designed an experiment that introduced fixed and growth theorists to topics that either matched or mismatched their core interests. They recruited college students who reported a well-developed interest in either the arts and humanities or science and technology in prescreening (those who reported interest in both or neither were not invited to participate). During the prescreen, they also measured students' implicit theory of interest by asking them to report their level of agreement with questions such as "You can be exposed to new things, but your core interests won't really change." At a later date, students came to the lab and read two articles taken from real academic journals. One was related to the arts and humanities and the other was related to science and technology. After reading each article, they rated their level of interest in it. The stronger students' fixed theory, the less interested they were in the mismatching article. For example, someone with a well-developed interest in the arts and humanities expressed relatively little interest in the science and technology article, as compared to students with a stronger growth theory. Both fixed and growth theorists, however, expressed the same amount of interest in the article that matched their area of well-developed interest. Critically, these findings held when controlling for the strength with which students held their core interest and the degree to which they were open to new experiences. These results were also replicated in a study that experimentally induced theories of interest by having participants first read a persuasive editorial-type article that either promoted a fixed or growth theory.

Another implication stemming from implicit theories of interest is that they will influence one's motivation to pursue a new, strong interest (i.e., a passion) in different ways. If interests are thought to be inherent, then when discovered, they should provide limitless motivation and be relatively easy to pursue. If an activity is difficult and one's motivation wavers, then it must not be a "true" interest after all. By contrast, if interests are developed, then they should grow over time, and the developmental process should be expected to present challenges along the way. Supporting these assertions, a survey in which undergraduates wrote about what it is like to find a passion showed that those with a stronger fixed theory were more likely to believe that passions would provide limitless motivation. By contrast, those with a stronger growth theory were more likely to mention that pursuing passions would be difficult at times.

If a fixed theory is associated with the belief that pursuing a new interest should be limitlessly motivating, then what happens when pursuing that interest actually becomes difficult? To answer this question, O'Keefe and his colleagues (2015) recruited undergraduates early in their college career—when students are "finding" their interests—and brought them to the lab. The students were first randomly induced to hold either a fixed or growth theory of interest. Then, to spark an interest, students watched a short, fun, animated video on Stephen Hawking's theories about black holes, which most (80%) found fascinating. Those participants moved on to the next part of the study, in which they read the first page of an article on black holes taken from *Science*—significantly more substantive and more difficult to understand than the video. Afterward, they rated their interest in black holes and also reported their perceived difficulty in understanding the article.

What happened to people's interest in black holes now that engaging in the topic became difficult? Would their motivational expectations be confirmed and affect their level of interest? For those who thought the article was easy to understand, there was no difference in the level of interest in the black holes article between those induced with a fixed or growth theory—after all, pursuing their new interest never became difficult. But for those who perceived the article to be difficult to understand, a different pattern emerged. For those induced with a fixed theory, their interest dropped dramatically. For those induced with a growth theory, their interest dropped a bit, but not nearly as much compared to those in the fixed condition. In fact, the mean for those in the fixed-theory condition was statistically significantly below the midpoint of the scale, suggesting that a topic they found fascinating approximately 5 min earlier was now uninteresting to them. In comparison, those in the growth condition maintained an interest in the topic, presumably because the difficulty they encountered did not conflict with their expectations or cause them to second-guess their initial excitement about the topic.

This research shows that people's basic beliefs about the nature of interest—whether interests are inherent or if they grow through a developmental process—have important consequences for motivation and engagement. A fixed theory limits the scope of possible interests and creates potentially maladaptive expectations about how easy it is to pursue "true" interests. By contrast, a growth theory is associated with a larger scope of interests and potentially adaptive motivational patterns once pursuing those interests becomes difficult.

The Role of Interest in Task Performance and Persistence

As we have discussed, interest can elicit intrinsic motivation, but does it facilitate effective goal pursuit? In a word, yes, but its relation to task performance and persistence is not straightforward. Because interest can narrow or broaden one's attention, it has the potential to increase or decrease task performance and persistence. As previously mentioned, broadened attention is associated with exploration, which can be critical for learning and other goal pursuits. It may, for example, increase persistence but decrease performance on a novel task because the individual might prioritize finding new strategies for solving problems over their actual performance on those problems. Narrowed attention, however, is usually associated with a clearly defined goal and a reasonable understanding of how to achieve it. Therefore, it can decrease time spent on the task but increase performance. In other words, interest can lead to different modes of engagement. In this section, we discuss research demonstrating this complex relation between interest and task performance and persistence.

Interest and Performance

To begin, it is well documented that interest can increase learning and performance (e.g., Durik, Shechter, Noh, Rozek, & Harackiewicz, 2015; Harackiewicz, Barron, Tauer, & Elliot, 2002; Hulleman, Godes, Hendricks, & Harackiewicz, 2010; O'Keefe & Linnenbrink-Garcia, 2014; Schiefele, Krapp, & Winteler, 1992). For example, in a study by Hulleman and Harackiewicz (2009), high school science students were asked to write about science topics throughout the semester. In a control condition, students periodically summarized what they were learning in their class—not dissimilar from what teachers typically ask their students to do. In the treatment condition, students periodically wrote about how what they were learning was relevant to their lives. In other words, the latter group made personal connections between the material and its usefulness. The benefits of the treatment condition were most apparent among students who had initially reported that they expected to perform relatively poorly in the course. After all, they had the most to gain from developing interest in science. At the end of the semester, those students not only reported increased interest in science, but also earned a higher grade—nearly a full letter grade higher—than those in the control condition who expected to perform poorly.

Interest, Performance, and Self-Regulation

How does interest increase performance? As previously mentioned, engagement driven by interest requires less attentional (or cognitive) resources. Conserving resources can help sustain engagement, especially during challenging tasks. Solving the Rubik's Cube, for example, could have a different effect on people depending on whether or not they find it interesting. Those with little interest might become mentally taxed in minutes and give up. Others who have a lot of interest might get deeply engaged, work on it for hours, and make good progress toward solving it. Rather than feeling mentally taxed, they might feel exhilarated by the experience.

Inspired by Csíkszentmihályi's (1990) work on flow, O'Keefe and Linnenbrink-Garcia (2014) sought to understand how people sustain deep levels of focused effort, perform at high levels, and feel energized by the task rather than mentally exhausted. They assumed that two facets of interest played an important role in maintaining mental energy during a task: affect-related interest and value-related interest. Affect-related interest refers to one's feelings of enjoyment, excitement, or fascination with regard to a particular activity, which plays a role in initiating and sustaining engagement. By contrast, value-related interest refers to how important the activity is to oneself or the personal connection one has with it. The researchers theorized that performance would be highest, and energy would be sustained rather than depleted, when both affect-related and value-related interest are high because the experience would be both positive and focused by the value of doing well on the task.

First, the researchers conducted a lab study to test the prediction that performance would be highest when both facets of interest are high. Undergraduates read instructions for a word puzzle they would work on next. After reading the task instructions, but before completing the task, they reported their level of affect-related interest. Afterward, the researchers manipulated participants' value-related interest by framing their performance on the task as either diagnostic of intellectual ability or not diagnostic. Subsequently, participants worked on each puzzle and could progress to the next one at any time until they were done with all five. As predicted, those in the high value condition who also reported high affect-related interest performed the best.

To test their second hypothesis—that high affect-related and high value-related interest would optimize performance while buffering against mental exhaustion—the researchers conducted a second study in which participants first read the instructions for an anagram task that was to follow. Before beginning, the task, participants reported their affect- and value-related interest for the task; then they worked on a set of 20 anagrams for 5 min. Up to this point, however, participants were under the impression that the anagrams were for an unrelated pilot study. This cover story was used to ensure that the anagram task was not framed as a challenge and that engagement would not be motivated by the desire for achievement, but instead by their interest in the task.

After the anagram task, the experimenter returned to inform the participants that they would now begin the "real" study, which involved holding a hand grip—the type used for exercise—closed for as long as they could. If they felt they had exhausted themselves on the anagram task, then they would be less able to override the impulse to let go of the grip when it became difficult. In other words, the longer participants were able to hold the grip closed, the more perceived resources they would have had left over from the prior task. As predicted, people who reported both high affect- and value-related interest solved among the most anagrams but showed the least depletion on the hand-grip task—their high performance did not come at the cost of mental exhaustion. On the whole, these findings suggest that the combination of high affect- and value-related interest buffers against depletion, which has important implications for the role of interest in sustaining engagement.

Modes of Engagement and Performance

The study by O'Keefe and Linnenbrink-Garcia (2014, Study 2) also found that different combinations of affect- and value-related interest impacted performance differently, which may have been influenced by variations in participants' mode of engagement. For example, engaging in a task that is high in affect-related interest but low in value-related interest led to relatively poor performance. This may not be detrimental, however. It might reflect a different mode of interested engagement—an exploratory mode—in which participants prioritized the experience of the task (such as their enjoyment and fascination with the task) and prioritized performing well to a lesser extent. Alternatively, these individuals might have been in another type of exploratory mode, in which they experimented with new strategies for completing the problems instead of prioritizing a high score on the task. By contrast, engaging in a task that was low in affect-related interest and high in value-related interest not only led to relatively poor performance, but was also depleting. This result may have stemmed from a different mode of interested engagement—a focused mode—such as when studying for an exam because you want to do well, but you do not enjoy the topic or activities. We encourage future research to empirically investigate how the affect- and value-related interest people hold for particular tasks give rise to different modes of engagement.

Modes of Engagement and the Trade-off Between Task Performance and Persistence

If one's interest is more exploratory in nature, then the purpose of one's engagement will likely be their experience (e.g., fascination, enjoyment) or to understand the task at hand. By contrast, if one's interest in an activity is more focused, performance will likely be of higher priority. This distinction between modes of interested engagement highlights a potential trade-off between task performance and persistence, such that performance may suffer if individuals persist on a task in order to enjoy themselves or hone their skills rather than immediately excel.

These trade-off effects would be expected to go in the opposite direction as well, such as when the needs of a given goal dictate the mode of engagement. In other words, when the purpose of engagement is the experience or to understand, an individual would likely enter into an exploratory mode; when the purpose of engagement is performing well, however, an individual would likely enter into a focused mode of engagement. Along these lines, in a study by Sansone and colleagues (1992), participants worked on a task that was either uninteresting (copying letter matrices) or interesting (searching for words in those matrices). Half of the participants in the uninteresting condition were also told that there were health benefits to copying the letter matrices, thereby giving them a reason to persist on the task. Those in the uninteresting condition who also had a reason to persist spent their time exploring ways to make it more interesting, such as varying the copying procedure, but copied fewer letters overall, suggesting that they had shifted toward an exploratory mode of engagement and prioritized the experiential aspect of the task over performance.

In another study conducted by Sansone, Smith, Thoman, and MacNamara (2012), undergraduates taking an upper-division course online (vs. on campus) tended to explore the online course materials to a greater extent than on-campus students, in an effort to make studying for an exam more enjoyable. Moreover, the subset of online students who reported greater exploration of course materials also reported just as much interest in the course as those who took it on campus, although they did not perform as well. Their efforts to increase their interest through exploration may have detracted from their goal to perform well in the course.

Therefore, interested engagement that is exploratory in nature can come at the cost of performance. But this is not necessarily a problem. Exploration can increase interest and aid learning, which can improve future performance.

Engagement Can Promote Interest

As we have seen, interest can spark intrinsic motivation. This spark can then lead to re-engagement over time, so it is important to consider what qualities of engagement best lead to interest. In this section, we discuss research from multiple theoretical approaches that demonstrates how interest can result from engagement.

Cognitive Dissonance, Insufficient Justification, and Overjustification

In their seminal study, Festinger and Carlsmith (1959) examined how cognitive dissonance could affect beliefs and ultimately one's interest in an activity. They had participants work on two boring tasks. In the first, participants put spools on a tray, one by one, then emptied the tray and repeated this process for half an hour. Next, they were presented with a grid of pegs and were asked to turn each a quarter of the way, one by one. When they finished all of the pegs in the grid, they started the procedure over again and repeated this process for another half an hour. Painfully boring, right? After completing the two tasks, the experimenter asked if the participant would be willing to tell the next participant—a confederate of the study—how great the tasks were. Depending on the condition, participants were told that they would be paid either $1 or $20 in return for their help. Those in the control condition were simply asked to wait in another room.

Afterward, participants were interviewed about their interest in the tasks and provided ratings. Those in the $1 (vs. $20) condition reported greater enjoyment and desire to re-engage in the activities (although this latter effect fell just short of statistical significance). Participants in the $20 condition had a strong justification for why they lied to the confederate—they were being paid quite well. In the $1 condition, however, there was insufficient justification. Participants did not have a good reason for claiming the tasks were fun, so their belief about the interestingness of the task changed to become more aligned with what they said, thereby resolving the dissonance.

Just as insufficient justification can increase interest, overjustification can decrease it. In a classic study, Lepper, Greene, and Nisbett (1973) examined the consequences of offering an external reason for doing what one would normally do for intrinsic reasons. In their study, children who had a preexisting interest in drawing were randomly assigned to one of three conditions. In one condition, children were told they would earn an award for drawing pictures. In the other conditions, they either earned an unexpected award after drawing some pictures or were not told anything about an award. What decreased interest in drawing? Earning an expected award. Expecting the award changed how children interpreted their engagement in the activity. It provided an external reason for doing what they already enjoyed, thereby decreasing their interest in the activity.

Making the Uninteresting Interesting

Aside from resolving dissonance, interest can result from motivated modifications of engagement. For example, when given an uninteresting task, people tend to develop strategies to make it interesting, thus helping them maintain engagement (Sansone et al., 1992; Sansone et al., 2012). Furthermore, when people are permitted to choose how long they work on an activity, they apply these strategies and persist longer (Sansone, Wiebe, & Morgan, 1999). As described earlier, a study by Sansone and colleagues (2012) showed that undergraduates who took a psychology course online—which yielded less overall interest in the course than for those who took it on campus—reported higher levels of interest if they had explored the material on the course website. Together, these studies suggest that people modify their behaviors in order to make engagement more interesting and to maintain motivation.

Social Engagement

Interest can also be sparked by social engagement. Humans are inherently social creatures, and over millennia, we have learned to cooperate and coordinate our collective behaviors. Doing so improved our evolutionary fitness. So it should not be surprising that interacting with others is often experienced positively. Notably, social interaction—whether real or imagined—can maintain or increase interest in particular activities. For example, when participants were led to believe they were working with another person on a challenging task, they persisted longer, reported higher interest and enjoyment in the task, and spent less self-regulatory resources while engaged (Carr & Walton, 2014). Other work by Plass, O'Keefe, and colleagues (2013) examined the effect of playing an educational math video game alone, in competition, or in cooperation with another student. In comparison to playing the game alone, both competition and cooperation—social modes of engagement—increased interest and enjoyment of the math game.

Another person's responsiveness during a social interaction can also influence interest. Pasupathi and Rich (2005) had pairs of friends participate in a study for which one was randomly assigned to play a game and the other was assigned to listen to the player's description of the game afterward. Unbeknownst to the players, these "listeners" were further instructed to be attentive, disagreeable, or distracted (i.e., unresponsive) while listening to their friend's description. Post-game interest was maintained for players whose friend was responsive to their description; that is, their friend was either attentive or disagreeable. When the listener appeared distracted, however, players' interest decreased. Thoman, Sansone, Fraughton, and Pasupathi (2012) found similar results when they examined structured discussions in a forum for an online psychology class. The frequency with which other students responded to students' posts was positively related to their interest in the course. In sum, social interaction can promote interest, and increase motivation and engagement.

Goal Orientations

People vary with regard to their reasons for engaging in particular activities, which color our interpretations of relevant events and how we respond to them. Generally speaking, these are known as goal orientations, which can play an important role in determining whether we sustain or lose interest.

Higgins (1997, 2000) posits that when people engage in a manner that supports rather than disrupts their goal orientation, they experience *regulatory fit*, which makes them "feel right" about their engagement. For example, a student eagerly working to earn an A in a course might do reading beyond what is required or visit a relevant museum. Because the student's eagerness supports the manner of her engagement, she would experience regulatory fit. If that same eager student instead focused on simply meeting the course requirements, she would experience regulatory nonfit. The experience of fit (vs. nonfit), in turn, has been shown to strengthen and sustain engagement (e.g., Freitas & Higgins, 2002; Higgins, Idson, Freitas, Spiegel, & Molden, 2003).

In a study examining the role of regulatory fit in promoting interest, Higgins, Cesario, Hagiwara, Spiegel, and Pittman (2010) had participants play a fun game, who were then given a reward contingent on their performance. Those who were given a reward in a fun and enjoyable way, as opposed to in a serious way, were more likely to voluntarily re-engage in the activity. The manner in which the reward was delivered fit with the participants' goal orientation, thereby sustaining their orientation to have fun. Conversely, the researchers also found increased likelihood of task re-engagement when a serious reward was provided after an important (vs. fun) task.

Research from a different theoretical perspective has also shown a reciprocal relation between the manner of engagement and interest. With regard to competency-related goals, achievement goal theory suggests that there are two main goal orientations that guide engagement. A *learning goal* (also known as a mastery goal) refers to a focus on learning and improvement. A *performance goal*, by contrast, refers to a focus on either demonstrating competencies when positive judgments are expected or avoiding appearing incompetent when negative judgments are expected. Harackiewicz, Durik, Barron, Linnenbrink-Garcia, and Taueret (2008) found a reciprocal relation between interest and a learning goal. Across a semester in an introductory psychology course, students' initial interest in the topic predicted their tendency to adopt a learning goal. That is, having an interest in psychology motivated them to learn more about the subject. In turn, delving into the material enriched their understanding of it, increasing their interest. Not only did engagement in the material lead to increased interest, but this recursive process also continued throughout the semester. Taken together, the various goal orientations we hold while engaged can powerfully shape our level of interest.

Personal Relevance and Utility Value

When one's engagement is personally relevant, interest can increase. As mentioned earlier, Hulleman and Harackiewicz (2009) demonstrated this by having students periodically write about the relevance of what they were learning in their science class to their lives. For students with low perceived competence, not only did writing about the class's relevance increase their interest in the subject, but it also increased their performance. Later, in a randomized controlled field study, researchers targeted high school students indirectly through their parents (Harackiewicz, Rozek, Hulleman, & Hyde, 2012), as parents are an often untapped resource for conveying the importance of science, technology, engineering, and math (STEM) to their children. Across 15 months, the researchers provided parents with brochures and a website with information about the usefulness of STEM in daily life and for various careers. The materials also included suggestions about how to talk with their children about the relevance of STEM to their lives. As compared to the control condition, in which parents did not receive any of the materials described above, the children in the intervention took, on average, nearly one more science and math course in the last two years of high school and reported greater utility value for STEM fields after graduation—both reliable indicators of interest.

Conclusion

Interest sparks a motivational process in which people become driven by what they *want* to do rather than what they feel they *must* do. This chapter has revealed ways in which interest can influence why we initiate, maintain, and re-engage in our goals over time. Because interest can be piqued either by encountering something new and unknown, or by feeling a personal connection to a content area or an activity, it can elicit intrinsic motivation. Moreover, interest can manifest itself in different modes of engagement that aid learning and performance; specifically, interest can either broaden attention, leading us to explore, or narrow attention, causing us to focus. Both modes can help individuals problem-solve and perform well.

That being said, much of the work examining the exploratory (e.g., Fredrickson, 1998; Izard, 1977) and focused (e.g., Csíkszentmihályi, 1990) modes of engagement elicited by interest has been theoretical, with limited empirical evidence. Given that interest serves these two functions, each with different associated outcomes, it is important for researchers to more clearly understand how and why they manifest. Such research will add to our understanding of interest's important role in problem solving and goal pursuit.

Researchers should also consider the role of implicit theories of interest (O'Keefe et al., 2015) in the development of interest. Hidi and Renninger (2006) proposed a four-phase model of interest development, beginning with triggered situational interest and transitioning into well-developed individual interest across several phases of increased stored knowledge, positive feelings associated with the content or activity, and personal relevance. Research on implicit theories of interest, however, suggests that the entire process might be thwarted if one does not believe that interests can be developed in the first place. Consequently, the research suggests that implicit theories of interest should be incorporated into the four-phase model.

More generally, we hope that insights from this chapter will inspire researchers to empirically investigate this important area of motivation science and will sharpen our understanding of the interplay between interest, motivation, and engagement. A clearer understanding of the multifaceted role of interest will help elucidate the functional role it plays in goal pursuit and how it is best promoted.

Acknowledgments We thank Gabriel Ibasco for his contributions to this manuscript.

References

Ainley, M., Hidi, S., & Berndorff, D. (2002). Interest, learning, and the psychological processes that mediate their relationship. *Journal of Educational Psychology, 94*(3), 545–561.

Anderson, R. C. (1982). Allocation of attention during reading. *Advances in Psychology, 8*, 292–305.

Berlyne, D. E. (1960). *Conflict, arousal, and curiosity*. New York: Mc-Graw-Hill.

Carr, P. B., & Walton, G. M. (2014). Cues of working together fuel intrinsic motivation. *Journal of Experimental Social Psychology, 53*, 169–184.

Carver, C. S. (2003). Pleasure as a sign you can attend to something else: Placing positive feelings within a general model of affect. *Cognition & Emotion, 17*(2), 241–261.

Carver, C. S., & Scheier, M. F. (2004). Self-regulation of action and affect. *Handbook of self-regulation: Research, theory, and applications*, 13–39.

Csíkszentmihályi, M. (1990). *Flow: The psychology of optimal performance*. New York: Cambridge University Press.

Csíkszentmihályi, M., Abuhamdeh, S., & Nakamura, J. (2005). In A. Elliot & C. Dweck (Eds.), *Flow. Handbook of competence and motivation* (pp. 598–623). New York: Guilford Press.

Deci, E. L., & Ryan, R. M. (2000). The "what" and "why" of goal pursuits: Human needs and the self-determination of behavior. *Psychological Inquiry, 11*, 227–268.

Durik, A. M., Shechter, O. G., Noh, M., Rozek, C. S., & Harackiewicz, J. M. (2015). What if I can't? Success expectancies moderate the effects of utility value information on situational interest and performance. *Motivation and Emotion, 39*(1), 104–118.

Festinger, L., & Carlsmith, J. M. (1959). Cognitive consequences of forced compliance. *The Journal of Abnormal and Social Psychology, 58*(2), 203.

Fredrickson, B. L. (1998). What good are positive emotions? *Review of General Psychology, 2*(3), 300.

Freitas, A. L., & Higgins, E. T. (2002). Enjoying goal-directed action: The role of regulatory fit. *Psychological Science, 13*, 1–6.

Harackiewicz, J. M., Barron, K. E., Tauer, J. M., & Elliot, A. J. (2002). Predicting success in college: A longitudinal study of achievement goals and ability measures as predictors of interest and performance from freshman year through graduation. *Journal of Educational Psychology, 94*(3), 562.

Harackiewicz, J. M., Durik, A. M., Barron, K. E., Linnenbrink-Garcia, L., & Tauer, J. M. (2008). The role of achievement goals in the development of interest: Reciprocal relations between achievement goals, interest, and performance. *Journal of Educational Psychology,* *100*(1), 105.

Harackiewicz, J. M., Rozek, C. S., Hulleman, C. S., & Hyde, J. S. (2012). Helping parents to motivate adolescents in mathematics and science an experimental test of a utility-value intervention. *Psychological Science, 23,* 899–906. doi:10.1177/0956797611435530.

Hidi, S. (1990). Interest and its contribution as a mental resource for learning. *Review of Educational Research, 60*(4), 549–571.

Hidi, S. E. (1995). A reexamination of the role of attention in learning from text. *Educational Psychology Review, 7*(4), 323–350.

Hidi, S., & Renninger, K. A. (2006). The four-phase model of interest development. *Educational Psychologist, 41*(2), 111–127.

Higgins, E. T. (1997). Beyond pleasure and pain. *American Psychologist, 52,* 1280–1300.

Higgins, E. T. (2000). Making a good decision: Value from fit. *American Psychologist, 55,* 1217–1230.

Higgins, E. T., Cesario, J., Hagiwara, N., Spiegel, S., & Pittman, T. (2010). Increasing or decreasing interest in activities: The role of regulatory fit. *Journal of Personality and Social Psychology, 98*(4), 559.

Higgins, E. T., Idson, L. C., Freitas, A. L., Spiegel, S., & Molden, D. C. (2003). Transfer of value from fit. *Journal of Personality and Social Psychology, 84,* 1140–1153.

Hulleman, C. S., Godes, O., Hendricks, B. L., & Harackiewicz, J. M. (2010). Enhancing interest and performance with a utility value intervention. *Journal of Educational Psychology, 102*(4), 880.

Hulleman, C. S., & Harackiewicz, J. M. (2009). Promoting interest and performance in high school science classes. *Science, 326*(5958), 1410–1412.

Izard, C. E. (1977). *Human emotions.* New York: Plenum Press.

Izard, C. E., & Ackerman, B. P. (2000). Motivational, organizational, and regulatory functions of discrete emotions. In M. Lewis & J. Haviland-Jones (Eds.), *Handbook of emotions* (2nd ed., pp. 253–322). New York: Guilford Press.

James, W. (1950). *The principles of psychology.* (Vols. 2). New York: Dover. (Original work published 1890).

Krapp, A. (1999). Interest, motivation and learning: An educational-psychological perspective. *European Journal of Psychology of Education, 14*(1), 23–40.

Lepper, M. R., Greene, D., & Nisbett, R. E. (1973). Undermining children's intrinsic interest with extrinsic reward: A test of the "overjustification" hypothesis. *Journal of Personality and Social Psychology, 28*(1), 129.

McDaniel, M. A., Waddill, P. J., Finstad, K., & Bourg, T. (2000). The effects of text-based interest on attention and recall. *Journal of Educational Psychology, 92*(3), 492.

Miller, W. I. (1998). *The anatomy of disgust.* Cambridge, MA: Harvard University Press.

O'Keefe, P. A., Dweck, C. S., & Walton, G. M. (2015). *Implicit theories of interest.* Paper presented at the annual meeting of the Academy of Management. Vancouver, BC.

O'Keefe, P. A., & Linnenbrink-Garcia, L. (2014). The role of interest in optimizing performance and self-regulation. *Journal of Experimental Social Psychology, 53,* 70–78.

Pasupathi, M., & Rich, B. (2005). Inattentive listening undermines self-verification in personal storytelling. *Journal of Personality, 73,* 1051–1086. doi:10.1111/j.1467-6494.2005.00338.x.

Plass, J. L., O'Keefe, P. A., Homer, B. D., Case, J., Hayward, E. O., Stein, M., & Perlin, K. (2013). The impact of individual, competitive, and collaborative mathematics game play on learning, performance, and motivation. *Journal of Educational Psychology, 105*(4), 1050.

Renninger, K. A., & Hidi, S. (2016). *The power of interest for motivation and learning.* New York: Routledge.

Sansone, C., & Harackiewicz, J. M. (2000). *Intrinsic and extrinsic motivation: The search for optimal motivation and performance.* San Diego: Academic Press.

Sansone, C., & Smith, J. L. (2000). Interest and self-regulation: The relation between having to and wanting to. In C. Sansone & J. M. Harackiewicz (Eds.), *Intrinsic and extrinsic motivation* (pp. 341–372). San Diego, CA: Academic Press.

Sansone, C., Smith, J. L., Thoman, D. B., & MacNamara, A. (2012). Regulating interest when learning online: Potential motivation and performance trade-offs. *The Internet and Higher Education, 15*, 141–149. doi:10.1016/j.iheduc.2011.10.004.

Sansone, C., Weir, C., Harpster, L., & Morgan, C. (1992). Once a boring task always a boring task? Interest as a self-regulatory mechanism. *Journal of Personality and Social Psychology, 63*(3), 379.

Sansone, C., Wiebe, D. J., & Morgan, C. (1999). Self-regulating interest: The moderating role of hardiness and conscientiousness. *Journal of Personality, 67*(4), 701–733.

Schiefele, U., & Krapp, A. (1996). Topic interest and free recall of expository text. *Learning and Individual Differences, 8*(2), 141–160.

Schiefele, U., Krapp, A., & Winteler, A. (1992). Interest as a predictor of academic achievement: A meta-analysis of research. In K. A. Renninger, S. Hidi, & A. Krapp (Eds.), *The role of interest in learning and development* (pp. 183–211). Hillsdale, NJ: Erlbaum.

Shirey, L. L., & Reynolds, R. E. (1988). Effect of interest on attention and learning. *Journal of Educational Psychology, 80*(2), 159.

Silvia, P. J. (2005). What is interesting? Exploring the appraisal structure of interest. *Emotion, 5*(1), 89.

Silvia, P. J. (2006). *Exploring the psychology of interest.* New York: Oxford University Press.

Silvia, P. J. (2008). Interest—The curious emotion. *Current Directions in Psychological Science, 17*(1), 57–60.

Thoman, D. B., Sansone, C., Fraughton, T., & Pasupathi, M. (2012). How students socially evaluate interest: Peer responsiveness influences evaluation and maintenance of interest. *Contemporary Educational Psychology, 37*, 254–265. doi:10.1016/j.cedpsych.2012.04.001.

Chapter 4
The Role of Interest in Learning: Knowledge Acquisition at the Intersection of Situational and Individual Interest

Jerome I. Rotgans and Henk G. Schmidt

Interest has always been conceived as an essential ingredient to spice up learning. Few educators would disagree that without capitalizing on students' preexisting interest for certain topics or presenting instructional materials to arouse students' interest, learning would be limited. Among the first educators to formally document the significance of interest in education was John Dewey. More than 100 years ago, he published a book entitled *Interest and Effort in Education* in which he portrayed interest as an internal motivational force that is more powerful than effort alone and results in meaningful learning (Dewey, 1913). His early writings are still relevant today, and many teachers echo his recommendations.

Despite being ahead of his time, Dewey did not go much beyond a descriptive account of how interest and learning are related, and it took some 70 years before researchers started to subject the concept of interest to systematic investigation. In the early 1990s, advancement came from researchers who were interested in how texts are processed. They noticed that certain textual manipulations and structural features of a text seem to arouse interest. For instance, when unexpected information was presented, the text was rated as more interesting (Hidi, 1990). This was also the case if a reader could identify with a main character in a story (Anderson, Shirey, Wilson, & Fielding, 1987). In addition, structural aspects of a text, such as coherence and completeness (Hidi & Baird, 1988; Schraw, Bruning, & Svoboda, 1995; Wade, 1992), informational complexity (van Dijk & Kintsch, 1999), suspense (Jose & Brewer, 1984), vividness (Garner, Brown, Sanders, & Menke, 1992), imagery (Goetz & Sadoski, 1995), and ease of comprehension (Schraw, 1997), seem to increase interest for the text in question.

J.I. Rotgans (✉)
Nanyang Technological University, Singapore, Singapore
e-mail: jerome.rotgans@ntu.edu.sg

H.G. Schmidt
Erasmus University Rotterdam, Rotterdam, The Netherlands

© Springer International Publishing AG 2017
P.A. O'Keefe, J.M. Harackiewicz (eds.), *The Science of Interest*,
DOI 10.1007/978-3-319-55509-6_4

It was at this point that researchers noticed that the kind of interest observed during text processing is qualitatively different from what Dewey describes as interest. Dewey conceived interest as a rather stable preexisting quality of an individual (Schraw & Lehman, 2001). Text-processing researchers however discovered that the interest they observed during reading individual text segments seemed less stable and rather fleeting and fluctuating—sometimes appearing and disappearing in a short time frame. It was from that moment onward that a distinction was made between two types of interest: stable *individual* interest (also referred to as personal interest) and fleeting *situational* interest (Schraw et al., 1995; Schraw, Flowerday, & Lehman, 2001). As we will elaborate in more detail below, this distinction between situational and individual interest is important and has caused, and still causes, confusion and misinterpretation of data in the interest literature.

Although the text-processing studies constituted an advancement for the field, researchers now realize that learning from texts only represents one facet of the collection of instructional interventions that can arouse interest. As a consequence, the last two decades have witnessed a surge in published studies that go beyond the processing of texts and include a wider variety of instructional tasks, such as science experiments, puzzles, or problems, that potentially can influence student interest in authentic classroom settings.

In this chapter, we will offer an overview of this current work. However, this overview will not constitute an attempt to provide a comprehensive summary of all studies. Rather, we will focus on the research that is concerned with the role of interest in knowledge acquisition. There are certainly different lenses through which one can look at interest, but since this chapter is about the role of interest in learning, arguably the acquisition of knowledge is its primary objective and desired outcome. In addition to discussing applications of interest research in the classroom setting, we will present results from *basic research*. That is, what is the science behind interest? How does interest work? We feel that interest research is in need of more experimental studies to help us understand its underlying psychological mechanisms. The observation that interest is aroused when students are provided with novel or surprising information only tells us *that* they are interested. It does not tell us *why* they are interested.

The chapter consists of three parts. First, we will discuss the science behind *situational interest*. Since this type of interest seems to be sensitive to instructional interventions, it has the greatest potential to make a difference for education. Thus, understanding how situational interest affects learning is important for both educators and researchers. Second, we will discuss what we know about the science behind *individual interest* and learning. And third, we will make an attempt to integrate the empirical findings discussed in this chapter in a model, outlining the different roles played by situational interest and individual interest in the acquisition of knowledge.

The Science of Situational Interest and Learning

Does Arousal of Situational Interest Lead to Knowledge Acquisition?

Most interest researchers would intuitively agree with the statement that situational interest has a role to play in knowledge acquisition and learning. There are numerous examples in the literature that support this notion (Alexander & Jetton, 1996; Alexander, Jetton, & Kulikowich, 1995; Alexander, Kulikowich, & Schulze, 1994; Schraw et al., 2001; Schraw & Lehman, 2001; Tobias, 1994). For instance, the early work by Hidi and Baird (1988) on text-based interest demonstrates that students' situational interest affected their understanding on a reading task and led to better recall of the text. Guthrie et al. (2006) provided students with stimulating tasks to arouse situational interest. This resulted in better learning as compared with students who did not receive the stimulating tasks. H. Kang, Scharmann, Kang, and Noh (2010) conducted a study in which they used a "discrepant event" regarding the concept of density. The discrepant event was described in the following scenario: "When two balls of the same size were dropped into the water, a small black ball weighing 100 g floated whereas a small gray ball weighing 500 g sank. Here is a 1,000 g large black ball made of the same material as the small black ball. Does it sink or float when it is dropped into the water" (p. 389)? The discrepant event resulted in the arousal of situational interest which, in turn, led to conceptual understanding.

However, other studies report outcomes that are not so clear-cut or even conflicting. For instance, Niemivirta and Tapola (2007) initially demonstrated that students' situational interest, aroused during a complex problem-solving task, predicted task performance. However, in subsequent studies, the same authors did not find significant correlations between situational interest and task performance (Tapola, Jaakkola, & Niemivirta, 2014; Tapola, Veermans, & Niemivirta, 2013). Similar conflicting findings were obtained in a study by Nieswandt (2007). They explored how students' situational interest in chemistry predicted their understanding of subject matter over the course of a school year and found no correlation between the two variables. Harackiewicz, Barron, Tauer, Carter, and Elliot (2000) also failed to find a relation between situational interest aroused and students' grade point average scores. However, in a subsequent study, Harackiewicz, Durik, Barron, Linnenbrink-Garcia, and Tauer (2008) found a significant positive effect of situational interest on grades. In summary, a positive relation between situational interest and learning is not always found. The issue is thus: How should these conflicting findings be understood?

We propose that these inconsistencies have their roots in at least three methodological problems: (1) inadequate operationalization of measurement; (2) lack of multiple measurements; and (3) lack of experimental manipulation. In the following three sections, we will discuss each of these issues consecutively. We take as a point of departure our own initial experiences with measuring interest in the context of learning.

Scope of Measurement: The Issue of Averaged Impressions

Upon entering the field of student motivation and learning as novices, we followed the example of others involved in this type of research: we selected a self-report instrument, administered it toward the end of a semester with the instruction to students to think back on what had happened during the semester, and correlated motivation with educational outcome measures. Our results agreed with other studies in the domain demonstrating correlations not surpassing the typical .30 mark and motivation constructs frequently explaining less than 10% of the variance in achievement measures (Rotgans & Schmidt, 2009, 2010, 2011a). It was at this point that we decided to change our approach because we felt that there may be a problem with asking students to retrospectively provide an accurate report of their motivational state over a relatively long period of time. We hypothesized that when students respond to such a questionnaire, they provide us with "averaged impressions" of what actually happened. For instance, a student may initially be quite motivated to learn because the teacher allowed them to work in small groups and to get actively involved. If, as the course progressed, his teacher would focus increasingly on what the students need to know for the final exam, perhaps resulting in more lecturing and less active involvement, motivation may drop. The "averaged impression" of the totality of experiences during the semester may not accurately represent the different motivational states experienced during the course. This may explain why some of the studies employing such approach do not report significant associations between situational interest (as a measure of motivation) and academic achievement (e.g., Harackiewicz et al., 2000; Nieswandt, 2007).

Based on our hypothesis that averaged impressions may not adequately represent the motivational states of the student, we decided to focus on the analysis of much smaller units of learning. Rather than measuring motivation over an entire semester, we began to measure student motivation during much shorter time frames, such as one lesson or even before and after critical events during one lesson. Focusing on situational interest as an indicator seemed a good idea, because as mentioned above, this construct is not considered a stable *trait* but a *state* measure determined by contextual and situational circumstances.

Microanalytical Measurement

Even if the granularity of the instructional event goes down from a course of several weeks to a lesson of a few hours, the problem of averaged impressions would probably persist when one confines oneself to measuring situational interest once (for instance, at the end of the lesson). A manner to deal with this problem is to measure situational interest *repeatedly* during the lesson. Following the terminology of Zimmerman, we adopted the term "microanalytical measurement" to describe this procedure (DiBenedetto & Zimmerman, 2010; Zimmerman & Kitsantas, 2005).

Table 4.1 Six-item situational interest questionnaire

1	I want to know more about this topic.	1 Not true at all	2 Not true for me	3 Neutral	4 True for me	5 Very true for me
2	I enjoy working on this topic.	1 Not true at all	2 Not true for me	3 Neutral	4 True for me	5 Very true for me
3	I think this topic is interesting.	1 Not true at all	2 Not true for me	3 Neutral	4 True for me	5 Very true for me
4	I expect to master this topic well.	1 Not true at all	2 Not true for me	3 Neutral	4 True for me	5 Very true for me
5	I am fully focused on this topic; I am not distracted by other things.	1 Not true at all	2 Not true for me	3 Neutral	4 True for me	5 Very true for me
6	Presently, I feel bored.	1 Not true at all	2 Not true for me	3 Neutral	4 True for me	5 Very true for me

Please indicate, on a scale from 1 (*not true at all for me*) to 5 (*very true for me*), how true the statements are for you *right now*.

Microanalytical measurements, we hypothesized, would give us the opportunity to observe how situational interest fluctuates as a function of instructional interventions and, because of the higher fidelity of measurement, would enable us to make more accurate predictions of performance.

To test this hypothesis, we conducted a study in which we measured situational interest five times at critical moments during a one-day problem-based learning session (O'Grady, Yew, Goh, & Schmidt, 2012; Rotgans, O'Grady, & Alwis, 2011; Rotgans & Schmidt, 2011b). The problem was about economics. We first developed and validated a short six-item situational interest questionnaire drawing upon existing conceptions of what situational interest according to others entails, an affective reaction caused by environmental stimuli, focused attention, and willingness to learn (Hidi, 2006; Krapp, 1999; Schraw & Lehman, 2001). See Table 4.1 for the items of the questionnaire.

This questionnaire takes only 30 sec to respond to. We assumed that it could therefore be administered several times during an instructional event, without disrupting the learning process or burdening students. Subsequently, we administered the questionnaire before and after students received a problem, immediately after initial discussion of the problem, after self-study, and finally after elaboration on what was learned during self-study. We then conducted a path analysis. The results revealed that situational interest predicted almost 20% of the variance in students' knowledge, twice the amount of variance explained in typical motivation-achievement studies, including our own. In addition to this outcome, we observed an interesting trend in situational interest over the course of the session: situational interest first increased when a problem was introduced, and students engaged in discussing it. However, as the students gained more knowledge about the problem in question, situational interest significantly decreased. Situational interest seemed to progress over the course of an instructional event in an inverted U-shape fashion.

The Significance of an Interest-Arousing Stimulus in Situational Interest Research

Applying repeated measurements in interest research is not new. Alexander et al. (1994) and Ainley, Hidi, and Berndorff (2002) were among the first to measure interest repeatedly while having students read expository texts. Most of these studies however, failed to find fluctuating pattern similar to the ones we found (Rotgans & Schmidt, 2011b, 2014). Tin (2008) conducted a study with postgraduate language teachers. She measured situational interest repeatedly during two-hour lectures. Her data did however not show significant fluctuations. Tapola et al. (2013) examined whether a concrete vs. an abstract science task differentially influenced situational interest. They measured situational interest three times during the task. Despite the fact that they found mean differences between both groups, they did not find significantly different patterns in situational interest between both conditions, and situational interest did not fluctuate significantly over time. Palmer (2009) measured students' interest six times during a science lesson. He found significant fluctuations in situational interest as the lesson progressed, but no distinct pattern emerged.

These findings are at odds with our own findings suggesting that situational interest first increases and then decreases over the course of an instructional event. A possible explanation for this discrepancy is that our studies always contained an instructional event that was aimed at *arousing* situational interest. Arousing situational interest may be a precondition for significant changes to occur over time. Appropriate arousal stimuli may be instructional problems, puzzles, counterintuitive science experiments, videos displaying difficult to understand phenomena or events, etc. An example of a history problem designed to arouse interest among Singapore secondary school children is depicted in Fig. 4.1. The problem is about the fall of Singapore to the Japanese during World War II. It contains information that students can easily relate to because they have sufficient prior knowledge that can be activated. For instance, students are expected to know what World War II is, and most students in Singapore should be aware of the fact that Singapore was conquered by the Japanese. However, what students may not know is that the British and allied forces outnumbered the Japanese Army 3:1 and that the Japanese General Yamashita therefore took a great gamble attacking Singapore.

To test the hypothesis that the presence of a precipitating event is a necessary condition for arousal of situational interest to occur, we conducted an experiment in which one group of students received a problem whereas another group did not receive a problem—all else being equal (Schmidt, Rotgans, & Yew, 2011). The students involved were primary school mathematics students studying the principle of

---

Bluff!

On 8 December 1941 the Japanese Imperial Army landed on the Northeast coast of Malaya. Under the command of General Yamashita, the Japanese Imperial Army rapidly advanced through Malaya destroying the British Army. On 8 February 1942 the Japanese invaded Singapore from Johor. Fierce fighting followed first in the North of the island and then in the Southwest. The fighting continued in Kranji, Pasir Panjang and Bukit Timah. By the morning of the Chinese New Year, 15 February 1942, the Japanese had broken through the last line of defense and the Allies were running out of food and ammunition. Shortly after 5:15 pm the British and Allied forces formally surrendered.

Several years after the fall of Singapore, General Yamashita revealed the following:

"My attack on Singapore was a bluff – a bluff that worked. I had 30 000 men and was outnumbered more than three to one. I knew that if I had to fight long for Singapore, I would be beaten. That was why the surrender had to be at once. I was very frightened all the time that the British would discover our numerical weakness and lack of supplies and force me into disastrous fighting."

If the British and Allied forces had known that Yamashita was bluffing, could the fall of Singapore be prevented?

Fig. 4.1 Example problem fall of Singapore during World War II

tessellation. Five measures of situational interest were administered at critical moments during the learning process. See Fig. 4.2 for an overview of the learning activities and measurement points for both conditions. The results revealed that situational interest for the group receiving the problem significantly increased after presentation of the problem and its subsequent discussion. Afterward, situational interest decreased according to the inverted U-shape pattern we had observed in previous studies.

For the group who did not receive a problem, no significant change in situational interest emerged (However, see the note accompanying Fig. 4.2). The latter finding seems to be a replication of the findings of the studies cited in this section that did not use instructional problems and did not observe significant changes in situational interest. We interpret these findings as supportive of the notion that situational interest must be aroused for learning to occur.

In summary, to do justice to the nature of situational interest, we propose that if one intends to measure situational interest, one has to choose a unit of analysis that is sufficiently small, such as one lesson or a short task. In our view, it makes no sense to measure situational interest as if it is a dispositional trait, only once or twice during a semester or school term, and expect to capture students' situational interest for the course in question. What one achieves with the latter approach is measurement of averaged impressions of situational interest. Situational interest, as the name implies, is situational and fleeting and needs to be measured in the situation as it happens. The best manner to operationalize this may be by means of repeated

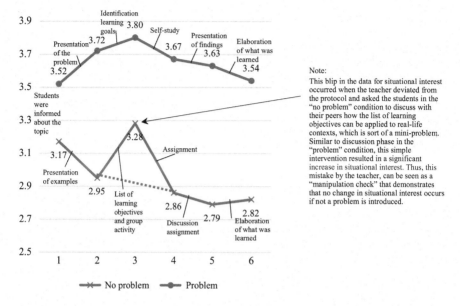

Fig. 4.2 Situational interest during a mathematics class, with and without a problem. Note: This blip in the data for situational interest occurred when the teacher deviated from the protocol and asked the students in the "no problem" condition to discuss with their peers how the list of learning objectives can be applied to real-life contexts, which is sort of a mini-problem. Similar to discussion phase in the "problem" condition, this simple intervention resulted in a significant increase in situational interest. Thus, this mistake by the teacher can be seen as a "manipulation check" that demonstrates that no change in situational interest occurs if not a problem is introduced

administrations of a situational interest questionnaire as the task unfolds. Third, without an arousing stimulus, such as an instructional problem, situational interest is not likely to emerge and measurement of it seems futile. However, if one succeeds in arousing situational interest, current research suggests that situational interest leads to knowledge acquisition and is a powerful motivational indicator of learning and engagement (Ainley, 2012; Alexander, 2003; Schmidt et al., 2011; Schraw et al., 1995, 2001; Schraw & Lehman, 2001).

The Knowledge-Deprivation Hypothesis of Situational Interest

That situational interest increases when students are confronted with an engaging problem is an empirical fact. However, this empirical fact does not in itself provide a clue as to what the psychological mechanism would be underlying this increase. In addition, what explains the *decrease* in interest observed when students engage with the subject matter relevant to the problem? The work of Berlyne may be particularly relevant to answer this question (Berlyne, 1954, 1962, 1978). Berlyne did not use the term situational interest but wrote about "epistemic curiosity," curiosity for knowledge. Epistemic curiosity and situational interest however seem to play similar roles in education; they are both aroused by instructional interventions and both are supposed to motivate the acquisition of knowledge. There is some evidence that these constructs are in fact identical, and we will treat them as such (Mussel, 2010). We will further use the term situational interest here for simplicity's sake. According to Berlyne (1954), the emergence of situational interest is the result of a gap between what one knows about a particular topic and what seemingly needs to be known; situational interest in this point of view is triggered by the experience of a knowledge deficit (see also Loewenstein, 1994). Berlyne (1954) referred to this process as a need for new information that motivates exploratory behavior and knowledge acquisition. In accordance with his work, we have proposed a drive-reduction explanation of situational interest, the "knowledge-deprivation hypothesis of situational interest" (Rotgans & Schmidt, 2014). Our proposal of how situational interest is aroused and satisfied has four elements: First, confronted with a problem not immediately understood, a person engages in an attempt to retrieve knowledge from long-term memory that may help him or her to interpret the problem. Second, if the retrieval from long-term memory fails, the person experiences a gap between what he or she knows and what he or she needs to know to understand the problem at hand. Third, this conscious realization of a knowledge deficit leads to the arousal of situational interest for information that may help eliminate the deficit ("I don't know this. Interesting! Let's find out more!"). Aroused situational interest is therefore a motivational indicator of the preparedness of the person to engage in processing such information. Fourth, the acquisition of new knowledge satisfies the drive to learn. If the knowledge gap is closed with regard to the problem, there is no further impetus to find out more about it. Hence, situational interest decreases and may even disappear.[1]

In our proposal, the failed attempt to retrieve relevant knowledge, necessary for understanding the problem, is crucial to the emergence of situational interest. Hence, our emphasis on the use of problems in education to create that awareness.

But how does this lead to deeper learning? Kornell, Hays, and Bjork (2009) have demonstrated that in particular *unsuccessful* knowledge retrieval attempts enhance learning. Their explanation for this positive effect of unsuccessful retrieval of knowledge on learning is that it encourages more extensive processing of what the learner knows relevant to the issue at hand. The attempt to retrieve the answer may enhance the activation of related concepts, which may, in turn, create a fertile con-

---

[1] Considering the notion that situational interest must necessarily decrease as knowledge is acquired, we are rather skeptical that the idea of "maintained" situational interest (or "hold" situational interest) is appropriate (Linnenbrink-Garcia et al., 2010; Mitchell, 1993). As we have suggested elsewhere, maintenance of situational interest should be conceived as repeated arousal of situational interest (Rotgans & Schmidt, 2014a). Related to this, it should be noted that some interest researchers wrongly state that "catch" and "hold" of situational interest was proposed by Dewey (1913). Dewey referred to "catch" only *once* in his book *Interest and Effort in Education* and stated "It is not enough to *catch* attention; it must be *held* (p.91)." It is questionable whether attention is identical to situational interest. Moreover, Dewey did not refer to situational interest but to individual interest (Schraw & Lehman, 2001).

text for encoding new information when it is presented. We propose therefore that unsuccessful retrieval also may lead to more extensive search for new information. The problem acts hereby as a catalyst; it makes the organism aware of a possible discrepancy between its understanding of the world and how the world really is [cf., incongruity theory (Berlyne, 1957, 1963)]. Since such discrepancy can have negative consequences for the organism, the drive to reduce the knowledge gap is, we suspect, a biological given (Kang et al., 2009). Situational interest is the red flag that signifies this undesirable state of affairs and is lowered when the informational needs are satisfied.

Empirical Evidence for the Knowledge-Deprivation Hypothesis

We conducted three studies to test the knowledge-deprivation hypothesis of situational interest (Rotgans & Schmidt, 2014). The first study was an experiment in which we presented Singapore secondary school students with the history problem depicted in Fig. 4.1 about the fall of Singapore during World War II. Prior to the problem, half of the participants received a text providing an explanation for this problem. The other half received unrelated information. By doing so, we manipulated their prior knowledge regarding the problem. Situational interest was measured both before and after the presentation of the problem. The participants who did not receive the explanatory information reported a significantly increased level of situational interest in the topic after the problem was presented; the group that was given the prior knowledge necessary to understand the problem beforehand did not show such change in situational interest. This finding demonstrates that situational interest is only aroused by a problem when a knowledge gap exists between what the learner knows about the problem and what needs to be known to understand it.

In a second study, participants were informed about a topic they were going to study (i.e., coastal erosion in Singapore), after which we measured both students' self-reported knowledge about this topic and their situational interest. We then presented them with a coastal erosion problem and recorded their self-reported knowledge and situational interest for a second time. Students who perceived a larger knowledge gap after introduction of the problem (as evidenced by the decrease in self-reported knowledge once the problem was presented) were shown to experience the largest increase in situational interest. These results suggests that participants have to be *consciously aware* that a gap exists between what they know and what they need to know to understand the problem at hand, to provoke situational interest.[2]

---

[2] Berlyne (1954) did not assume that the person should be consciously aware of a gap between what he or she knows and what should be known. For him, the existence of a knowledge deficit is sufficient for situational interest to occur. We, however, noticed that students often are not metacognitively aware that they lack knowledge and therefore do not indicate higher levels of situational interest.

In a third study, we investigated the trade-off between situational interest and knowledge acquisition over the duration of three lessons in a natural classroom setting. In this study, we administered measures of situational interest and knowledge acquisition repeatedly, which enabled us to observe how both develop over the course of a learning event. The results of the study confirmed and extended the findings from the first two studies. Initially, when the problem was presented, participants responded with a significant increase in situational interest. Subsequently, however, while participants gained knowledge during self-study and knowledge consolidation, their situational interest in the topic decreased significantly. This outcome supports the idea that situational interest emerges from lack of knowledge and disappears when sufficient new knowledge is acquired.

Can the Knowledge-Deprivation Hypothesis Explain Other Situational Interest Findings?

The knowledge-deprivation hypothesis appears to provide the most parsimonious account of our data and has potential in explaining a number of other instructional interventions that are known to increase situational interest. Among them, *novelty* has been proposed as a variable that positively influences situational interest (Fulmer, D'Mello, Strain, & Graesser, 2015; Kashdan & Silvia, 2009; Krapp, 2007). If something is considered "novel," it is by definition unknown to the person, and therefore the realization of one's ignorance regarding the topic at hand arouses situational interest, as the knowledge-deprivation hypothesis would predict. Other researchers have proposed that complexity, unexpectedness, expectancy violations, surprise, suspense etc., lead to situational interest as well (Berlyne & McDonnell, 1965; Dohn, 2011; Iran-Nejad, 1987; Jirout & Klahr, 2012; Loewenstein, 1994). Clearly, these characteristics of materials presented to students lead to increased situational interest because they all signify lack of knowledge. If something is considered complex, there is missing knowledge about how different knowledge units are linked to each other. Similarly, unexpectedness, expectancy violations, and surprise lead to situational interest because they are excellent means to make a person more consciously aware that he or she lacks knowledge regarding the topic in question (the person was under the impression that he or she did know, when in fact he or she does not). Suspense is another variable that has been used to arouse situational interest in text-processing studies (Alexander & Jetton, 1996; Jose & Brewer, 1984; Schraw, 1997). Suspense, we argue, is the result of withholding information, which makes the person in question aware of his or her knowledge gap. This may also explain why seductive details (interesting but irrelevant information) arouse situational interest in text-processing studies (Schraw, 1998). The discrepancy between irrelevant information and useful information conveyed in the text may represent the knowledge gap that leads to situational interest.

Needless to say that the above explanations are tentative and possibly a simplified application of the knowledge-deprivation hypothesis, what is needed is more basic research to systematically test these assumptions.

In the previous sections, we have attempted to provide an account of the nature of situational interest and how it leads to knowledge acquisition. The knowledge-deprivation hypothesis presents a possible mechanism for the underlying psychological process. This process perhaps explains why instructional approaches that incorporate problems or puzzles to activate learning are successful in motivating and engaging students in deep learning, such as problem-based learning, inquiry teaching, and team-based learning (Abdelkhalek, Hussein, Gibbs, & Hamdy, 2010; Rotgans et al., 2011; Rotgans & Schmidt, 2012; Schmidt et al., 2011; Schmidt, Van der Molen, Te Winkel, & Wijnen, 2009). These instructional approaches have in common that they start with a problem or puzzle to arouse students' interest. Furthermore, they allow for ample self-study opportunities which may have an additional motivational effect due to the fact that students can make choices of what they study (Flowerday, Schraw, & Stevens, 2004; Flowerday & Shell, 2015; Høgheim & Reber, 2015), which may result in feeling of being empowered and autonomous (Deci, 1992; Deci & Ryan, 2004; Deci, Vallerand, Pelletier, & Ryan, 1991). Collaborative peer learning characterizing these approaches may also facilitate and enhance the motivational experience (Sungur & Tekkaya, 2006).

We will now turn to the question of what happens with knowledge, once it has been acquired, and how it is related to the second type of interest: individual interest, the stable and dispositional interest of a person with regard to a domain.

The Science of Individual Interest and Learning

The Issue of Causation: Does Individual Interest Cause Knowledge or Does Knowledge Cause Individual Interest?

The close association between knowledge and individual interest is widely acknowledged in the literature. For instance, Schiefele and Rheinberg (1997) postulate that individual interest should only refer to knowledge domains and not activities or events (as it is the case with situational interest). Similarly, Hidi and Renninger (2006) conceived individual interest to be associated with knowledge and value. The latter part, "value," is an additional component that echoes Schiefele and Krapp's characterization that interest consists of value- and feeling-related valences (Krapp, 2007; Schiefele, 1991, 1999). This is in line with ideas of researchers who conceptualize interest as an emotion (Ainley, 2008, 2012; Ainley et al., 2002; Silvia, 2008). In short, there is general agreement that knowledge is closely related to individual interest, and it appears that value and feelings are attached to it.

In addition, there is almost universal agreement that individual interest is a causal factor in learning; interest is the independent variable whereas knowledge is the dependent variable (Ainley, 2012; Ainley et al., 2002; Hidi, 2001; Koller, Baumert, & Schnabel, 2001; Krapp, 1999; Schiefele, 1999; Schraw & Lehman, 2001, 2009). A fitting example of this point of view is the meta-analysis conducted by Schiefele, Krapp, and Winteler (1992). Summarizing 121 studies carried out between 1965 and 1992, they found a mean correlation coefficient between individual interest and academic achievement of .31. They interpreted this mean correlation coefficient as the best estimate of the influence that individual interest exerts on knowledge acquisition.

But is this the only possibility? A problem with the type of correlational analysis employed by most of these studies is that not much can be said about the directionality of influence, and thus it is not clear if interest does indeed *cause* learning. Establishing the causal direction between these variables is important, not only for gaining a better understanding of the nature of the interest construct itself but also because of its instructional implications. The pedagogical literature is full of suggestions that learning should start with the arousal of curiosity (Reio, 2004), that teachers should seek to instruct in line with student interests in mind (Reid, 1987), and that learning should be fun (Barab, Thomas, Dodge, Carteaux, & Tuzun, 2005). But assume for a moment that the relation between the two is the other way around: that it is increased knowledge that leads to increased interest. Under this account, interest is not the driver of knowledge but its by-product.

Is there any evidence for this possibility? Only a few researchers have pursued this idea, and there are currently only a limited number of empirical studies available that have systematically explored this option. For instance, Iran-Nejad and Cecil (1992) propose that knowledge determines interest. Empirical support for this point of view is however limited. Iran-Nejad and Cecil refer to one study in which they used two different types of stories, with some having a congruent ending and some having an incongruent ending. They found that only when story endings resolved incongruity, it resulted in increased interest. They claimed that these findings suggested that if incongruity could not be resolved, participants were not able to acquire knowledge (no "theme integration" and "categorical completion" could be achieved), which did not change interest, whereas for congruent endings interest increased. They interpreted these findings as supportive for the knowledge-causes-interest hypothesis.

More recently, in the field of science education, researchers conducted a meta-analysis to investigate how attitudes toward science are related to students' science knowledge. Mattern and Schau (2002) examined the causal relation between student attitudes toward science and their achievement in science using cross-lagged panel analysis. This analysis entails that students' attitudes and achievement are measured simultaneously at two points in time (Kenny, 2005). It is then possible to examine how attitudes and achievement are directionally related (i.e., cross-effects of pre- and post-measures can be examined). Their results suggest that achievement was a predictor of students' attitudes toward science and not the other way around. Translated to the interest context, these findings seem to suggest that if it is increased learning that causes interest to accumulate, then individual interest must be considered an affective by-product of an increase in knowledge. It is easy to see that such state of affairs would lead to quite different instructional recommendations for pedagogical practice. Considering the significant implications of the matter for educational practice, we recently conducted a study to examine how individual interest and knowledge are causally related (Rotgans & Schmidt, 2016b).

Empirical Evidence of the Causal Relation Between Knowledge and Individual Interest

To test whether a causal relation between knowledge and individual interest exists, we conducted a cross-lagged panel analysis. In the study, we measured individual interest and knowledge at two points in time in a group of primary school science students. A model with the pre- and post-measures of individual interest (I) and knowledge (K) was tested using a structural equation modeling approach. See Fig. 4.3 for an overview of the conceptual model with its relations.

Individual interest measures are symbolized by circles and are labeled I_1 and I_2 (i.e., latent variables for individual interest at time 1 and time 2 1 week later) and rectangles for the two observed achievement measures (i.e., K_1 knowledge at time 1 and K_2 knowledge at time 2). The test-retest correlations of individual interest and achievement are represented by $rI_1 \cdot I_2$ and $rK_1 \cdot K_2$.

The relation between individual interest at time 1 and knowledge at time 2 ($rI_1 \cdot K_2$) versus the relation of knowledge at time 1 and individual interest at time 2 ($rK_1 \cdot I_2$) is the critical coefficients and central to the analysis. If individual interest is the precursor of knowledge, then $rI_1 \cdot K_2$ should exceed $rK_1 \cdot I_2$. In contrast, $rK_1 \cdot I_2$ should be greater than $rI_1 \cdot K_2$ if knowledge is a precursor to individual interest. If both are significantly different from zero and nonsignificantly different from each

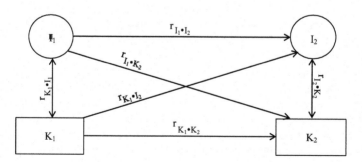

Fig. 4.3 Conceptual model of a cross-lag design for individual interest and achievement measures on two sequential occasions

other, then this can be read as support for a reciprocal influence of both variables. Finally, if both would be nonsignificantly different from zero, one would have to conclude that no causal relation exists or that other, unobserved, variables influence individual interest and achievement.

The results of the analysis revealed that interest measured at an earlier point in time was unrelated to knowledge measured at a later point (the regression coefficient was nonsignificantly different from zero). On the other hand, knowledge measured earlier was significantly related to interest measured later. We consider these findings to be initial support for the hypothesis that the growth of interest in a domain must be seen as a consequence, an offshoot, of growing knowledge of that domain: knowledge measured at an early point in time *did* predict subsequent individual interest (standardized regression coefficient $\beta = .20$, $p < .05$). For the hypothesis that interest and learning influence each other reciprocally, we found no evidence.

To further elaborate on the above findings, we conducted two follow-up experiments involving secondary school students with either low or high individual interest in science. Prior knowledge of these students was assessed preceding the experiment, and knowledge gains were measured after a learning exercise. Interest had only an influence on knowledge acquisition when preexisting differences in prior knowledge were ignored. In an ANCOVA, factoring out prior knowledge, no influence of individual interest on knowledge acquisition remained.

In a second experiment, using a similar logic, secondary school science students with low versus high prior knowledge engaged in a learning task. Prior to the experiment, individual interest in the subject was measured. At the end of the learning task, statistically significant differences in individual interest emerged. After factoring out possible influences of prior individual interest through an ANCOVA, the initial effect of knowledge differences on interest survived, providing support for the hypothesis that interest should be considered a by-product rather than a cause of knowledge gains.

In sum, our findings provide some empirical evidence that pointing at interest as a causal source of learning may have less validity than generally expected. Rather, our data show that with growing knowledge, individual interest develops. A possible explanation would involve the concept of mastery. Knowledge changes our view of the world. What appeared previously undifferentiated and bland becomes a source of excitement and opportunity. Understanding the world produces the sensation of fulfillment because we experience mastery and competence (Deci, 1992; Ryan & Deci, 2000). This experience of mastery expresses itself in positive feelings with regard to, and liking for, the topic mastered (Ainley & Patrick, 2006; Hulleman, Durik, Schweigert, & Harackiewicz, 2008). These feelings of liking express themselves as individual interest in the domain. It takes much effort to accumulate new knowledge and develop an understanding of a domain. Therefore, individual interest is expected to increase slowly, with increasing knowledge.

An Epistemic Model of Interest in Education

How are situational interest, knowledge acquisition, and individual interest related? Two theories relating these concepts dominate the field: "the three-phase" (respectively, four-phase) model on interest development (Hidi & Renninger, 2006; Krapp, 2003) and the model of domain learning (Alexander et al., 1994). The three-phase model proposed by Krapp assumes that interest development starts with the arousal of situational interest, which then slowly transforms into a more stable form over time. Krapp (2003) distinguishes between three (possibly overlapping) phases or stages: (1) triggered situational interest, (2) stabilized situational interest, and (3) individual interest. Hidi and Renninger (2006) extended Krapp's model by subdividing the development of individual interest into two phases: (1) emerging individual interest and (2) well-developed individual interest. Their developmental model is depicted in Fig. 4.4.

This model has two shortcomings. Although the authors state that knowledge acquisition plays a role in this developmental process, its role is underspecified. In particular, the interaction between the various forms of interest and the process of knowledge acquisition (if any) is unclear. Second, how are these various phases to be distinguished? When does triggered situational interest transform into maintained situational interest? How can emerging individual interest be distinguished from well-developed individual interest? How can they be measured as separate entities? What is the time frame within which these transformations take place? Weeks? Months? Years? Is the whole process dependent on the development of knowledge of a domain or an issue of maturation?

Patricia Alexander's model of domain learning (Alexander, 2004; Alexander et al., 1995; Alexander, Sperl, Buehl, Fives, & Chiu, 2004) gives the acquisition of knowledge a more central role. According to Alexander, knowledge and interest (together with strategic processing) interact differently as a student develops expertise in a domain. Their model proposes that expertise develops along three stages. The first stage is acclimation, then competency, and finally proficiency/expertise. The model suggests that in the early stage of expertise development (acclimation), learners have only limited knowledge and individual interest and have to rely predominantly on situational interest to engage in learning. As learners become more competent, more knowledge develops, situational interest decreases, and individual

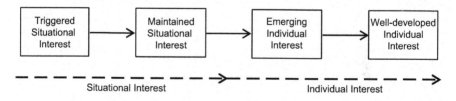

Fig. 4.4 Schematic representation of the four-phase model of interest development (Hidi & Renninger, 2006)

INTEREST AND KNOWLEDGE ACQUISITION

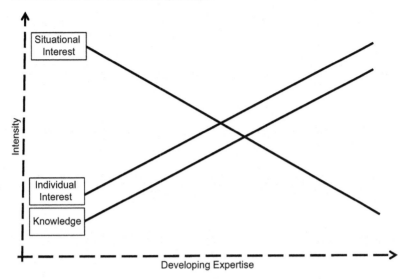

Fig. 4.5 Schematic representation of the model of domain learning (Alexander et al., 1994)

interest increases. Finally, as learners reach proficiency, they have gained a substantive amount of knowledge, have high levels of individual interest and depend less on situational interest. See Fig. 4.5 for a simplified depiction of the model.

The authors propose that novelty and challenge of new learning materials are the drivers of situational interest but do not provide a detailed account of why that would happen; the emergence of situational interest seems more or less self-evident in their analyses. In addition, how situational interest and early knowledge gains are related is unclear. Is it a causal process (as assumed in Fig. 4.5) or a reciprocal process? Second, like most other authors in the field, Alexander sees individual interest as the precursor of knowledge acquisition, rather than an outcome, a point of view at variance with the findings we presented in the previous section.

The model that we propose here, the *epistemic model of interest in education*, has at its core the acquisition of knowledge. It emphasizes education's primary objective as helping learners acquire knowledge needed to make sense of the world around them and the supporting role of interest and its development. Arousal of situational interest is considered the driver of this learning process, and growing individual interest can be seen as its by-product: the more people learn, the more extensive their interest becomes. We believe that this model has the potential to explain many of the empirical phenomena belonging to the interest field while being psychologically plausible. See Fig. 4.6 for a visual overview of the model.

The model also points at an issue overlooked by the other models. It concerns the influence of individual interest on situational interest. Most models follow the logic that situational interest develops into individual interest. We do not believe that students are "blank slates" with regard to their individual interest when approaching

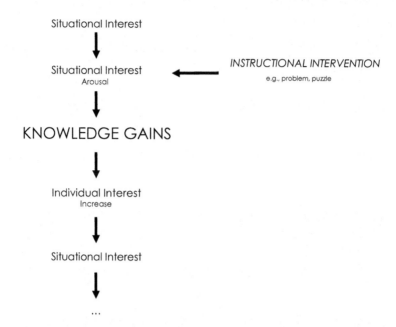

Fig. 4.6 A schematic overview of the epistemic model of interest in education

a learning task. We and others have argued that some individual interest is always present when students encounter a learning situational because there is always some (perhaps superficial) knowledge available. As Bergin (1999) put it, "*It is important to recognize that personal or individual factors always interact with situational factors to create interest or lack of interest*" (p. 89). In line with this statement, we propose that whatever school subject is presented to students, there will always be some value (even if negative) attached to it. For instance, if students are presented with a new mathematics topic that they never encountered before, they may not have stored knowledge about that particular topic, but they have knowledge about mathematics in general. Consequently, the students with relatively higher knowledge and thus individual interest for mathematics will have more initial situational interest in the topic when they first encounter the new topic as compared to students who have relatively little individual interest for mathematics. Our model represents this idea by assuming that situational interest does not emerge out of the blue but always is partly dependent on preexisting individual interest; however superficial, and perhaps negative, this individual interest may be. This is another element that distinguishes the epistemic model of interest in education from its predecessors.

There is ample empirical evidence to support this point of view (Harackiewicz, Barron, Tauer, & Elliot, 2002; Harackiewicz et al., 2008; Tapola et al., 2014). Tsai, Kunter, Lüdtke, Trautwein, and Ryan (2008), for instance, conducted a study in which they investigated the extent to which individual interest influences situational interest at the beginning of a three-week period in three different school subjects. Their findings suggest that individual interest explained about 20% of the variance in situational interest at the beginning of the three-week period for all three school subjects. A similar result was obtained by Harackiewicz et al. (2008) in a study in which they examined the extent to which initial interest in an introductory psychology course predicted situational interest, academic performance, as well as course choices and academic major seven semesters later. Their findings also suggest that almost 20% of the variance in situational interest could be explained by initial interest. Tapola et al. (2013) conducted a study in which they investigated the predictors and outcome of situational interest during a science task. Their findings also suggest that students' situational interest at the beginning of the task was determined by preexisting individual interest.

The results of these studies suggest that individual interest indeed influences students' situational interest at the beginning of a task. However, they provide no information on the pervasiveness of this effect. Is the influence of differences in individual interest still traceable once an instructional event is introduced to arouse students' situational interest? This is an important issue because if the influence of individual interest diminishes over time and students' learning is predominantly driven by situational interest, it would suggest that personal characteristics of learners (i.e., how much individual interest they bring to class) are far less important than generally assumed.

There is some evidence in the Harackiewicz et al. (2008) study which suggests that situational and individual interest are both predictors of learning. However, in the study, they only measured situational interest at two time points over an entire semester, which does not allow for examining if the effect of individual interest diminishes over time. To further test this, we recently conducted a study in which we measured the influence of individual interest on situational interest not only at the very start and end of an intervention but throughout: after an instructional problem was introduced, after discussion of the problem, after self-study, etc. (Rotgans & Schmidt, 2016a). Our study demonstrated that individual interest significantly influences situational interest at the beginning of the learning task; its influence on subsequent measurements of situational interest wanes and eventually dwindles into nonsignificance. The learning outcomes were only dependent on situational interest; individual interest was immaterial to its emergence.

In sum, the extent to which a student has knowledge about a subject determines his or her level of experienced individual interest. Individual interest in turn determines the extent to which a student feels situationally interested when he or she is confronted with a particular topic with which he or she is expected to engage. However, as soon as a problem or another instructional event aimed at the arousal of situational interest is introduced, the influence of preexisting individual interest on situational interest decreases and eventually disappears. It seems that aroused situational interest emerges in response to the problem and is independent of preexisting dispositional interest: even students who are not really interested in the topic may become situationally interested when challenged by a problem. This outcome also demonstrates once again the important role that instructional problems play in arousing situational interest and subsequent knowledge acquisition.

Concluding Remarks

How should we proceed from here? Before attempting to study substantive hypotheses about how interest plays its part in the game of schooling, it is essential that we clean up the mess that results from the idiosyncratic research practices that dominate the field. First, we should agree on the definitions of situational and individual interest. Some define interest as an emotion (Silvia, 2008), others equate it to curiosity (Rotgans & Schmidt, 2014), and again others see it as a person-object interaction (Krapp, 2007). Second, we should begin to use the same instruments. Some use surveys, some prefer a single item, and others use direct observations. The result is that we do not really know what we compare when we try to make sense of contradictory findings. Third, it would support the generalizability of our findings if we try to find alternatives for the self-report measures we tend to use. There are examples of behavioral measures that may suit our purposes, such as the willingness to engage in exploratory behavior. Fourth, if one studies situational interest, one should not treat the construct as a dispositional entity but as an undulating phenomenon. Using a microanalytic approach to its measurement is therefore a logical necessity. Fifth, the study of situational interest would profit from the explicit introduction of instructional events that have the potential to arouse it. Without aroused situational interest, one cannot expect learning to be affected. The absence of such interventions is perhaps the main reason that so many studies fail to demonstrate effects of interest on learning. Sixth, instructional interventions that arouse situational interest should be studied in their own right. The educational community would be served with a better understanding of what stimulates situational interest and why. Finally, the knowledge-deprivation hypothesis of situational interest deserves further scrutiny. A deeper grasp on *why* problems induce interest arousal would advance the science of interest.

References

Abdelkhalek, N., Hussein, A., Gibbs, T., & Hamdy, H. (2010). Using team-based learning to prepare medical students for future problem-based learning. *Medical Teacher, 32*(2), 123–129. doi:10.3109/01421590903548539.

Ainley, M. (2008). Interest: A significant thread binding cognition and affect in the regulation of learning. *International Journal of Psychology, 43*(3–4), 17–18.

Ainley, M. (2012). Students' interest and engagement in classroom activities. In S. L. Christenson, A. L. Reschly, & C. Wylie (Eds.), *Handbook of research on student engagement* (pp. 283–302). New York: Springer Science + Business Media.

Ainley, M., Hidi, S., & Berndorff, D. (2002). Interest, learning, and the psychological processes that mediate their relationship. *Journal of Educational Psychology, 94*(3), 545–561.

Ainley, M., & Patrick, L. (2006). Measuring self-regulated learning processes through tracking patterns of student interaction with achievement activities. *Educational Psychology Review, 18*(3), 267–286. doi:10.1007/s10648-006-9018-z.

Alexander, P. A. (2003). The development of expertise: The journey from acclimation to proficiency. *Educational Researcher, 32*(8), 10–14.

Alexander, P. A. (2004). A model of domain learning: Reinterpreting expertise as a multidimensional, multistage process. In *Motivation, emotion, and cognition: Integrative perspectives on intellectual functioning and development* (pp. 273–298). Mahwah, NJ: N.J Lawrence Erlbaum Associates.

Alexander, P. A., & Jetton, T. L. (1996). The role of importance and interest in the processing of text. *Educational Psychology Review, 8*(1), 89–121. doi:10.1007/BF01761832.

Alexander, P. A., Jetton, T. L., & Kulikowich, J. M. (1995). Interrelationship of knowledge, interest, and recall: Assessing a model of domain learning. *Journal of Educational Psychology, 87*(4), 559–575.

Alexander, P. A., Kulikowich, J. M., & Schulze, S. K. (1994). How subject-matter knowledge affects recall and interest. *American Educational Research Journal, 31*(2), 313–337.

Alexander, P. A., Sperl, C. T., Buehl, M. M., Fives, H., & Chiu, S. (2004). Modeling domain learning: Profiles from the field of special education. *Journal of Educational Psychology, 96*(3), 545.

Anderson, R. C., Shirey, L. L., Wilson, P. T., & Fielding, L. G. (Eds.). (1987). *Interestingness of children's reading material*. Hillsdale, NJ: Erlbaum.

Barab, S., Thomas, M., Dodge, T., Carteaux, R., & Tuzun, H. (2005). Making learning fun: Quest Atlantis, a game without guns. *Educational Technology Research and Development, 53*(1), 86–107.

Bergin, D. A. (1999). Influences on classroom interest. *Educational Psychologist, 34*(2), 87–98. doi:10.1207/s15326985ep3402_2.

Berlyne, D. E. (1954). A theory of human curiosity. *British Journal of Psychology, 45*(3), 180–191.

Berlyne, D. E. (1957). Conflict and information-theory variables as determinants of human perceptual curiosity. *Journal of Experimental Psychology, 53*(6), 399–404.

Berlyne, D. E. (1962). Uncertainty and epistemic curiosity. *British Journal of Psychology, 53*(1), 27–34.

Berlyne, D. E. (1963). Complexity and incongruity variables as determinants of exploratory choice and evaluative ratings. *Canadian Journal of Psychology/Revue canadienne de psychologie, 17*(3), 274–290.

Berlyne, D. E. (1978). Curiosity and learning. *Motivation and Emotion, 2*(2), 97–175.

Berlyne, D. E., & McDonnell, P. (1965). Effects of stimulus complexity and incongruity on duration of EEG desynchronization. *Electroencephalography and Clinical Neurophysiology, 18*(2), 156–161.

Deci, E. L. (1992). The relation of interest to the motivation of behavior: A self-determination theory perspective. In K. A. Renninger, S. Hidi, & A. Krapp (Eds.), *The role of interest in learning and development* (pp. 43–70). Hillsdale, NJ: Lawrence Erlbaum Associates.

Deci, E. L., & Ryan, R. M. (2004). *Handbook of self-determination research*. Rochester, NY: University of Rochester Press.

Deci, E. L., Vallerand, R. J., Pelletier, L. G., & Ryan, R. M. (1991). Motivation and education: The self-determination perspective. *Educational Psychologist, 26*(3&4), 325–346.

Dewey, J. (1913). *Interest and effort in education*. Cambridge, MA: Riverside Press.

DiBenedetto, M. K., & Zimmerman, B. J. (2010). Differences in self-regulatory processes among students studying science: A microanalytic investigation. *The International Journal of Educational and Psychological Assessment, 5*, 2–24.

Dohn, N. B. (2011). Situational interest of high school students who visit an aquarium. *Science Education, 95*(2), 337–357. doi:10.1002/Sce.20425.

Flowerday, T., Schraw, G., & Stevens, J. (2004). The role of choice and interest in reader engagement. *Journal of Experimental Education, 72*(2), 93–114.

Flowerday, T., & Shell, D. F. (2015). Disentangling the effects of interest and choice on learning, engagement, and attitude. *Learning and Individual Differences, 40*, 134–140. doi:10.1016/j.lindif.2015.05.003.

Fulmer, S. M., D'Mello, S. K., Strain, A., & Graesser, A. C. (2015). Interest-based text preference moderates the effect of text difficulty on engagement and learning. *Contemporary Educational Psychology, 41*, 98–110. doi:10.1016/j.cedpsych.2014.12.005.

Garner, R., Brown, R., Sanders, S., & Menke, D. J. (1992). "Seductive details" and learning from text. In K. A. Renninger, S. Hidi, & A. Krapp (Eds.), *The role of interest in learning and development* (pp. 239–254). Hillsdale, NJ: Erlbaum.

Goetz, E. T., & Sadoski, M. (1995). The perils of seduction: Distracting details or incomprehensible abstractions? *Reading Research Quarterly, 30*(3), 500–511.

Guthrie, J. T., Wigfield, A., Humenick, N. M., Perencevich, K. C., Taboada, A., & Barbosa, P. (2006). Influences of stimulating tasks on reading motivation and comprehension. *Journal of Educational Research, 99*(4), 232–245.

Harackiewicz, J. M., Barron, K. E., Tauer, J. M., Carter, S. M., & Elliot, A. J. (2000). Short-term and long-term consequences of achievement goals: Predicting interest and performance over time. *Journal of Educational Psychology, 92*(2), 316–330. doi:10.1037//0022-0663.92.2.316.

Harackiewicz, J. M., Barron, K. E., Tauer, J. M., & Elliot, A. J. (2002). Predicting success in college: A longitudinal study of achievement goals and ability measures as predictors of interest and performance from freshman year through graduation. *Journal of Educational Psychology, 94*(3), 562–575. doi:10.1037//0022-0663.94.3.562.

Harackiewicz, J. M., Durik, A. M., Barron, K. E., Linnenbrink-Garcia, L., & Tauer, J. M. (2008). The role of achievement goals in the development of interest: Reciprocal relations between achievement goals, interest, and performance. *Journal of Educational Psychology, 100*(1), 105–122. doi:10.1037/0022-0663.100.1.105.

Hidi, S. (1990). Interest and its contribution as a mental resource for learning. *Review of Educational Research, 60*(4), 549–571.

Hidi, S. (2001). Interest, reading, and learning: Theoretical and practical considerations. *Journal of Educational Psychology Review, 13*(3), 191–209.

Hidi, S. (2006). Interest: A unique motivational variable. *Educational Research Review, 1*(2), 69–82.

Hidi, S., & Baird, W. (1988). Strategies for increasing text-based interest and students' recall of expository texts. *Reading Research Quarterly, 23*(4), 465–483. doi:10.2307/747644.

Hidi, S., & Renninger, K. A. (2006). The four-phase model of interest development. *Educational Psychologist, 41*(2), 111–127.

Høgheim, S., & Reber, R. (2015). Supporting interest of middle school students in mathematics through context personalization and example choice. *Contemporary Educational Psychology, 42*, 17–25.

Hulleman, C. S., Durik, A. M., Schweigert, S. A., & Harackiewicz, J. M. (2008). Task values, achievement goals, and interest: An integrative analysis. *Journal of Educational Psychology, 100*(2), 398–416. doi:10.1037/0022-0663.100.2.398.

Iran-Nejad, A. (1987). Cognitive and affective causes of interest and liking. *Journal of Educational Psychology, 79*(2), 120.

Iran-Nejad, A., & Cecil, C. (1992). Interest and learning: A biofunctional perspective. In K. A. Renninger, S. Hidi, & A. Krapp (Eds.), *The role of interest in learning and development* (pp. 297–329). Hillsdale, NJ: Lawrence Erlbaum Associates.

Jerome I. Rotgans, Henk G. Schmidt, (2017) The relation between individual interest and knowledge acquisition. British Educational Research Journal 43 (2):350–371.

Jirout, J., & Klahr, D. (2012). Children's scientific curiosity: In search of an operational definition of an elusive concept. *Developmental Review, 32*(2), 125–160.

Jose, P. E., & Brewer, W. F. (1984). Development of story liking: Character identification, suspense, and outcome resolution. *Developmental Psychology, 20*(5), 911–924.

Kang, H., Scharmann, L. C., Kang, S., & Noh, T. (2010). Cognitive conflict and situational interest as factors influencing conceptual change. *International Journal of Environmental and Science Education, 5*(4), 383–405.

Kang, M. J., Hsu, M., Krajbich, I. M., Loewenstein, G., McClure, S. M., Wang, J. T. Y., & Camerer, C. F. (2009). The wick in the candle of learning: Epistemic curiosity activates reward circuitry and enhances memory. *Psychological Science, 20*(8), 963–973.

Kashdan, T. B., & Silvia, P. (Eds.). (2009). *Curiosity and interest: The benefits of thriving on novelty and challenge* (2nd ed.). New York: Oxford University Press.

Kenny, D. A. (2005). *Cross-Lagged panel design*. New York: Wiley Online Library.

Koller, O., Baumert, J., & Schnabel, K. (2001). Does interest matter? The relationship between academic interest and achievement in mathematics. *Journal for Research in Mathematics Education, 32*(5), 448–470. doi:10.2307/749801.

Kornell, N., Hays, M. J., & Bjork, R. A. (2009). Unsuccessful retrieval attempts enhance subsequent learning. *Journal of Experimental Psychology: Learning, Memory, and Cognition, 35*(4), 989–998.

Krapp, A. (1999). Interest, motivation and learning: An educational-psychological perspective. *European Journal of Psychology of Education, 14*(1), 23–40.

Krapp, A. (2003). Interest and human development: An educational-psychological perspective. Development and motivation. *British Journal of Educational Psychology, Monograph Series, II*(2), 57–84.

Krapp, A. (2007). An educational–psychological conceptualisation of interest. *International Journal for Educational & Vocational Guidance, 7*(1), 5–21. doi:10.1007/s10775-007-9113-9.

Linnenbrink-Garcia, L., Durik, A. M., Conley, A. M., Barron, K. E., Tauer, J. M., Karabenick, S. A., & Harackiewicz, J. M. (2010). Measuring situational interest in academic domains. *Educational and Psychological Measurement, 70*(4), 647–671. doi:10.1177/0013164409355699.

Loewenstein, G. (1994). The psychology of curiosity: A review and reinterpretation. *Psychological Bulletin, 116*(1), 75–98.

Mattern, N., & Schau, C. (2002). Gender differences in science attitude-achievement relationships over time among white middle-school students. *Journal of Research in Science Teaching, 39*(4), 324–340.

Mitchell, M. (1993). Situational interest: Its multifaceted structure in the secondary mathematics classroom. *Journal of Educational Psychology, 85*(3), 424–436.

Mussel, P. (2010). Epistemic curiosity and related constructs: Lacking evidence of discriminant validity. *Personality and Individual Differences, 49*(5), 506–510. doi:10.1016/J. Paid.2010.05.014.

Niemivirta, M., & Tapola, A. (2007). Self-efficacy, interest, and task performance: Within-task changes, mutual relationships, and predictive effects. *Zeitschrift Fur Padagogische Psychologie, 21*(3–4), 241–250. doi:10.1024/1010-0652.21.3.241.

Nieswandt, M. (2007). Student affect and conceptual understanding in learning chemistry. *Journal of Research in Science Teaching, 44*(7), 908–937. doi:10.1002/tea.20169.

O'Grady, G., Yew, E., Goh, K. P. L., & Schmidt, H. G. (2012). *One-day, one-problem: An approach to problem-based learning*. New York: Springer.

Palmer, D. H. (2009). Student interest generated during an inquiry skills lesson. *Journal of Research in Science Teaching, 46*(2), 147–165. doi:10.1002/Tea.20263.

Reid, J. M. (1987). The learning style preferences of ESL students. *TESOL Quarterly, 21*(1), 87–111.

Reio, T. G. (2004). Prior knowledge, self-directed learning readiness, and curiosity: Antecedents to classroom learning performance. *International Journal of Self-directed learning, 1*(1), 18–25.

Rotgans, J. I., O'Grady, G., & Alwis, W. A. M. (2011). Introduction: Studies on the learning process in the one-day, one-problem approach to problem-based learning. *Advances in Health Sciences Education, 16*(4), 443–448. doi:10.1007/s10459-011-9299-y.

Rotgans, J. I., & Schmidt, H. G. (2009). Examination of the context-specific nature of self-regulated learning. *Educational Studies, 35*(3), 239–253. doi:10.1080/03055690802648051.

Rotgans, J. I., & Schmidt, H. G. (2010). The motivated strategies for learning questionnaire: A measure for students' general motivational beliefs and learning strategies? *The Asia-Pacific Education Researcher, 19*(2), 357–369. doi:10.3860/taper.v19i2.1603.

Rotgans, J. I., & Schmidt, H. G. (2011a). The intricate relationship between motivation and achievement: Examining the links between motivation, self-regulated learning, classroom behaviors, and academic achievement. *International Journal of Teaching and Learning in Higher Education, 24*, 197–208.

Rotgans, J. I., & Schmidt, H. G. (2011b). Situational interest and academic achievement in the active-learning classroom. *Learning and Instruction, 21*(1), 58–67. doi:10.1016/J. Learninstruc.2009.11.001.

Rotgans, J. I., & Schmidt, H. G. (2012). Problem-based learning and student motivation: The role of interest in learning and achievement. In G. O'Grady, E. H. J. Yew, P. L. G. Goh, & H. G. Schmidt (Eds.), *One-day, one-problem: An approach to problem-based learning* (pp. 85–101). Singapore: Springer.

Rotgans, J. I., & Schmidt, H. G. (2014). Situational interest and learning: Thirst for knoweldge. *Learning and Instruction, 32*(August), 37–50. doi:10.1016/j.learninstruc.2014.01.002.

Rotgans, J. I., & Schmidt, H. G. (2016). *How Individual Interest Influences Situational Interest and How Both are Related to Knowledge Acquisition: A Micro-Analytical Investigation*. In Press.

Rotgans, J. I., & Schmidt, H. G. (2017). The relationship between individual interest and knowledge acquisition. *British Educational Research Journal, 43*(2), 350–371.

Ryan, R. M., & Deci, E. L. (2000). Self-determination theory and the facilitation of intrinsic motivation, social development, and well-being. *American Psychologist, 55*(1), 68–78.

Schiefele, U. (1991). Interest, learning, and motivation. *Educational Psychologist, 26*(3&4), 299–323.

Schiefele, U. (1999). Interest and learning from text. *Scientific Studies of Reading, 3*(3), 257–279.

Schiefele, U., Krapp, A., & Winteler, A. (1992). Interest as a predictor of academic achievement: A meta-analysis of research. In K. A. Renninger, S. Hidi, & A. Krapp (Eds.), *The role of interest in learning and development* (pp. 183–212). Hillsdale, NJ: Lawrence Erlbaum Associates.

Schiefele, U., & Rheinberg, F. (1997). Motivation and knowledge acquisition: Searching for mediating processes. In M. L. Maehr & P. R. Pintrich (Eds.), *Advances in motivation and achievement* (Vol. 10, pp. 251–301). London: Jai Press Inc..

Schmidt, H. G., Rotgans, J. I., & Yew, E. H. J. (2011). The process of problem-based learning: What works and why. *Medical Education, 45*(8), 792–806. doi:10.1111/j.1365-2923.2011.04035.x.

Schmidt, H. G., Van der Molen, H. T., Te Winkel, W. W. R., & Wijnen, W. H. F. W. (2009). Constructivist, problem-based learning does work: A meta-analysis of curricular comparisons involving a single medical school. *Educational Psychologist, 44*(4), 227–249.

Schraw, G. (1997). Situational interest in literary text. *Contemporary Educational Psychology, 22*(4), 436–456.

Schraw, G. (1998). Processing and recall differences among seductive details. *Journal of Educational Psychology, 90*(1), 3–12. doi:10.1037//0022-0663.90.1.3.

Schraw, G., Bruning, R., & Svoboda, C. (1995). Sources of situational interest. *Journal of Reading Behavior, 27*(1), 1–17.

Schraw, G., Flowerday, T., & Lehman, S. (2001). Increasing situational interest in the classroom. *Educational Psychology Review, 13*(3), 211–224.

Schraw, G., & Lehman, S. (2001). Situational interest: A review of the literature and directions for future research. *Educational Psychology Review, 13*(1), 23–52. doi:10.1023/a:1009004801455.

Schraw, G., & Lehman, S. (2009). *Interest*. Retrieved from http://www.education.com/reference/article/interest/

Silvia, P. J. (2008). Interest – The curious emotion. *Current Directions in Psychological Science, 17*(1), 57–60.

Sungur, S., & Tekkaya, C. (2006). Effects of problem-based learning and traditional instruction on self-regulated learning. *Journal of Educational Research, 99*(5), 307–317. doi:10.3200/JOER.99.5.307-320.

Tapola, A., Jaakkola, T., & Niemivirta, M. (2014). The influence of achievement goal orientations and task concreteness on situational interest. *The Journal of Experimental Education, 82*(4), 455–479.

Tapola, A., Veermans, M., & Niemivirta, M. (2013). Predictors and outcomes of situational interest during a science learning task. *Instructional Science, 41*(6), 1047–1064. doi:10.1007/s11251-013-9273-6.

Tin, T. B. (2008). Exploring the nature of the relation between interest and comprehension. *Teaching in Higher Education, 13*(5), 525–536. doi:10.1080/13562510802334764.

Tobias, S. (1994). Interest, prior knowledge, and learning. *Review of Educational Research, 64*(1), 37–54.

Tsai, Y., Kunter, M., Lüdtke, O., Trautwein, U., & Ryan, R. M. (2008). What makes lessons interesting? The role of situational and individual factors in three school subjects. *Journal of Educational Psychology, 100*(2), 460–472. doi:10.1037/0022-0663.100.2.460.

van Dijk, T. A., & Kintsch, W. (1999). *Strategies of discourse comprehension*. New York: Academic Press.

Wade, S. E. (1992). How interest affects learning from text. In K. A. Renninger, S. Hidi, & A. Krapp (Eds.), *The role of interest in learning and developmentt* (pp. 281–296). Hillsdale, NJ: Lawrence Erlbaum Associates.

Zimmerman, B. J., & Kitsantas, A. (2005). The hidden dimension of personal competence: Self-regulated learning and practice. In A. J. Elliot & C. S. Dweck (Eds.), *Handbook of competence and motivation* (pp. 509–526). New York: The Guilford Press.

Part III
The Interest Spectrum

Chapter 5
Curiosity

Paul J. Silvia

Curiosity

If anything defines the human condition, it is our ability to immerse ourselves in inane and nonsensical things. Unlike other animals, we can be motivated to spend our energy and hours on the hopelessly impractical things that will never put money in our wallets, food in our tummies, or mates in our beds. Much of what we do and learn is practical, of course, but unlike almost all other animals, people can transcend daily life's practical problems when investing their time and brainpower.

As the history of research on human motivation shows (Bolles, 1967; Silvia, 2012), scientists have grappled with the family of concepts captured by *curiosity* since psychology's early days. In modern times, concepts related to interest, curiosity, and learning motivation appear in a wide swath of scholarship, from genetics to classroom instruction to literary analysis (Silvia, 2006). In this chapter, I step back to look at the bigger picture of curiosity. My aim is not to review or integrate such disparate fields. Instead, I want to discuss a perspective on curiosity that is grounded in modern models of motivation and emotion. These models do not solve all the problems that human curiosity poses, but they do try to analyze curiosity at a fundamental and general level instead of within a narrow domain (e.g., vocational decisions or classroom learning).

After considering how the modern science of motivation and emotion views curiosity, we will consider some of its implications. Some definitional issues that have bedeviled research on interest and curiosity, for example, can be clarified by a basic analysis of how curiosity works. Likewise, the thorny nature of individual differences in interest and curiosity can be unpacked and illuminated.

P.J. Silvia (✉)
Department of Psychology, University of North Carolina at Greensboro,
Greensboro, NC 27402-6170, USA
e-mail: p_silvia@uncg.edu

© Springer International Publishing AG 2017   97
P.A. O'Keefe, J.M. Harackiewicz (eds.), *The Science of Interest*,
DOI 10.1007/978-3-319-55509-6_5

Why Are People so Curious? A Functional Analysis

Why are humans curious at all? Plenty of the world's creatures seem wholly incurious: they eat, sleep, and mate. Many animals, particularly mammals, show behavioral expressions of curiosity that we humans recognize (e.g., Darwin, 1872/1998), such as experimenting with objects, exploring new places and things, and playing. But all of us animals are the product of a long evolutionary process, so the distribution of curiosity as a motivational system across species must tell us something fundamental about it.

This is the starting point of a *functional approach*, which seeks to understand human curiosity in terms of the functions it serves for near-term adaptation and long-term human development (Keltner & Gross, 1999; Parrott, 2001). My ideas about the functions of curiosity are heavily influenced by Izard's (1977) model of human emotions, which views emotions as evolved psychobiological systems that have adaptive roles in human development. His functional view is widespread in modern emotion science. Most modern theories view emotions as having motivational qualities that organize behaviors necessary to confront humans' major adaptational challenges (Frijda, 1986; Lazarus, 1991; Panksepp, 1998; Scherer, 2001; Tomkins, 1962).

Curiosity, in Izard's view, is captured by the basic emotion of *interest–excitement*. (Curiosity and interest are essentially synonymous in this model.) Like all the basic emotions, interest is innate, in the sense of being unlearned and universal—people are not taught to be curious. And like all emotions, interest accomplishes something for people. Some emotions have obvious functions, such as fear's preparation for fighting or fleeing, but others have more subtle functions that reflect long-range social or developmental goals (Abe & Izard, 1999). Interest's functions are both obvious and subtle, and they can be viewed as a family of intertwined functions.

Function 1: Interest Motivates Learning

Some species have little need for learning: many animals, from seahorses to salamanders, are born more or less ready for the challenges they will face in their environments. Being born ready has its virtues, but the trade-off is behavioral rigidity. Such creatures are behaviorally inflexible, and their limited ability to learn prevents them from capitalizing on acquired experience. On the other hand, other creatures, such as humans, are born ignorant but with an awe-inspiring ability to learn. Here we see the other side of the trade-off. Humans are born helpless and incompetent, and we remain dependent on adults for an unusually long developmental period. But our ability to learn allows us to capitalize on experience, act flexibly, and leverage cultural knowledge passed along from adults.

The emotion of interest, in Izard's view, is an engine of learning. Curiosity is what gives us our hungry minds. It is the motivational system that ensures that humans will engage with the environment, enjoy learning, and seek out new experiences and ideas (Abe & Izard, 1999). If they have a system that motivates learning for its own sake, people do not need to be born with much innate knowledge—they will inevitably want to learn because they are easily bored and will enjoy exploring new things.

It is telling that the emotion of interest appears so early in development. Developmental research on emotion shows that, across the globe, emotions appear in a fixed order during infancy (Izard, 1978). At birth, newborns show—as all parents know—an eerily effective distress system. But they also show a nascent form of disgust (e.g., rejecting bad-tasting objects from the mouth) and a well-developed form of interest. At birth, infants show selective attention, both to human faces (aiding social bonding and social learning) and to events that are novel and changing. From the beginning, the human baby's mind is hungry.

Across the lifespan, our curious minds motivate us to learn. The allure of the new, the vexation of boredom, and the desire to learn foster long-term developmental projects, such as acquiring complex skills and mastering large bodies of knowledge (Fiske & Maddi, 1961). Without the intrinsic motivation to explore inherent in curiosity, it would be hard to acquire the complex competencies that adults have.

Function 2: Interest Serves as a Motivational Counterweight to Anxiety

The emotion of fear serves the noble goal of keeping us safe by promoting caution and wariness (Lazarus, 1991). It is not irrational to fear new foods, new places, new things, and new people. New things can be, and quite often are, harmful to us. Feelings of fear thus motivate avoidance: anxious people do not approach, seek out, or engage with unfamiliar things. But what would happen if we always avoided unfamiliar things? New foods, new places, new things, and new people can be fascinating and rewarding, so our wariness would make us miss out.

Motivation science has a long history of emphasizing push–pull conflicts between motivational states (Atkinson, 1964; Bolles, 1967). The tension between anxiety and curiosity is a classic case, one emphasized by most of the theories of curiosity that come from motivation science (e.g., Berlyne, 1960, 1971; Kashdan, 2004, 2009; Spielberger & Starr, 1994; Tomkins, 1962). Avoiding new things keeps us safe, but it prevents us from cultivating knowledge and expertise: we cannot learn new things without trying new things. Conversely, curiosity motivates us to explore new things, but it exposes us to their real risks.

One of the functions of interest, then, is to serve as a counterweight to anxiety. Because new things can be scary, the motivational system needs an appetitive, approach-oriented mechanism for overcoming wariness and making new things appealing.

Function 3: Interest Serves as a Motivational Counterweight to Enjoyment

Fear of the unfamiliar is not the only barrier to exploring new things. Attachments to the familiar are a less obvious but probably stronger barrier to engaging with novelty. The emotion of happiness does many things (Fredrickson, 1998), but a key function is to build attachments to people and things that evoke it (Tomkins, 1962). When an activity is enjoyable, people develop positive attitudes toward it and expect that doing it again will evoke similar happy feelings. A tension thus exists between trying something new and trying something that has always been fun.

The motivational conflict between interest and enjoyment is fascinating. It has been discussed by several emotion theories (Izard, 1977; Tomkins, 1962), but it is counterintuitive and has not received much attention in the study of curiosity and interest (Turner & Silvia, 2006). Happiness motivates people to stick with the sure bet, to go with what was safe and fun and rewarding the last time. Interest, in contrast, motivates people to go out on a limb, to try something new.

One way to see the conflict between interest and enjoyment is to expose people to creepy and unseemly things. In one of our studies (Turner & Silvia, 2006), we asked the participants to view a broad set of Western paintings. Some of the images were familiar and calming, such as nature landscapes or impressionistic art. Other images, however, were disturbing, creepy, or upsetting (e.g., Francisco Goya's *Saturn Devouring His Children* and Francis Bacon's *Head Surrounded by Sides of Beef*). For each painting, people rated their feelings of interest and enjoyment as well as ratings of the images' familiarity, novelty, and disturbingness. Overall, interest and enjoyment were unrelated. Appraising images as new and unfamiliar predicted higher interest but lower enjoyment—unfamiliar things were interesting but not pleasant. Likewise, the disturbing images were much more interesting—but much less pleasant—than the conventional ones. Thus, while interest and enjoyment commonly go together, they represent different emotions with distinct functions.

The tug of the familiar versus the allure of the new appears whenever people have to choose between what they like and what they not yet tried. When people want to go out to eat, do they go to their favorite place that they always enjoy, or do they try the new place that just opened next door? The new place might be better, so trying something new could uncover a new source of reward. But it might be disappointing or foul, so trying something new has a big opportunity cost when there is a sure thing. Even when people choose their favorite restaurant, do they pick what they always pick, or do they try something new?

As a pair, fear and enjoyment are major barriers to trying new things. Fear motivates wariness and avoidance of unfamiliar things; happiness motivates attachments to tried-and-true sources of pleasure. Curiosity thus motivates people to engage in new things despite both the potential cost of the action (i.e., it could be harmful) and the opportunity cost of forsaking the sure thing.

Curiosity's Conceptual Cousins

Viewing curiosity as an evolved psychobiological emotional-motivational system relocates it. Researchers have tended to group curiosity together with the family of positive emotions (Ellsworth & Smith, 1988). This is sensible because both interest and enjoyment are appetitive and approach-oriented emotions, and the subjective experience of curiosity is a pleasing feeling of being activated, immersed, and absorbed (Izard, 1977).

But one could also view curiosity as a member of the family of *knowledge emotions*, a group of emotions associated with learning and exploring (Keltner & Shiota, 2003; Silvia, 2010). Some emotions have metacognitive roots: they are evoked when people appraise aspects of their knowledge. Surprise, for example, stems from appraising an event as unexpected (Scherer, 2001), and interest follows when people further appraise the unexpected thing as within their capacity to understand (Silvia, 2005, 2008). Confusion stems from appraising an unexpected, unfamiliar thing as essentially beyond one's ability to master or understand (Silvia, 2010, 2013). And awe, perhaps the most obscure of the knowledge emotions, comes from encountering something that cannot be assimilated to existing knowledge and thus requires accommodation (Keltner & Haidt, 2003; Nusbaum & Silvia, 2014).

One virtue of thinking of curiosity as a member of an emotion family is that it highlights its similarities with other motivational states. I find the relationship between interest and awe particularly intriguing. One possibility is that awe is simply the most intense pole of interest. Izard (1977) labeled the intense form of interest *fascination*, and some researchers have speculated that feelings of awe and wonder are what intense interest feels like (Campos, Shiota, Keltner, Gonzaga, & Goetz, 2013; Silvia, Fayn, Nusbaum, & Beaty, 2015). The subjective experience of awe—a feeling of being absorbed, immersed, and captivated—certainly has the hallmarks of interest's motivational function of exploration and engagement. On the other hand, perhaps awe represents a family of states that are sufficiently different in their origins and functions. For example, part of awe is a transcendent experience of feeling moved and touched (Bonner & Friedman, 2011; Nusbaum & Silvia, 2014), which seems outside of our common understanding of interest and curiosity. In any case, the relationships between curiosity and other emotions deserve more attention.

Implications for Concepts and Terms

We noted earlier that a functional analysis of curiosity is fundamental: it seeks to explain it using basic science models of motivation and emotion. Such models view curiosity as an innate system that motivates learning and exploration for its own sake. Thinking of curiosity as part of humanity's evolved motivational architecture can shed some light on how we define and talk about it.

In particular, some domains of interest research have drawn some sharp differences between curiosity and interest (for a review, see Grossnickle, 2016) or between types of interest (e.g., cognitive vs. emotional; Harp & Meyer, 1997). In motivation research, however, curiosity and interest are seen as synonymous, and I think a unitary view is more fruitful for understanding curiosity across all of psychology's domains. The English language gives different senses to these words, to be sure, but we should not be led astray by our lexicon. People tend to use *curious* to describe upcoming events ("I am curious to hear what he has to say") or to refer to a stable quality of a person ("She is such a curious child"). *Interest* seems to appear more often to refer to ongoing or past experiences ("That was just so interesting!"). Usage has changed over time, however, which is a clue that we should not read too much into words. *Curious*, for example, was once common in contexts in which now only *interesting, amazing,* or *puzzling* would appear (e.g., "What a curious spectacle!" or "I saw the most curious thing on the tram this morning"; see "curious, adj.," entry 16a, OED, 2016), and *interest* is still an allowable word for stable dispositions ("My daughter is interested in so many things").

The psychobiology of curiosity does not support the notion of distinct interest and curiosity systems (DeYoung, 2013; Panksepp, 1998; Zuckerman, 1994). Instead, I think that curiosity—like all things that are profoundly important to people—is widely lexicalized in language so that people can talk flexibly about a complex and pressing topic (Cruse, 2011).

Stable Aspects of Curiosity: The Specific and the General

Stable aspects of curiosity are tackled in other chapters in this volume, but they are worth mentioning here. In my own work, I have argued that a comprehensive analysis of interest should have something to say both about momentary emotional states (e.g., finding things interesting and feeling curious in the moment) and about stable aspects of motivation (Silvia, 2006; Silvia & Kashdan, 2009, in press). Curiosity can be stable in two senses: a concrete one and a general one. For the most part, researchers in education have focused on the former, and researchers in personality and neuroscience have focused on the latter.

In the concrete sense of stable, we have people's unique and specific "interests." Education researchers have been the most forward-looking in this respect, having emphasized the difference between *situational interest* and *individual interest* several decades ago (e.g., Renninger, Hidi, & Krapp, 1992). Individual interests are narrow domains of activity that people find interesting, valuable, and rewarding. Hobbies are perhaps the best example of how idiosyncratic such interests can be, such as when one meets people who collect Waltham 1883 model pocket watches, participate in Civil War reenactments, or develop recipes for fermenting their own kombucha. More widely studied, however, are academic and occupational interests. Interest researchers view individual interests as having a cluster of features: finding the domain interesting is clearly one, but valuing and knowing a lot about the domain are just as central (Hidi & Renninger, 2006; Schiefele, 2009). Individual interests essentially resemble concepts from other sides of psychology, such as the *personal goals* and *personal strivings* discussed in research on personality and motivation (Emmons, 1986, 1999). How people's quirky hobbies and interests develop is a vexing problem that has bedeviled theories of motivation (for a review, see Silvia, 2006).

The general sense in which curiosity is stable—variation in "trait curiosity"—is much easier to study and understand. In this approach, researchers have identified and studied broad between-person individual differences in curiosity. The trait approach assumes that some people are more curious than others, although this could mean many things: they experience curiosity more often (frequency), they experience curiosity more strongly when they feel it (intensity), or they need less input for curiosity to be sparked (sensitivity).

A small but intriguing strand of research on trait curiosity has examined the genetics and neuroscience of curiosity, often in nonhuman animals. This line of work has explored heritable variation in genes related to novelty seeking, such as variants in the family of dopamine receptor genes (DeYoung, 2013). Traits associated with curiosity show substantial heritability in behavioral genetics studies (Bouchard & Loehlin, 2001; Zuckerman, 1994). These differences are in turn apparent in the brain when people do tasks involving imagination, novelty, and exploration (e.g., Beaty et al., 2016).

The larger strand of research on trait curiosity, however, has sought to identify traits related to curiosity, develop valid measures of them, and then understand their meaning and implications. Some researchers have focused simply on trait-like curiosity (e.g., Kashdan et al., 2009; Spielberger & Starr, 1994). Other researchers have funneled in on likely facets of trait curiosity, such as facets reflecting specific or diverse curiosity, or facets reflecting exploration motivated by interest versus uncertainty (e.g., Litman & Jimerson, 2004; Litman & Spielberger, 2003).

More commonly, however, researchers have examined broader traits in which curiosity is a facet. The Big Five tradition, for example, locates curiosity within *openness to experience*, one of the major dimensions of personality (Goldberg, 1990; McCrae, 1994). There are many models of openness to experience (for reviews, see Oleynick et al., 2017; Nusbaum & Silvia, 2017), but curiosity is important to all of them. Central to openness to experience is an interest in new things, a willingness to explore new ideas, people, and places.

People high in openness to experience show higher curiosity in a wide range of contexts. They are more likely to find unusual art and music interesting, to try foreign food, to visit other countries, to enjoy intellectual ideas, and to seek gradu-ate education, among other things (e.g., McCrae & Sutin, 2009). Similarly, people high in openness to experience are much more likely to generate new things. Openness to experience strongly predicts everyday creativity. In experience sam-pling (Silvia et al., 2014) and daily diary (Conner & Silvia, 2015) studies, for exam-ple, people high in openness are much more likely to be spending time on creative goals and hobbies. And openness predicts creativity at the sociocultural level as well: people high in openness to experience have more creative accomplishments over the lifespan (Feist & Barron, 2003). Curious people thus seek out, enjoy, and create novelty.

We can think of traits like openness to experience as parameters that tilt the scales of curiosity versus anxiety. In their model, Spielberger and Starr (1994) pro-posed that personality traits shift the relative weight of approach and avoidance motivation when people are faced with new things. Traits like openness to experi-ence and sensation seeking, for example, incline people toward exploration; traits like anxiety and neuroticism, in contrast, incline people toward avoidance. By inclining people toward exploration, openness to experience fosters learning and creativity. At the same time, some things in life should be left unexplored, and open-ness to experience does increase the likelihood that people will delve into behaviors and situations that are unproductive or maladaptive (see Kashdan, 2009; Chap. 8).

Conclusion

Wanting to know something for its own sake, wanting to do something simply because it is interesting—this is part of human nature. In this chapter, we explored a functional analysis of curiosity. Modern models of motivation and emotion have much to say about the role of interest in learning, adaptation, and development. Fundamentally, curiosity motivates the enormous amount of learning that people need to do. Over time, people develop the skills and knowledge needed to flourish because they enjoy learning and are easily bored. Although some people are more curious than others, and people's quirky interests will vary, all people are essentially curious creatures.

References

Abe, J. A., & Izard, C. E. (1999). The developmental functions of emotions: An analysis in terms of differential emotions theory. *Cognition and Emotion, 13*, 523–549.

Atkinson, J. W. (1964). *An introduction to motivation.* New York: Van Nostrand.

Beaty, R. E., Kaufman, S. B., Benedek, M., Jung, R. E., Kenett, Y. N., Jauk, E., et al. (2016). Personality and complex brain networks: The role of openness to experience in default network activity. *Human Brain Mapping, 37*, 773–779.

Berlyne, D. E. (1960). *Conflict, arousal, and curiosity.* New York: McGraw–Hill.

Berlyne, D. E. (1971). *Aesthetics and psychobiology*. New York: Appleton-Century-Crofts.

Bolles, R. C. (1967). *Theory of motivation*. New York: Harper & Row.

Bonner, E. T., & Friedman, H. L. (2011). A conceptual clarification of the experience of awe: An interpretative phenomenological analysis. *The Humanistic Psychologist, 39*, 222–235.

Bouchard, T. J., & Loehlin, J. C. (2001). Genes, evolution, and personality. *Behavior Genetics, 31*, 243–273.

Campos, B., Shiota, M. N., Keltner, D., Gonzaga, G. C., & Goetz, J. L. (2013). What is shared, what is different? Core relational themes and expressive displays of eight positive emotions. *Cognition and Emotion, 27*, 37–52.

Conner, T. S., & Silvia, P. J. (2015). Creative days: A daily diary study of emotion, personality, and everyday creativity. *Psychology of Aesthetics, Creativity, and the Arts, 9*, 463–470.

Cruse, A. (2011). *Meaning in language: An introduction to semantics and pragmatics* (3rd ed.). New York: Oxford University Press.

curious, adj. (2016). *Oxford English Dictionary Online*. New York: Oxford University Press. Retrieved online 5 May 2016.

Darwin, C. (1872/1998). *The expression of the emotions in man and animals* (3rd ed.). New York: Oxford University Press.

DeYoung, C. G. (2013). The neuromodulator of exploration: A unifying theory of the role of dopamine in personality. *Frontiers in Human Neuroscience, 7*(762).

Ellsworth, P. C., & Smith, C. A. (1988). Shades of joy: Patterns of appraisal differentiating positive emotions. *Cognition and Emotion, 2*, 301–331.

Emmons, R. A. (1986). Personal strivings: An approach to personality and subjective well-being. *Journal of Personality and Social Psychology, 51*, 1058–1068.

Emmons, R. A. (1999). *The psychology of ultimate concerns: Motivation and spirituality in personality*. New York: Guilford.

Feist, G. J., & Barron, F. X. (2003). Predicting creativity from early to late adulthood: Intellect, potential, and personality. *Journal of Research in Personality, 37*, 62–88.

Fiske, D. W., & Maddi, S. R. (1961). A conceptual framework. In D. W. Fiske & S. R. Maddi (Eds.), *Functions of varied experience* (pp. 11–56). Homewood, IL: Dorsey.

Fredrickson, B. L. (1998). What good are positive emotions? *Review of General Psychology, 2*, 300–319.

Frijda, N. H. (1986). *The emotions*. Cambridge: Cambridge University Press.

Goldberg, L. R. (1990). An alternative "description of personality": The big five factor structure. *Journal of Personality and Social Psychology, 59*, 1216–1229.

Grossnickle, E. M. (2016). Disentangling curiosity: Dimensionality, definitions, and distinctions from interest in educational contexts. *Educational Psychology Review, 28*, 23–60.

Harp, S. F., & Mayer, R. E. (1997). The role of interest in learning from scientific text and illustrations: On the distinction between emotional interest and cognitive interest. *Journal of Educational Psychology, 89*, 92–102.

Hidi, S., & Renninger, K. A. (2006). The four-phase model of interest development. *Educational Psychologist, 41*, 111–127.

Izard, C. E. (1977). *Human emotions*. New York: Plenum.

Izard, C. E. (1978). On the development of emotions and emotion–cognition relationships in infancy. In M. Lewis & L. A. Rosenblum (Eds.), *The development of affect* (pp. 389–413). New York: Plenum.

Kashdan, T. B. (2004). Curiosity. In C. Peterson & M. E. P. Seligman (Eds.), *Character strengths and virtues: A handbook and classification* (pp. 125–141). New York: Oxford University Press.

Kashdan, T. B. (2009). *Curious? Discover the missing ingredient to a fulfilling life*. New York: William Morrow.

Kashdan, T. B., Gallagher, M. W., Silvia, P. J., Winterstein, B. P., Breen, W. E., Terhar, D., et al. (2009). The curiosity and exploration inventory–II: Development, factor structure, and psychometrics. *Journal of Research in Personality, 43*, 987–998.

Keltner, D., & Gross, J. J. (1999). Functional accounts of emotions. *Cognition and Emotion, 13*, 467–480.

Keltner, D., & Haidt, J. (2003). Approaching awe, a moral, spiritual, and aesthetic emotion. *Cognition and Emotion, 17*, 297–314.

Keltner, D., & Shiota, M. N. (2003). New displays and new emotions: A commentary on Rozin and Cohen (2003). *Emotion, 3*, 86–91.

Lazarus, R. S. (1991). *Emotion and adaptation.* New York: Oxford University Press.

Litman, J. A., & Jimerson, T. L. (2004). The measurement of curiosity as a feeling of deprivation. *Journal of Personality Assessment, 82*, 147–157.

Litman, J. A., & Spielberger, C. D. (2003). Measuring epistemic curiosity and its diversive and specific components. *Journal of Personality Assessment, 80*, 75–86.

McCrae, R. R. (1994). Openness to experience: Expanding the boundaries of factor V. *European Journal of Personality, 8*, 251–272.

McCrae, R. R., & Sutin, A. R. (2009). Openness to experience. In M. R. Leary & R. H. Hoyle (Eds.), *Handbook of individual differences in social behavior* (pp. 257–273). New York: Guilford.

Nusbaum, E. C., & Silvia, P. J. (2014). Unusual aesthetic states. In P. P. L. Tinio & J. K. Smith (Eds.), *The Cambridge handbook of the psychology of aesthetics and the arts* (pp. 519–539). Cambridge, UK: Cambridge University Press.

Nusbaum, E. C., & Silvia, P. J. (2017). What are funny people like? Exploring the crossroads of humor ability and openness to experience. In G. J. Feist, R. Reiter-Palmon, & J. C. Kaufman (Eds.), *Cambridge handbook of creativity and personality research* (pp. 294–322). New York, NY: Cambridge University Press.

Oleynick, V. C., DeYoung, C. G., Hyde, E., Kaufman, S. B., Beaty, R. E., & Silvia, P. J. (2017). Openness/intellect: The core of the creative personality. In G. J. Feist, R. Reiter-Palmon, & J. C. Kaufman (Eds.), *Cambridge handbook of creativity and personality research* (pp. 9–27). New York, NY: Cambridge University Press.

Panksepp, J. (1998). *Affective neuroscience: The foundations of human and animal emotions.* New York: Oxford University Press.

Parrott, W. G. (2001). Implications of dysfunctional emotions for understanding how emotions function. *Review of General Psychology, 5*, 180–186.

Renninger, K. A., Hidi, S., & Krapp, A. (Eds.). (1992). *The role of interest in learning and development.* Hillsdale, NJ: Lawrence Erlbaum Associates.

Scherer, K. R. (2001). Appraisal considered as a process of multilevel sequential checking. In K. R. Scherer, A. Schorr, & T. Johnstone (Eds.), *Appraisal processes in emotion: Theory, methods, research* (pp. 92–120). New York: Oxford University Press.

Schiefele, U. (2009). Situational and individual interest. In K. R. Wenzel & A. Wigfield (Eds.), *Handbook of motivation at school* (pp. 197–222). New York: Routledge.

Silvia, P. J. (2005). What is interesting? Exploring the appraisal structure of interest. *Emotion, 5*, 89–102.

Silvia, P. J. (2006). *Exploring the psychology of interest.* New York: Oxford University Press.

Silvia, P. J. (2008). Interest—The curious emotion. *Current Directions in Psychological Science, 17*, 57–60.

Silvia, P. J. (2010). Confusion and interest: The role of knowledge emotions in aesthetic experience. *Psychology of Aesthetics, Creativity, and the Arts, 4*, 75–80.

Silvia, P. J. (2012). Curiosity and motivation. In R. M. Ryan (Ed.), *The Oxford handbook of human motivation* (pp. 157–166). New York: Oxford University Press.

Silvia, P. J. (2013). Interested experts, confused novices: Art expertise and the knowledge emotions. *Empirical Studies of the Arts, 31*, 107–116.

Silvia, P. J., Beaty, R. E., Nusbaum, E. C., Eddington, K. M., Levin-Aspenson, H., & Kwapil, T. R. (2014). Everyday creativity in daily life: An experience-sampling study of "little c" creativity. *Psychology of Aesthetics, Creativity, and the Arts, 8*, 183–188.

Silvia, P. J., Fayn, K., Nusbaum, E. C., & Beaty, R. E. (2015). Openness to experience and awe in response to nature and music: Personality and profound aesthetic experiences. *Psychology of Aesthetics, Creativity, and the Arts, 9*, 376–384.

Silvia, P. J., & Kashdan, T. B. (2009). Interesting things and curious people: Exploration and engagement as transient states and enduring strengths. *Social and Personality Psychology Compass, 3*, 785–797.

Silvia, P. J., & Kashdan, T. B. (in press). Curiosity and interest: The benefits of thriving on novelty and challenge. In S. J. Lopez, L. M. Edwards, & S. C. Marques (Eds.), *Handbook of positive psychology* (3rd ed.). New York: Oxford University Press.

Spielberger, C. D., & Starr, L. M. (1994). Curiosity and exploratory behavior. In H. F. O'Neil Jr. & M. Drillings (Eds.), *Motivation: Theory and research* (pp. 221–243). Hillsdale, NJ: Lawrence Erlbaum Associates.

Tomkins, S. S. (1962). *Affect, imagery, consciousness: Vol. 1, the positive affects.* New York: Springer.

Turner Jr., S. A., & Silvia, P. J. (2006). Must interesting things be pleasant? A test of competing appraisal structures. *Emotion, 6,* 670–674.

Zuckerman, M. (1994). *Behavioral expressions and biosocial bases of sensation seeking.* New York: Cambridge University Press.

Chapter 6
Situational Interest: A Proposal to Enhance Conceptual Clarity

Maximilian Knogler

Situations powerfully influence peoples' state of mind and behavior (Nisbett & Ross, 1991). This is not just a disciplinary tenet promoted by social psychologists but a well-established empirical fact verified by decades of rigorous research in psychological science (Reis, 2008). Accordingly, the concept of a "situation" cuts through many theories of psychological science, extending and complementing dispositional views and explanations for peoples' actions or their lack of actions (Mischel & Shoda, 1995). Yet despite the widely acknowledged importance of situational influences on human behavior, some of the most recent publications on the study of situations arrive at the conclusion that there is currently no consensual definition or framework for what situations are and how they operate (Rauthmann & Sherman, 2016; Rauthmann, Sherman, & Funder, 2015). Thus, whereas psychological research on people and their psychologically important characteristics are relatively advanced, with widely accepted definitions, taxonomies, and inventories (e.g., Funder, 2001), there is much less agreement on how *situations* are described, measured, and taxonomized (Rauthmann et al., 2014). Consequently, the recent resurgence in the general study of psychological situations, which sets out to tackle these important issues (e.g., Rauthmann et al., 2015), can also be expected to significantly influence research in different subdisciplines of psychological science, including educational psychology and motivation science.

What currently unites the different disciplines in psychological science in their view on situations and person-situation relationships has recently been referred to as the "processing principle" (Rauthmann et al., 2015). This principle states that although situations are made of relatively objective elements of the physical world (persons, objects, events, location, and time), these situational elements or cues do not possess intrinsic meaning. Rather, they require active processing by the individual to become psychologically powerful and effective (Rauthmann & Sherman, 2016).

M. Knogler (✉)
Technical University of Munich, TUM School of Education, Munich, Germany
e-mail: maximilian.knogler@tum.de

© Springer International Publishing AG 2017
P.A. O'Keefe, J.M. Harackiewicz (eds.), *The Science of Interest*,
DOI 10.1007/978-3-319-55509-6_6

In that sense, "activated person factors and situation cues 'feed into' a person's psychological representation of a situation and how the situation is experienced will determine what the person thinks, wants and acts upon within it" (Rauthmann et al., 2015, p. 371). Hence, following a long debate about the prevalence of person vs. situation influences, it is now widely accepted that situations as well as persons are integral elements of *person-situation transactions*, meaning that individuals construe and influence situations just as situations influence peoples' behavior and personalities (Fleeson & Noftle, 2009).

In motivation science, interest theories, such as the Person-Object Theory of interest (POI) (Krapp, 2000, 2002) or the Four-Phase Model of Interest Development (FPM) (Hidi & Renninger, 2006; Renninger & Hidi, 2016), offer an adaptive conceptualization for such person-situation transactions: interest as a relational construct. There is strong agreement in the research literature that interest is a motivational phenomenon that emerges from an individual's interaction with his or her environment (Renninger & Hidi, 2011). This interactionist view identifies interest as a relational construct that consists of a more or less enduring relationship between a person and an object (Krapp 2002; Schiefele, 2009). Consequently, interested individuals are always interested *in* something, and this "something" or "object" is a rather broad category encompassing content, activities, events, ideas, etc.

Further, it is important to note that interest as a person-object relationship manifests itself on different time scales. People may *momentarily* be interested in a certain topic (e.g., Greek philosophy) while doing something (e.g., watching a documentary about Greek philosophers) and thus be in a *state of interest*. On such a microscopic (moment-to-moment) scale, interest is a dynamic and malleable experiential phenomenon. For example, an individual is very likely to perceive some parts of a documentary as more interesting than others (intraindividual variance), and this dynamic also varies across individuals (interindividual variance). According to this momentary perspective, individuals are in a state of interest to varying degrees; this variance and its antecedents, correlates, and consequences are an important area of current interest research. This perspective and related research will be further elaborated in the following section about state interest.

Moreover, any interaction with some content (e.g., watching a documentary about Greek philosophers) can be part of a long-term process of interest development. This process is located on a macroscopic time scale, because interest development unfolds over more extended time periods (ranging from several moments up to many years) and through continued and repeated interaction with the interest object (Krapp, 2002). Over time, individuals can move from having a less-developed interest to having a well-developed interest. Thus, according to this developmental perspective, individuals differ with regard to the developmental level or developmental phase (e.g., triggered situational interest) they are in (Hidi & Renninger, 2006). The differences between these phases manifest themselves on several dimensions associated with interest development. After having spent a substantial amount of time repeatedly interacting with content, individuals with a well-developed interest usually have more knowledge, better skills, and a higher degree of identification with this content than individuals with less-developed interest (e.g., Renninger & Hidi, 2016). The empirical identification of different developmental phases, their thresholds, and the differential characteristics of individuals belonging to these phases is another crucial area of current interest research (Renninger & Su, 2012). This developmental perspective and related research will be further discussed in the following section, with a particular focus on less-developed interest.

As research in psychological science is still seeking a consensus definition of what situations are and how they operate, the concept of *situational* interest cannot be clearly defined on the basis of a general theory of situations. Interest research has therefore defined situational interest in its own terms. According to prominent interest theories, such as POI (Krapp, 2000, 2002) and the FPM (Hidi & Renninger, 2006; Renninger & Hidi, 2016), the relational nature of interest allows for a dynamic conceptualization of motivation in person-situation transactions at a particular moment in time *and* across time. This chapter describes and analyzes the most prominent definition of situational interest as conceived by the FPM. The model seeks to integrate a momentary notion of situational interest as "state interest," which people experience while interacting, and a long-term developmental notion of situational interest as "less-developed interest." In line with these two notions, the chapter provides a short review of recent research on situational interest separately for these two perspectives and demonstrates that research has implicitly embraced this separation. Finally, it offers some conclusions for the future use of terminology.

Situational Interest in the Four-Phase Model of Interest Development

Currently, situational interest is most prominently described in the FPM (Hidi & Renninger, 2006). Hidi and Renninger's publication is one of the most cited papers in the history of interest theory and research. With its more than 1600 citations, it has gathered more references in 10 years than Dewey's *Interest and Effort in Education* (1913) or Krapp, Renninger, and Hidi's *The Role of Interest in Learning and Development* (1992) (according to Google Scholar, as of November 2016). Therefore, it is not surprising that many, if not most, interest researchers refer to the FPM when defining their constructs and deriving their research questions. Within the FPM, situational interest is embedded in a rather complex semantic and conceptual field. Each of the model's two signature constructs (situational and individual interest) refers to two different concepts depending on the time scale considered (see Table 6.1). Situational interest refers to state interest *and* less-developed interest.[1] Individual interest refers to both state interest and well-developed interest. Conversely, state interest refers to both situational interest and individual interest.

---

[1] Less-developed interest is a summary term which describes individuals at the initial phases of interest development (i.e., first two phases of interest development: triggered situational interest and maintained situational interest).

Table 6.1 Overview of terminology

	Momentary process	Long-term development
Situational interest	State interest	Less-developed interest
Individual interest		Well-developed interest

This overlapping terminology carries a number of complications. State interest and less-developed interest, which operate on different levels and time scales, can both be referred to as "situational interest." Whereas state interest refers to an action-related, in-the-moment experience (microscopic time scale), "less-developed interest" marks the initial phases of a long-term development of interest (macroscopic time scale). In that sense, situational interest can be a fleeting and a malleable experience or refers to less-developed phases of interest, which can last for months and even years (Renninger & Hidi, 2002). While less-developed interest can always be referred to as "situational interest," state interest can only be called "situational interest" if it is predominantly environmentally supported, which is usually the case in earlier phases of development. If state interest is more internally supported, then it represents an in-the-moment manifestation of individual interest. In other words, situational interest and individual interest share the same state (Renninger & Hidi, 2016; Schiefele, 2009), which means that the in-the-moment experience of situational interest and individual interest feels the same.

In short, according to the FPM, situational interest may refer to a particular psychological state *or* to the beginning of interest development as less-developed interest. Semantically, this has led to ambiguity and may at least partly explain why researchers struggle to agree on a single definition and operationalization of situational interest (Renninger & Hidi, 2011). Consequently, there is not currently a single instrument to measure situational interest but many different instruments (e.g., Knogler, Harackiewicz, Gegenfurtner, & Lewalter, 2015; Linnenbrink-Garcia et al., 2010; Lipstein & Renninger, 2007; Tsai, Kunter, Trautwein, & Lüdtke, 2008). Thus, even though researchers frequently refer to one and the same model to define "situational interest," there are still varying interpretations of the concept and its operationalization in empirical studies. Some of this variance is due to the fact that situational interest combines the two notions of situational interest as state interest and situational interest as less-developed interest. Thus, the following sections review research on situational interest separately for both perspectives. These two perspectives are similar to what Krapp referred to as actual genetic and ontogenetic perspectives on interest development (e.g., Krapp, 2002).

Situational Interest as State Interest: A Momentary Process Perspective

The momentary process perspective focuses on the in-the-moment experience of interest (state interest), while someone is reading an interesting text, solving a challenging problem, or having a good conversation. Individuals experience state interest as a result of their momentary interaction with a particular environment. As such, state interest may depend on whether there is a match between the person's characteristics and the environmental affordances present in a certain situation or moment. For example, an engineering student who is fascinated by technology but does not like mathematics has to attend an advanced mathematics seminar as part of his or her undergraduate studies. As there is a mismatch between the student's (prior) interest in math and the seminar situation, chances are that the student experiences low levels of state interest during the seminar. However, it could also be that the student's state interest levels are high despite low prior interest. This would likely be due to powerful situational cues, such as an inspiring teacher or an intriguing math task, which trigger his or her interest in advanced mathematics.

As the example shows, state interest is an amalgamation of the interest individuals bring to situations and the interest triggered by situational cues, which is focused on the experience and behavior during the activity. According to theoretical explanations (Hidi & Renninger, 2006; Krapp, 2002), the interest individuals bring to situations can have a strong organizing function in relation to interest states (Ainley, 2006). This may be the case when individuals enter an activity, often deliberately chosen, with well-developed interest for the activity, like how a passionate chess player enters a chess game. Then the interest experience during the game may be attributed to the player's well-developed prior interest in chess. In that sense, "the personal is expressed as state" (Ainley, 2006, p. 394) and according to the FPM should be referred to as "individual interest." Conversely, state interest can only be referred to as "situational interest" when it is (mostly) environmentally triggered (or maintained) (Hidi & Renninger, 2006), and the relative influence of students' individual interest is rather low. Practically, however, the label "situational interest" is frequently used for state measurements of interest without testing this assumption (Ainley & Hidi, 2002). Strictly speaking, research using state measures of interest should not automatically label them as "situational interest," because the influence of certain person characteristics, including prior interest, may be equally strong or stronger than the influence of situational cues. This is why some researchers prefer to use "interest experience" or "state interest" when measuring momentary experiences of interest (e.g., Tanaka & Murayama, 2014; Tsai et al., 2008).

In order to shed further light on the issue of relative influence of person and situation factors on state interest Knogler et al. (2015), recently conducted a study with a fixed situation design. They repeatedly measured high school students' states of interest after short instructional activities during an educational intervention. The problem-based instructional design of the intervention offered a relatively heterogeneous and yet coherent set of activities (briefing, inquiry, discussion, reflection) around a single topic. In addition to the several state measures, the researchers also collected self-reported data on students' prior interest in the focal topic of the intervention before students began to engage in problem-solving activities. For data analysis, they employed a latent variable approach based on latent state-trait theory, which allows disentangling variance proportions that are occasion-specific vs. variance proportions that are stable across multiple measurement occasions (see Geiser & Lockhart, 2012). The specific combination of study design and data-analytic strategy provided some new and nuanced findings. These indicated that about half of the variance in state interest was occasion-specific and that the other half of the variance was stable across all measures. These substantial proportions of occasion-specific variance underlined the transient and malleable character of state interest, which in turn reinforces the recent trend of using repeated measures at short time intervals. Importantly, the results also revealed that the students' prior interest significantly predicted cross-situationally stable state variance components. This provides more evidence that prior individual interest indeed may have an organizing and supportive role in the experience of state interest during some interest-related activities. At the same time, the study found the prior interest to be unrelated to occasion-specific state variance components. Thus, due to the substantial proportions of state variance, which were both situation-specific and unrelated to initial interest, the authors concluded that under the specific circumstances of this study, state measurements can be referred to as situational interest.

For thorough coverage of the entire process, investigations typically monitor interest levels (and other relevant variables) at the beginning, middle, and end of an activity or event (Ainley, 2006). In order to capture the influence of person characteristics on state interest, researchers assess individual differences on relevant trait dimensions prior to engagement. In educational settings, for example, these often include prior knowledge, achievement or mastery goals, a sense of value, or a self-concept of ability (Brophy, 2008; Hidi & Harackiewicz, 2000). These particular configurations of person characteristics are likely to have an impact on the individual's level of engagement and experience of interest during the activity (Durik, Shechter, Noh, Rozek, & Harackiewicz, 2015; Tapola, Jaakkola, & Niemivirta, 2014). As there is currently no instrument available that can differentiate between individuals according to the four different phases of interest development (Renninger & Hidi, 2011), investigators frequently use multiple-item scales to assess individual interest, for example, as a relatively stable affective-evaluative orientation toward a particular topic (e.g., energy transformation) or a certain domain (e.g., physics) (based on Krapp's (2002) conceptualization) (e.g., Knogler et al., 2015; Tsai et al., 2008).

The momentary process perspective conceives of state interest on the level of current processes as the interest people experience while interacting with their environment during an activity. Depending on the length and variability of the activity (or of multiple activities), people may experience state interest at different levels of intensity across time. To capture this within-person variation in state interest, multiple assessments are required. Deciding on assessment intervals can be an easy task when dealing with a sequence of clear-cut activities (fixed situation design) where participating individuals have a clear sense of which time episodes they are rating. However, it can pose some difficulty when there is no particular activity or event structure but a continuous flow of situations typical for daily life (random situation design). The question of how and when one situation ends and another one begins is difficult to address and central to the current debate about a general theory of situations (Rauthmann & Sherman, 2016).

In terms of construct content, investigations often use individuals' reports of their level of attention and their positive feeling with regard to particular activities or events to identify the cognitive and affective aspects of state interest (e.g., Rotgans & Schmidt, 2014). In addition, researchers have also used indicators for perceived value (Linnenbrink-Garcia et al., 2010; Linnenbrink-Garcia, Patall, & Messersmith, 2012) and individuals' intention to further explore content (Knogler et al., 2015) as indicators for state interest. The idea of these multifaceted state measures is to integrate markers of development. In that sense they seek to combine state and development perspectives, as these markers acknowledge that development can also be captured on the level of concurrent experiences. In order to mark developmental differences, these measures include experiences that are prototypical for different developmental phases (i.e., triggered and maintained situational interest). Knogler et al., for example, used items that refer to individuals' evaluation of their attention and positive affect and thus reflect prototypical experiences during the first phase of interest development (triggered situational interest). Prototypical experiences of the second phase (maintained situational interest) may not just be indicated by constant or increasingly high levels of attention and positive affect (e.g., Chen et al., 2016) but also include self-reports of personal significance of content and spontaneous intentions to further explore the content (Knogler et al., 2015). These experiences may be seen as driving forces of underlying maintenance processes. This is in line with the FPM, as Renninger and Su argued "that as interest develops and deepens, the desire for knowledge and value develop concurrently, while affect continues to be an important aspect" (Renninger & Su, 2012, p. 169). Presently, however, "it is not clear whether and how the experience of interest varies with development" (Renninger & Su, 2012, p. 169).

In line with the momentary process perspective, more and more studies are examining interest at the level of current processes. The temporal design of these studies (see below) typically involves relatively short time frames—ranging from several minutes to several weeks—and frequent probes. The methodology is quantitative in nature and is based on self-reports of subjective experiences ranging from single-item measures of state interest (e.g., Fulmer & Tulis, 2013; Palmer, 2009; Tapola, Veermans, & Niemivierta, 2013) to multiple-item questionnaires (e.g., Holstermann, Ainley, Grube, Roick, & Bögeholz, 2012; Knogler et al., 2015; Rotgans & Schmidt, 2011, 2014). The studies are conducted in learning and instructional contexts, while students are working on text-based or mathematical tasks (e.g., Ainley & Hidi, 2002; Fulmer & Tulis, 2013; Tulis & Fulmer 2013), play instructional games or simulations (Chen et al., 2016; Knogler et al., 2015; Tapola et al., 2014), work on projects (Minnaert, Boekaerts, & DeBrabander, 2007; Minnaert, Boekaerts, DeBrabander, & Opdenakker, 2011), or receive classroom-based instruction (Holstermann et al., 2012; Palmer, 2009; Randler & Bogner, 2007; Rotgans & Schmidt, 2011, 2014; Schmidt, Rotgans, & Yew, 2011; Tanaka & Murayama, 2014; Tsai et al., 2008).

For the statistical modeling of these repeated measures data, researchers often use latent variable approaches based on longitudinal structural equation modeling (e.g., Chen et al., 2016; Knogler et al., 2015) or hierarchical linear modeling (e.g., Tanaka & Murayama, 2014; Tsai et al., 2008) to investigate both inter- and intrain-dividual variances or mean changes in individuals' state interest. The results indi-cate substantial intra- and interindividual variance in the repeated experience of interest, suggesting that both environmental circumstances and person-level factors influence the experience of state interest. This has been further confirmed through additional use of occasion-specific predictors. For example, in several studies stu-dents were asked to report on their current levels of autonomy, competence, and relatedness—self-determination theory's three basic needs—at different phases of project work or during different classroom lessons (e.g., Minnaert et al., 2007, 2011; Tsai et al., 2008). The results showed that basic need satisfaction on one occasion also predicted students' state of interest on another occasion. At the same time, person characteristics such as prior knowledge (Rotgans & Schmidt, 2011, 2014), gender (Chen & Darst, 2002; Holsterman et al. 2012), particular goal orientations (Tanaka & Murayama, 2014), and prior interest (Chen et al., 2016; Knogler et al., 2015) were associated with variance in state interest.

Considered together, these studies indicate that both occasion-specific and person-specific factors determine individuals' experiences of interest at certain moments in time (state interest). This is in line with intervention research on enhanc-ing state interest, which typically makes use of mechanisms based on person factors or specific situational cues (Harackiewicz & Knogler, 2017). Thus, designers create environments that either explicitly adapt and connect to learners' prior interests (Walkington & Bernacki, 2014) or include structural or content features (e.g., intriguing questions) that trigger state interest in many individuals (Rotgans & Schmidt, 2014). Consequently, research on promoting interest, which often uses the term "situational interest," actually measures interest in a particular moment, which may reflect situational interest *or* individual interest, but more likely both, to vary-ing degrees. Hence, the most appropriate way to refer to the short-term measures used in intervention research may be simply "state interest."

Situational Interest as Less-Developed Interest: A Long-Term Development Perspective

Situational interest as defined by the FPM is not just a particular state at a certain moment in time but also a variable that can develop over time (Renninger & Hidi, 2016). Whereas situational interest as a state is primarily defined by the characteris-tics of a certain experience, situational interest as less-developed interest is primar-ily defined as a certain phase in a long-term developmental process. Situational interest as less-developed interest reflects the spectrum concept that has been elabo-rated in this section of this volume. From a long-term development perspective, situational interest is located on the less-developed end of the developmental continuum, which spans from a "potential interest" to a "well-developed interest." As a developmental trajectory, interest starts from a single situation-specific person-object relation (Krapp, Hidi & Renninger, 1992). For example, a young boy or girl sees people playing in a band for the first time in his or her life and is immediately fascinated by the sound, the atmosphere, and the skills of the musicians. Once such an interest in music, for instance, is triggered (Phase 1) and the child gets further opportunities and support in interacting with the object, he or she may move further along the developmental continuum, allowing the connection to transcend the boundaries of a single situation. In that sense, an individual's interest is maintained (Phase 2), and the connection gains further temporal stability and strength (Phase 3). Eventually, a well-developed interest (Phase 4) is formed; this refers to a person's long-term relationship with a specific domain or object that portrays a high level of stability across situations and contexts (Renninger, 2009).

From a developmental perspective, there are important questions concerning the nature and dimensions of the change that occurs with regard to the person-object relationship as interest develops (e.g., Frenzel et al., 2012). It is also important to define some of the critical thresholds along this continuum that separate one phase of development from another (e.g., the difference between less-developed and well-developed interest). This is linked to the question of how individuals differ in their experiences and behaviors at different phases of development and what factors are most beneficial to this development. These important questions are only beginning to receive empirical attention, as research on interest development is still in its infancy (Hofer, 2010; Krapp, 2002; Renninger & Su, 2012). As a consequence, there are currently no instruments available that would allow the measurement of interest development (Renninger & Hidi, 2011) or the identification of the four phases of development proposed by the FPM. The following paragraphs describe theory and some findings addressing these questions, with a specific focus on less-developed interest and how it differs from well-developed interest.

There are large quantitative differences between less-developed and well-developed interest. As essentially any interaction with objects in our environment has at least the potential to turn into a well-developed interest, the number of potential interests is as large as the number of objects we encounter and interact with in our lives (Hofer, 2010). However, only a very small percentage of all these interactions and potential interests actually become a well-developed interest. Thus, there is a strong selection mechanism underlying interest development, as individuals only have enough resources to entertain a rather small number of well-developed interests. That is why the further one moves from the less-developed to the well-developed end of the continuum, there are fewer and fewer person-object relationships in people's lives that meet the criteria to be well developed. At the same time, the accumulated amount of resources (e.g., time) spent on these fewer but well-developed interests is much larger compared to the few minutes spent on a short-term engagement with an object that did not develop into anything longer-lasting. One can easily imagine a person with a well-developed interest in music having devoted thousands of hours to playing an instrument or listening, talking, thinking, and reading about music. Since a well-developed interest can only evolve through continued interactions or engagement with the interest object, the resources spent on an object of interest are an important indicator of its developmental phase.

Coinciding with quantitative differences and changes, the development from less-developed interest to well-developed interest is also marked by qualitative changes such as an underlying shift in agency or regulatory style as well as an increasing metacognitive awareness of one's own interest. Behavior based on less-developed interest tends to be externally regulated and emerges as a response to features in the environment (Hidi & Anderson, 1992). Individuals with a less-developed interest are often not explicitly aware of their interest (Hidi & Renninger, 2006; Renninger & Hidi, 2016). In contrast, well-developed interest is mainly internally regulated and follows an individual's impulse to interact with the interest object (e.g., based on self-generated curiosity). Thus, whereas interest in its early phases largely depends on external resources for support in the form of attention-grabbing stimuli, individuals with well-developed interest rely on their own resources and independently seek opportunities to interact with their interest object on their own volition. Krapp (2002, 2005, 2007) proposed that an underlying process of internalization or integration of the interest object into one's value system may explain this gradual shift, in a manner similar to self-determination theory (Ryan & Deci, 2000). As a result, individuals with well-developed interest are usually more aware of their interest and have stronger intentions of engaging with their interest objects and persevering through challenges and frustrations in pursuing interest-related goals than individuals whose interest is less developed (Hofer, 2010).

Moreover, qualitative changes affect the quality of the relationship as well as the structure of individuals' internal representations of their interest object. Hidi and Renninger (2006) proposed that each of the developmental phases of the FPM is characterized by varying amounts of knowledge, value, and affect. According to the model, interest in early phases may be considered primarily an affective reaction at the initial triggering but evolves into a relationship marked by a greater emphasis on knowledge and value components in later phases (Hidi, 2006). These qualitative changes become apparent when investigators focus on qualitative, structural aspects of the construct and its measurement instead of mere indicators of intensity (e.g., mean changes). For example, Frenzel et al. (2012) investigated high school students' interpretations of interest measures over the course of 5 school years (grades 5–9). They found that the measurement model of students' interest in mathematics varied across time, demonstrating a qualitative shift from a more affect-based notion of interest to a more value-based notion. They concluded that with increasing grade levels, students appear to become increasingly aware that being interested is not just about having fun while doing math "but also involves the desire to learn more and autonomously choose to reengage in the respective domain" (p. 129). Renninger (2000, 2009) emphasized changes in levels of stored domain knowledge as an important indicator for interest development. According to Renninger, a person's developing understanding of the procedures and discourse knowledge of particular activities or ideas clearly signal progress in interest development. A similar point was made by Krapp (2002), who suggested that interest development is very likely to alter the structure of an individual's internal representation of an interest object, resulting in a more elaborated and sophisticated representation. Thus, individuals with more developed interest are characterized by higher values, deeper knowledge, and a stronger tendency to voluntarily reengage compared to individuals with less-developed interest.

These quantitative and qualitative changes, which characterize interest as a relational and dynamic variable, do not occur in a vacuum. Interest development at all phases is reciprocally related to the development of other psychological constructs (Harackiewicz, Barron, Tauer, Carter, & Elliot, 2000; Harackiewicz, Barron, Tauer, & Elliot, 2002; Harackiewicz, Durik, Barron, Linnenbrink-Garcia, & Tauer, 2008; Marsh, Trautwein, Lüdtke, Köller & Baumert, 2005). Interest can act as a facilitator to goal adoption (Harackiewicz et al., 2008), self-regulation (O'Keefe & Linnenbrink-Garcia, 2014; Sansone & Thoman, 2005; Sansone, Smith, Thoman, & MacNamara, 2012), self-efficacy (Durik et al., 2015; Hidi & Ainley, 2007), the use of learning strategies (Krapp & Prenzel, 2011), and performance (Eccles, 2009; Harackiewicz et al., 2008; O'Keefe & Linnenbrink-Garcia, 2014). Conversely, all of these variables can influence interest, resulting in a cyclical or reciprocal development, whereby an initial interest in a task can foster the adoption of mastery goals, which in turn may positively influence the development and deepening of interest (e.g., Harackiewicz et al., 2008). This means that characterizing individuals as belonging to certain phases of interest development, such as less-developed interest, is a difficult task, not just because interest development involves several dimensions of change but also because the development is embedded in a complex dynamic system of interactions with other variables. Nevertheless, in order to generate a better understanding of situational interest as less-developed interest (and interest development in general), it is crucial to establish a clear set of characteristics that apply to individuals with less-developed interest as opposed to individuals with well-developed interest. These efforts are particularly important to the study of developing interest over extended time periods. Changes in individuals and in their connections to certain content have multiple dimensions and distinct developmental thresholds that cannot be sufficiently captured with regular trait or state measures (Krapp, 2002). Figure 6.1 depicts a hypothetical multidimensional model of interest development. The model is based on the research elaborated above and shows that individuals need to be characterized along several dimensions to judge their level of interest. According to the FPM, individuals can be allocated into four different groups as a function of the developmental phase of interest (toward a particular object) they are in. Individuals in later phases of development are supposed to show higher values on all dimensions (the dimension of positive emotion may be an exception) compared to individuals in earlier phases. An empirically sound allocation of an individual to a particular group, however, requires reliable and valid measurement for all dimensions considered and well-defined thresholds for discerning individuals in different phases. Thus, for the empirical advancement of models of interest development, researchers will have to move beyond one- or two-dimensional trait measures and engage in concerted efforts to develop more multidimensional measurement tools. These are required and can lay the ground for truly capturing interest development. Because, as their interest develops, individuals change in several ways resulting in a complex process of interrelated development on multiple dimensions. Current empirical research is only beginning to explore this process in sufficient detail (Renninger & Su, 2012).

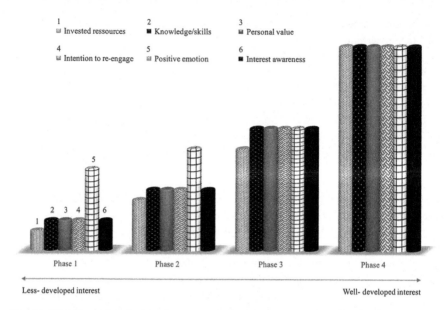

Fig. 6.1 Multidimensional model of interest development

In an effort to summarize and integrate research findings on differences and changes related to interest development as a four-phase process, Renninger and colleagues have recently created a schematic overview (see, e.g., Renninger & Hidi, 2016; Renninger & Riley, 2013; Renninger & Su, 2012). This schematic specifies learner characteristics and beneficial contextual affordances for each of the four phases. Most of these characteristics are based on longer-term studies (e.g., Hidi & Renninger, 2002; Lipstein & Renninger, 2007) and include qualitative and mixed-method data, which is necessary to capture change on different levels as well as change that individuals might not be aware of themselves (Renninger & Bachrach, 2015). Learner characteristics at each phase highlight different experiential or behavioral aspects and knowledge requirements that are common to individuals in a certain phase. Such a schematic also helps to identify developmental thresholds between phases. For example, learners who display a strong focus on their curiosity questions by definition have reached a more developed phase of interest development than learners who do not (see, e.g., Renninger & Su, 2012). Such a schematic is both the result and the facilitator of research on interest development. For example, it may help establish clear guidelines for multidimensional measures that are able to distinguish between individuals with less-developed and well-developed interest.

Considered together, the main purpose of research on interest development is to better describe the continuum and the complex processes that move individuals from the less-developed end to the well-developed end. To this end, it seems most productive to define and empirically validate person characteristics and critical leverages for support as a function of different phases. At all phases, the role (and the match) of both person characteristics *and* environmental affordances is critical for development. Thus, it is not clear why two phases should be highlighted as "situational" and two phases should be highlighted as "individual." "Less-developed" and "well-developed" seem to be more appropriate and less ambiguous labels.

Conclusion

Current psychological science is still seeking a consensual definition of what situations are and how they operate. Thus, in order to define the concept of "situational interest," interest research could not build on a general theory of situations but had to specify the meaning of "situational" on its own terms. Within the FPM, which is the most frequently used theoretical underpinning of research on interest and interest development today, situational interest refers to both state interest and less-developed interest. While state interest is an experience of interest in the moment, less-developed interest describes individuals at the initial phases of a developing interest. Research on situational interest has implicitly embraced these different meanings by investigating different phenomena (experience vs. person characteristics) on different time scales (micro vs. macro). In both lines of research, the distinction between situation categories and person categories is not clear-cut. This echoes the main point of the long-standing person-situation debate in personality and social psychology: namely, that persons and situations are inextricably linked, which renders distinctions between person and situation constructs difficult and imprecise. Among the major motivational frameworks and theories, interest theory is the only theory that explicitly uses the labels "person" and "situation" to denote its core constructs. At the end of this chapter about situational interest, there seems to be no added value in doing so. State interest and less-developed interest are the more parsimonious and less ambiguous options.

References

Ainley, M. (2006). Connecting with learning: Motivation, affect and cognition in interest processes. *Educational Psychological Review, 18*, 391–405.

Ainley, M., & Hidi, S. (2002). Dynamic measures for studying interest and learning. In P. R. Pintrich & M. L. Maehr (Eds.), *Advances in motivation and achievement: New directions in measures and methods* (Vol. 12, pp. 43–76). Amsterdam: JAI.

Brophy, J. (2008). Developing students' appreciation for what is taught in school. *Educational Psychologist, 43*(3), 132–141.

Chen, A., & Darst, P. W. (2002). Individual and situational interest: The role of gender and skill. *Contemporary Educational Psychology, 27*(2), 250–269.

Chen, J. A., Tutwiler, M. S., Metcalf, S. J., Kamarainen, A., Grotzer, T., & Dede, C. (2016). A multi-user virtual environment to support students' self-efficacy and interest in science: A latent growth model analysis. *Learning and Instruction, 41*, 11–22.

Dewey, J. (1913). *Interest and effort in education*. Boston: Houghton Mifflin.

Durik, A. M., Shechter, O., Noh, M. S., Rozek, C. R., & Harackiewicz, J. M. (2015). What if I can't? Perceived competence as a moderator of the effects of utility value information on situational interest and performance. *Motivation and Emotion, 39*, 104–118.

Durik, A. M., Hulleman, C. S., & Harackiewicz, J. M. (2015). One size fits some: Instructional enhancements to promote interest don't work the same for everyone. In K. A. Renninger, M. Nieswandt, & S. Hidi (Eds.), *Interest in mathematics and science learning* (pp. 49–62). Washington, DC: American Educational Research Association.

Eccles, J. S. (2009). Who am I and what am I going to do with my life? Personal and collective identities as motivators of action. *Educational Psychologist, 44*, 78–89.

Fleeson, W., & Noftle, E. E. (2009). In favor of the synthetic resolution to the person–situation debate. *Journal of Research in Personality, 43*(2), 150–154.

Frenzel, A. C., Pekrun, R., Dicke, A. L., & Goetz, T. (2012). Beyond quantitative decline: Conceptual shifts in adolescents' development of interest in mathematics. *Developmental Psychology, 48*(4), 1069–1082.

Funder, D. C. (2001). Personality. *Annual Review of Psychology, 52*, 197–221.

Fulmer, S. M., & Tulis, M. (2013). Changes in interest and affect during a difficult reading task: Relationships with perceived difficulty and reading fluency. *Learning and Instruction, 27*, 11–20.

Geiser, C., & Lockhart, G. (2012). A comparison of four approaches to account for method effects in latent state-trait analyses. *Psychological Methods, 17*(2), 255–283.

Harackiewicz, J. M., Barron, K. E., Tauer, J. M., Carter, S. M., & Elliot, A. J. (2000). Short-term and long-term consequences of achievement goals: Predicting interest and performance over time. *Journal of Educational Psychology, 92*, 316–330.

Harackiewicz, J. M., Barron, K. E., Tauer, J. M., & Elliot, A. J. (2002). Predicting success in college: A longitudinal study of achievement goals and ability measures as predictors of interest and performance from freshman year through graduation. *Journal of Educational Psychology, 94*(3), 562.

Harackiewicz, J. M., Durik, A. M., Barron, K. E., Linnenbrink-Garcia, L., & Tauer, J. M. (2008). The role of achievement goals in the development of interest: Reciprocal relations between achievement goals, interest, and performance. *Journal of Educational Psychology, 100*, 105–122.

Harackiewicz, J. M., & Knogler, M. (2017). Interest: Theory and application. In A. J. Elliot, C. S. Dweck, & D. S. Yaeger (Eds.), *Handbook of competence and motivation* (pp. 334–352). New York: Guilford Press.

Hidi, S., & Anderson, V. (1992). Situational interest and its impact on reading and expository writing. In K. A. Renninger, S. Hidi, & A. Krapp (Eds.), *The role of interest in learning and development* (pp. 215–238). Hillsdale, NJ: Erlbaum.

Hidi, S. (2006). Interest: A unique motivational variable. *Educational Research Review, 1*(2), 69–82.

Hidi, S., & Ainley, M. (2008). Interest and self-regulation: Relationships between two variables that influence learning. In B. J. Zimmerman & D. H. Schunk (Eds.), *Motivation and self-regulated learning: Theory, research, and applications.* (pp. 77–109). Mahwah, NJ: Erlbaum.

Hidi, S., & Harackiewicz, J. M. (2000). Motivating the academically unmotivated: A critical issue for the 21st century. *Review of Educational Research, 79*(2), 151–179.

Hidi, S., & Renninger, K. A. (2006). The four-phase model of interest development. *Educational Psychologist, 41*(2), 111–127.

Hofer, M. (2010). Adolescents' development of individual interests: A product of multiple goal regulation? *Educational Psychologist, 45*(3), 149–166.

Holstermann, N., Ainley, M., Grube, D., Roick, T., & Bögeholz, S. (2012). The specific relationship between disgust and interest: Relevance during biology class dissections and gender differences. *Learning and Instruction, 22*(3), 185–192.

Knogler, M., Harackiewicz, J. M., Gegenfurtner, A., & Lewalter, D. (2015). How situational is situational interest? Investigating the longitudinal structure of situational interest. *Contemporary Educational Psychology, 43*, 39–50.

Krapp, A. (2000). Interest and human development during adolescence: An educational-psychological approach. In H. Heckhausen (Ed.), *Motivational psychology of human development* (pp. 109–128). London: Elsevier.

Krapp, A. (2002). Structural and dynamic aspects of interest development: Theoretical considerations from an ontogenetic perspective. *Learning and Instruction, 13*(4), 383–409.

Krapp, A. (2005). Basic needs and the development of interest and intrinsic motivational orientations. *Learning and Instruction, 15*(5), 381–395.

Krapp, A. (2007). An educational–psychological conceptualisation of interest. *International Journal for Educational and Vocational Guidance, 7*(1), 5–21.

Krapp, A., Hidi, S., & Renninger, K. A. (1992). Interest, learning, and development. In K. A. Renninger, S. Hidi, & A. Krapp (Eds.), *The role of interest in learning and development* (pp. 3–25). Hillsdale: Erlbaum.

Krapp, A., & Prenzel, M. (2011). Research on interest in science: Theories, methods, and findings. *International Journal of Science Education, 33*(1), 27–50.

Linnenbrink-Garcia, L., Durik, A. M., Conley, A. M., Barron, K. E., Tauer, J. M., Karabenick, S. A., et al. (2010). Measuring situational interest in academic domains. *Educational and Psychological Measurement, 70*, 647–671.

Linnenbrink-Garcia, L., Patall, E. A., & Messersmith, E. E. (2012). Antecedents and consequences of situational interest. *British Journal of Educational Psychology, 83*(4), 591–614.

Lipstein, R. L., & Renninger, K. A. (2007). Putting things into words: The development of 12-15 year olds' interest for writing. In P. Boscolo & S. Hidi (Eds.), *Motivation and writing: Research and school practice* (pp. 113–140). New York: Kluwer Academic/Plenum.

Lipstein, R. L., & Renninger, K. A. (2007). Interest for writing: How teachers can make a difference. *English Journal, 96*, 79–85.

Marsh, H. W., Trautwein, U., Lüdtke, O., Köller, O., & Baumert, J. (2005). Academic self-concept, interest, grades, and standardized test scores: Reciprocal effects models of causal ordering. *Child Development, 76*(2), 397–416.

Minnaert, A., Boekaerts, M., & De Brabander, C. (2007). Autonomy, competence, and social relatedness in task interest within project-based education. *Psychological Reports, 101*(2), 574–586.

Minnaert, A., Boekaerts, M., De Brabander, C., & Opdenakker, M. C. (2011). Students' experiences of autonomy, competence, social relatedness and interest within a CSCL environment in vocational education: The case of commerce and business administration. *Vocations and Learning, 4*(3), 175–190.

Mischel, W., & Shoda, Y. (1995). A cognitive-affective system theory of personality: reconceptualizing situations, dispositions, dynamics, and invariance in personality structure. *Psychological Review, 102*(2), 246.

Nisbett, R., & Ross, L. (1991). *The person and the situation.* New York: McGraw Hill.

O'Keefe, P. A., & Linnenbrink-Garcia, L. (2014). The role of interest in optimizing performance and self-regulation. *Journal of Experimental Social Psychology, 53*, 70–78.

Palmer, D. H. (2009). Student interest generated during an inquiry skills lesson. *Journal of Research in Science Teaching, 46*(2), 147–165.

Randler, C., & Bogner, F. X. (2007). Pupils' interest before, during, and after a curriculum dealing with ecological topics and its relationship with achievement. *Educational Research and Evaluation, 13*(5), 463–478.

Rauthmann, J. F., Sherman, R. A., & Funder, D. C. (2015). New horizons in research on psychological situations and environments. *European Journal of Personality, 29*, 382–432.

Rauthmann, J. F., Gallardo-Pujol, D., Guillaume, E. M., Todd, E., Nave, C. S., Sherman, R. A., et al. (2014). The Situational Eight DIAMONDS: A taxonomy of major dimensions of situation characteristics. *Journal of Personality and Social Psychology, 107*(4), 677.

Rauthmann, J. F., & Sherman, R. A. (2016). Situation change: stability and change of situation variables between and within persons. *Frontiers in Psychology, 6*, 1938–1956.

Reis, H. T. (2008). Reinvigorating the concept of situation in social psychology. *Personality and Social Psychology Review, 12*(4), 311–329.

Renninger, K. (2000). Individual interest and its implications for understanding intrinsic motivation. In C. Sansone & J. M. Harackiewicz (Eds.), *Intrinsic and extrinsic motivation* (pp. 373–404). San Diego: Academic.

Renninger, K. A. (2009). Interest and identity development in instruction: An inductive model. *Educational Psychologist, 44*(2), 105–118.

Renninger, K. A., & Bachrach, J. E. (2015). Studying triggers for interest and engagement using observational methods. *Educational Psychologist, 50*(1), 58–69.

Renninger, K., & Hidi, S. (2002). Student interest and achievement: Developmental issues raised by a case study. In A. Wigfield & J. S. Eccles (Eds.), *Development of achievement motivation* (pp. 173–195). San Diego, CA: Academic Press.

Renninger, K. A., & Hidi, S. (2011). Revisiting the conceptualization, measurement, and generation of interest. *Educational Psychologist, 46*(3), 168–184.

Renninger, K. A., & Hidi, S. (2016). *The power of interest for motivation and engagement.* New York: Routledge.

Renninger, K. A., & Riley, K. R. (2013). Interest, cognition and case of L-and science. In *Cognition and motivation: Forging an interdisciplinary perspective* (pp. 352–382). Cambridge, MA: Cambridge University Press.

Renninger, K. A., & Su, S. (2012). Interest and its development. In R. Ryan (Ed.), *The Oxford handbook of human motivation* (pp. 167–187). Oxford: Oxford University Press.

Rotgans, J. I., & Schmidt, H. G. (2011). Situational interest and academic achievement in the active-learning classroom. *Learning and Instruction, 21*(1), 58–67.

Rotgans, J. I., & Schmidt, H. G. (2014). Situational interest and learning: Thirst for knowledge. *Learning and Instruction, 32*, 37–50.

Ryan, R. M., & Deci, E. L. (2000). Self-determination theory and the facilitation of intrinsic motivation, social development, and well-being. *American Psychologist, 55*(1), 68.

Sansone, C., & Thoman, D. B. (2005). Interest as the missing motivator in self-regulation. *European Psychologist, 10*(3), 175–186. doi:10.1027/1016-9040.10.3.175.

Sansone, C., Smith, J. L., Thoman, D. B., & MacNamara, A. (2012). Regulating interest when learning online: Potential motivation and performance trade-offs. *The Internet and Higher Education, 15*(3), 141–149.

Schiefele, U. (2009). Situational and individual interest. In K. Wentzel & A. Wigfield (Eds.), *Handbook of motivation at school* (pp. 197–222). New York, NY: Routledge.

Schmidt, H. G., Rotgans, J. I., & Yew, E. H. J. (2011). The process of problem-based learning: what works and why. *Medical Education, 45*(8), 792–806.

Tanaka, A., & Murayama, K. (2014). Within-person analyses of situational interest and boredom: Interactions between task-specific perceptions and achievement goals. *Journal of Educational Psychology, 106*(4), 1122–1134.

Tapola, A., Jaakkola, T., & Niemivirta, M. (2014). The influence of achievement goal orientations and task concreteness on situational interest. *The Journal of Experimental Education, 82*(4), 455–479.

Tapola, A., Veermans, M., & Niemivirta, M. (2013). Predictors and outcomes of situational interest during a science learning task. *Instructional Science, 41*(6), 1047–1064.

Tulis, M., & Fulmer, S. M. (2013). Students' motivational and emotional experiences and their relationship to persistence during academic challenge in mathematics and reading. *Learning and Individual Differences, 27*, 35–46.

Tsai, Y. M., Kunter, M., Lütke, O., Trautwein, U., & Ryan, M. R. (2008). What makes lessons interesting? The roles of situational and individual factors in three school subjects. *Journal of Educational Psychology, 100*, 460–472.

Walkington, C., & Bernacki, M. L. (2014). Motivating students by "personalizing" learning around individual interests: A consideration of theory, design, and implementation issues. *Advances in Motivation and Achievement, 18*, 139–176.

Chapter 7
The Power Within: How Individual Interest Promotes Domain-Relevant Task Engagement

Amanda M. Durik, Meghan Huntoon Lindeman, and Sarah L. Coley

Imagine two students who are taking a history class together. One claims to be "very interested in history," and the other claims to be "not interested in history at all." How might these students differ? It is likely that the very interested student has prior knowledge of history, values the knowledge, and can envision herself elaborating upon her domain knowledge. She probably embraced the opportunity to take the course and may have even sought it out. Once in the course, she is likely to care about doing well, feel confident in navigating the course challenges, easily become involved, and find the material interesting. These experiences may motivate her to continue engaging with the material after the course is over. This example demonstrates the self-sustaining cycle of individual interest and task engagement. Meanwhile, the uninterested student enters the class without inspiration. Although the student may care about competence, it is not because of the content itself, and the student will likely lack confidence and find it very difficult to become and stay involved in the course material. Although this student might perform okay in the course, the student is not likely to engage with the material again.

As these examples suggest, individual interest motivates individuals to engage over time with content from a particular domain (Ainley & Ainley, 2011; Deci, 1992; Hidi & Renninger, 2006; Krapp, 2002; Prenzel, 1992; Renninger & Hidi, 2011; Renninger, Hidi, & Krapp, 1992; Schiefele, 1991; Silvia, 2006). It includes both cognitive and affective features that are focused on the domain content. Those with a well-developed individual interest have both stored knowledge and stored value associated with the domain of interest (Hidi & Renninger, 2006). Stored knowledge represents a schema for the content itself, including how ideas within the domain fit together and are organized (Alexander, Jetton, & Kulikowich, 1995; Alexander, Murphy, Woods, Duhon, & Parker, 1997; Tobias, 1994). Stored value refers to the positive valence and meaning that individuals attach to the stored knowledge. Stored

A.M. Durik (✉) • M.H. Lindeman • S.L. Coley
Department of Psychology, Northern Illinois University, DeKalb, IL, USA
e-mail: adurik@niu.edu; meg.huntoon@gmail.com; scoleypsychology@gmail.com

© Springer International Publishing AG 2017
P.A. O'Keefe, J.M. Harackiewicz (eds.), *The Science of Interest*,
DOI 10.1007/978-3-319-55509-6_7

value also includes affective experiences of enjoyment and excitement that come to be associated with the domain, as well as the sense of meaning that emanates from the association between the domain and an individual's developing sense of self (Eccles, 2009). Both knowledge and value contribute to choices to engage in the activity as well as the experience of interest during task engagement.

Individual interest develops over time and is a relatively enduring aspect of a person. This is in contrast to situational interest, which is a temporary experience of interest in a particular situation that arises in response to cues in the environment (see Chap. 6). Those with individual interest are still responsive to situations and can experience situational interest when interacting with domain content, but individual interest is fueled largely by internal processes (Hidi & Renninger, 2006). Moreover, the internal processes that define individual interest may foster interest in a given situation to the extent that those processes guide individuals to select relevant opportunities to engage with content and manipulate content so that their situational interest is maintained.

The purpose of this chapter is to outline the internal processes that lead people to choose activities from a domain of individual interest, and then to articulate how these same processes manifest during task engagement, in response to situational factors. We divide our treatment of this topic into three segments. The first segment outlines our causal theoretical model about how the internal factors associated with individual interest unfold to support the choice to engage in domain-relevant content. In the second segment, we draw on and extend Harackiewicz and Sansone's (1991) process model of intrinsic motivation to specify how individual interest might affect the dynamics of task engagement while in contact with domain content. We argue that the processes that underlie intrinsic motivation specified in this model can also guide our understanding of how individual interest can translate into the experience of situational interest. The description rests on how internal resources can foster the importance of doing well, a secure self-concept of ability, and the extent to which individuals can become wholly absorbed in the task. We also highlight ways in which those without individual interest may be vulnerable to disruptions in these processes. In the third and final segment, we briefly consider how those with individual interest may reflect on prior task experiences and come to view domain-relevant task engagement as meaningful and worth pursuing again. Finally, we conclude by considering how and when targeted external supports may be important for those with individual interest.

When Choosing What to Do

Individual interest does not simply lie dormant as a static characteristic of a person. Instead, it motivates and sustains engagement in domain content over time (e.g., Harackiewicz, Durik, Barron, Linnenbrink-Garcia, & Tauer, 2008; Renninger, 1990; Simpkins, Davis-Kean, & Eccles, 2006). As such, individual interest must involve processes that lead to the decision to engage. We put forth a theoretical

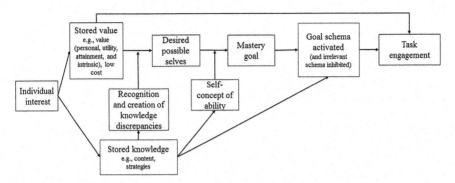

Fig. 7.1 Diagram depicting causal relations hypothesized to link components of individual interest (stored value and knowledge) in a domain to choices to engage in domain-relevant task

model (see Fig. 7.1) that outlines how individual interest might affect decisions to engage in particular content. We describe in detail these internal processes that lead to task choice because they are also relevant to the experience of situational interest, once engaged in the task.

Stored Knowledge and Stored Value

Individual interest is theorized to include both stored knowledge and stored value about a given domain (Hidi & Renninger, 2006). Stored value can take many forms (e.g., Eccles et al., 1983; Feather, 1988; Wigfield & Eccles, 2000). For example, achievement tasks are often valued because they are enjoyable (intrinsic value), useful for achieving other goals (utility value), or important for an individual's sense of identity (attainment value). For instance, the student who is highly interested in history might value the information from a course on American history because she perceives the material as useful for accomplishing her future goals, such as obtaining a graduate degree in history (high utility value), or because the course provides an opportunity to learn and think about history, which she finds enjoyable (high intrinsic value). In contrast, the student who is uninterested in history might not plan to pursue further study in history, and therefore might not perceive the course as useful (low utility value), and might not enjoy learning or thinking about history (low intrinsic value).

At a broader level, tasks or domains may take on more general personal values, such as when individuals are prompted to consider, in the context of achievement, what is important to them, such as helping others or being self-disciplined (Cohen, Garcia, Apfel, & Master, 2006; Miyake et al., 2010; Schwartz, 1992). When a domain is associated with personal value, the task is significant to the person and is a source of meaning that can support achievement and interest (Harackiewicz, Tibbetts, Canning, & Hyde, 2014). Stored value is an important part of individual interest because the domain can affirm individuals' beliefs about themselves (Hidi & Renninger, 2006). Finally, at the highest level, individuals may perceive a task as affirming a deep sense of satisfaction (Sheldon & Elliot, 1999). In other words, engaging in the domain is an extension of who they are; it is simply what they do. The student who is deeply interested in history may come to know herself and the world more completely through her interaction with and understanding of history.

Stored knowledge refers to amassed knowledge and skills that the person has acquired over time through contact with the domain. The stored knowledge is a resource for individuals because it is organized in long-term memory and gives individuals access to core features of the domain in order to facilitate global as well as fine-tuned understanding (see Chi, Glaser, & Rees, 1982; Ericsson & Kintsch, 1995 for reviews). This allows them to work with a larger quantity of information at a given time and to employ well-practiced strategies. The accumulation of knowledge can also foster interest because it allows individuals both to perceive complexity in the content and to cope with the complexity (Alexander et al. 1995; Durik & Matarazzo, 2009; Silvia, 2006; Tobias, 1994). Stored knowledge may also contribute to the experience of curiosity (see Chap. 5). Curiosity is theorized to emerge when individuals perceive a gap in their knowledge, and this is heightened when the gap is small (Litman, Hutchins, & Russon, 2005; Loewenstein, 1994). When individuals have little knowledge of a domain, the gap is vast and unspecific; however, when they have a lot of knowledge, their attention can turn to the smaller pieces of information that would lead to greater completeness and coherence. When individuals identify small gaps in their knowledge, they may be motivated to seek out additional knowledge. The development of knowledge and expertise tends to prompt individuals to continue to develop in that domain (e.g., Alexander, 1997). For example, consider the student from our opening example who is very interested in history and, therefore, likely has a well-developed knowledge base of history. This student might realize that, while she knows that Benjamin Franklin signed both the Declaration of Independence and the US Constitution, she does not know if anyone else signed both of those documents. She might use her history textbook to fill this knowledge gap by looking up if any other individuals, aside from Benjamin Franklin, signed both documents. This question might not even occur to someone with less integrated knowledge.

Both stored knowledge and stored value have been associated with choices to reengage in domain content over time. However, it is helpful to consider the mechanisms by which this occurs. It seems possible that stored knowledge and stored value alone could exist without motivating subsequent engagement. For example, a diligent student who learned a lot in a course, upon finishing the course, may have no desire to continue studying in the domain. In this sense, individuals may value knowledge that they have already acquired and be satisfied in their current level of understanding without a desire to continue in the domain. In other words, it may be possible for stored knowledge and stored value to be perceived as complete. In contrast, if stored knowledge and stored value are going to prompt subsequent task choices, they may need to be linked to individuals' futures (DeVolder & Lens, 1982; Husman & Lens, 1999; Simons, Dewitte, & Lens, 2000).

Interest, by definition, requires the thirst for additional personal development within the domain. Therefore, a thorough discussion of the internal processes that sustain individual interest across time requires consideration of a mechanism that will put stored knowledge and stored value in motion, toward a future that involves engagement in the domain.

Possible Selves and Mastery Goals

Both stored knowledge and stored value need to be connected to the future possibilities that individuals desire for themselves (Renninger, 2009). Stored knowledge can help individuals to identify what they do not yet know and to imagine what they could understand more completely. However, the potential for new knowledge would not move the person forward, toward domain content, without stored value and the belief that the knowledge can be gained. Stored value must be present to transform the potential for acquiring new knowledge into a possible desired self that has additional knowledge. Without stored value, a person may recognize a discrepancy but have no motivation to reduce it. However, if a person recognizes knowledge that could be acquired, and values it, then a desired possible self emerges: a possible self who has that knowledge. As this example suggests, a possible self is an imagined state that guides a person's striving (Markus & Nurius, 1986; Markus & Ruvolo, 1989). Possible selves embody the potential realities that individuals hold for themselves and can be either desired or feared. For instance, a student taking a history course may consider a possible self who understands the antecedents of World War II (a desired possible self), which is to be approached, or the student might consider a possible self who fails the course (a feared possible self), which is to be avoided. Possible selves emerge from individuals' self-knowledge of who they can imagine themselves to be in the future (Markus & Nurius, 1986).

Possible selves are a special type of self-knowledge and serve as links between the self-concept and motivation (Markus & Nurius, 1986). Although all possible selves link the self-concept to motivation, some are stronger and more motivating than others (Markus & Ruvolo, 1989). Those possible selves that are most defined and integrated within the self-concept (i.e., central to the self-concept) are given priority over other less central possible selves. In this way, the possible selves that are most personally important to the individual are most likely to be pursued by the individual (Oyserman, Bybee, & Terry, 2006). It is likely that possible selves for domains in which individuals are interested are more likely to be desired selves that are personally important and therefore central to the self-concept. As such, those possible selves may be prioritized.

Desired possible selves are not just musings about the self. Instead, they energize goal-directed behavior. First, they set a clear standard for organizing behavior (Markus & Nurius, 1986). A desired possible self provides individuals with a specific and well-defined end state, which aids in appropriate goal setting and successful goal pursuit. Indeed, research shows that goals with specific criteria are more likely to be achieved than vague general intentions (Locke & Latham, 1985). Second, because the possible self is linked to the self-concept, it provides an incentive for action (Markus & Ruvolo, 1989). Finally, if difficulty is encountered, possible selves that are well-integrated into the self-concept can help foster individuals' sense of personal importance (Smith & Oyserman, 2015).

Applied to individual interest, the identification and integration of desired possible selves relevant to a domain can set the stage for the adoption of a goal that is focused on knowledge acquisition and domain mastery. Mastery goals (or learning goals) specify desired end states related to knowledge or skill acquisition that is not yet realized (Dweck & Leggett, 1988; Nicholls, 1984). A person with individual interest can envision a desired possible self that is more expert than the current self, which can lead this individual to adopt a mastery goal to continue to learn in the domain. Although individual interest has been strongly linked to the adoption of mastery goals (e.g., Harackiewicz et al., 2008), this relationship is clarified by the presence of a desired possible self. The desired possible self also provides a mechanism whereby stored knowledge and stored value both can contribute to the adoption of a mastery goal. For example, participants who were prompted to think about achievement tasks in terms of future outcomes were more motivated to learn (Simons et al., 2000). Possible selves have the potential to clarify how stored knowledge and stored value might lead to the desire to acquire more domain knowledge. The adoption of mastery goals is central to the forward propulsion of individuals toward knowledge acquisition.

To this discussion, it is necessary to add a description of how beliefs about self-concept of ability within the domain play out. Self-concept of ability refers to how individuals conceptualize their current knowledge and skills as well as their expectations of success for future attempts at task engagement (Bandura, 1986; Eccles et al., 1983; Nicholls, 1984). Researchers have found that, at the domain level, very few distinctions between perceived competence and expectancies for success emerge (Eccles & Wigfield, 1995). Therefore, for a specified domain, we will treat self-concept of ability and perceived competence as a single entity. Indeed, perceived competence and success expectancies in a domain are likely to be tightly coupled among those with a well-developed individual interest (Hidi & Renninger, 2006; Koller, Baumert, & Schnabel, 2001; Krapp, 2000; Marsh, Trautwein, Ludtke, Koller, & Baumert, 2005).

It is likely that those with a well-developed individual interest have a secure self-concept of ability. In other words, they might recognize that they have considerable knowledge yet to gain (i.e., they lack current knowledge and skills and can imagine developing more expertise), yet they believe that they can overcome various barriers toward acquiring knowledge and skills. Self-concept of ability is relevant to the current model because it may moderate the extent to which a possible self is translated into a mastery goal. Not all possible selves will lead to mastery goals. However, this process may be especially likely for those who have high self-concept of ability in the domain. This process may be illustrated with evidence from research on role models and features that make them more or less inspiring. Role models may provide a concrete example of a possible self for a given individual. However, whether that role model is motivating depends on whether it provides a standard that is perceived to be within the person's capacities (Lockwood & Kunda, 1997). Those with a more secure self-concept of ability are more likely to see desired possible selves as attainable. Consequently, the translation from a possible self to a mastery goal may not be as direct for those with a less secure self-concept of ability, even if they have domain knowledge and value. For instance, imagine two students who hear from a peer that a particular Japanese history class was extremely difficult but very rewarding. Both students can envision a desired possible self that understands Japanese history; however one student has a more secure self-concept of ability than the other. The student with a less secure self-concept of ability may not enroll in the course due to concerns that they may not be successful.

Mastery Goals and Goal Schemas

Once a goal has been adopted, both conscious and nonconscious processes are put in motion that can facilitate goal pursuit. In the case of individual interest, the mastery goal to learn and master domain content can trigger processes that promote choices to engage in domain-relevant tasks. Research on self-regulatory processes in the service of goal attainment clarifies how this occurs. These processes depend on a social cognitive conceptualization of goals and related stimuli as an associated network of constructs that are subject to spreading activation (Kruglanski & Kopetz, 2009). To engage in behaviors aimed at goal attainment, individuals must identify and select a means for achieving the goal, avoid other distracting goals, and evaluate the goal positively (Kruglanski & Kopetz, 2009).

Once a goal becomes activated, constructs that are associated with the goal tend to become activated and are evaluated positively. Meanwhile, other constructs that are inconsistent with the goal tend to be deactivated and are evaluated negatively (Ferguson & Bargh, 2004). For example, when individuals are pursuing a goal, then means, or the specific ways to pursue the goal, are more accessible (Shah, Friedman, & Kruglanski, 2002; Shah & Kruglanski, 2003). Not only are goal-relevant stimuli more likely to be at the front of consciousness for important goals, but the goal-relevant stimuli are also more likely to evoke positive affect (Ferguson & Bargh, 2004; Fishbach & Shah, 2006). Moreover, when stimuli are not relevant to a current goal, individuals can actively employ an avoidance orientation toward such stimuli (Fishbach & Shah, 2006). Applied to individual interest, it is reasonable to predict that those with individual interest in a given domain who adopt mastery goals are prepared to respond with an approach tendency to domain content and to actively avoid distractions, both of which will facilitate task choice.

Moreover, the process of highlighting and responding positively to goal-relevant content while inhibiting distractions will likely be fueled by the connection between mastery goals, personal value, and the self. Individuals who are pursuing goals for purposes that are of high value and are central to the self are likely to think about the choice to engage in an activity at a high level of construal (for a review, see Trope

& Liberman, 2010). When people think at a high level of construal, they focus on the abstract essence of objects, choices, and behaviors and dismiss the low-level, concrete details (Trope & Liberman, 2010). For example, the interested history student thinking at a high level of construal will be able to view events holistically and connect them to other events, whereas the disinterested history student might only memorize disconnected, concrete facts to pass their in-class tests. In addition to improving the way individuals think about a domain, a high level of construal can also facilitate goal striving because the importance of the goal-related features of available options is more salient (Fujita, Eyal, Chaiken, Trope & Liberman, 2008; Trope & Liberman, 2000). High levels of construal during goal striving can also help individuals avoid temptations that might otherwise derail goal pursuit. For instance, one study demonstrated that when thinking at a high level of construal, individuals filtered secondary goals, which benefitted pursuit of the primary goal (Freitas, Gollwitzer, & Trope, 2004). These results suggest that thinking at a high level of construal promotes primary goal pursuit and inhibits secondary goals.

Applied to individual interest, it is plausible that mastery goals extending from possible selves are particularly likely to be construed at high levels. As such, mastery goals are adopted for developing the self in those domains that hold personal value (Pintrich, 2000). Mastery goals that are rooted in desired possible selves fit a similar role, in that they tend to be high-level, abstract conceptualizations that persist across time and contexts. Given their high level of construal, mastery goals are likely to help individuals notice opportunities to engage with domain-relevant content and to ignore other less salient pursuits. For instance, the interested student from our earlier example might have a choice between studying one evening or watching television. If that student is thinking at a high level of construal, she might be particularly likely to study and ignore the temptation to watch television.

At the Moment of Choice

In summary, these processes help explain how individuals with a developed individual interest might select to engage in an activity that allows for continued development of knowledge and skills in the domain of interest. Specifically, the stored knowledge and stored value associated with the domain allow individuals to imagine desired possible selves that are not yet realized. Additionally, developed individual interest, along with a secure self-concept of ability, supports the adoption of mastery goals focused on learning and mastering domain content. Further, striving toward these adopted mastery goals may be facilitated by processes that make goal-relevant options stand out as attractive and that also inhibit goal-irrelevant options. Together, these processes lay fertile soil in which engagement can bloom.

Finally, at the moment of task choice, when an individual has the opportunity to engage, one final consideration may push them toward the activity versus away. The individual will be more likely to choose the task if they expect it to be intrinsically valuable (Sansone & Harackiewicz, 1996; Sansone & Thoman, 2005) and not costly (Eccles et al., 1983). Two elements of stored value may play a role at this late stage of the process, prior to task choice. Specifically, individuals will be more likely to choose task engagement if they feel like doing the task (it has intrinsic value) and believe that the choice will not lead to other negative consequences (low cost). For example, our very interested history student may have the choice to watch a 2-hour documentary about World War II one evening. At the moment of choice, she will do so if she has enjoyed similar documentaries in the past (high intrinsic value) and if she does not have other more pressing activities (no exams for which to study; low cost).

When Task Engagement Begins

According to our model of task choice, those with individual interest have several resources that lead them to choose the task (stored knowledge and stored value, a desired possible self that is relevant to the domain, a goal to develop knowledge and skills, an active goal schema, and the anticipation of enjoyment). These resources are still present once task engagement begins, but have unique implications for how individual interest affects situational interest once an individual is in contact with domain content.

Harackiewicz and Sansone (1991) presented a model to explain and predict how goals play out in the context of achievement activities and how goals incite motivational processes that lead to the promotion or undermining of situational interest. According to the model, many factors can affect the goals that individuals adopt during a given achievement activity, including both personal factors and situational factors. There is strong evidence that those with individual interest are especially likely to experience situational interest during task engagement (Ainley, Hidi, & Berndorff, 2002; Harackiewicz et al., 2008; Linnenbrink-Garcia et al., 2013). We follow this individual difference variable through the process model to outline how it would be expected to lead to the adoption of goals and key process variables outlined in the model: task involvement, competence valuation, and perceived competence.

Individual Interest and Goals

Purpose Goals According to the model, purpose goals describe the reason why a person is engaging in a particular achievement activity (Harackiewicz & Sansone, 1991). Not surprisingly, people with an individual interest in the domain are likely to be engaged in the task, at least in part, to master the material or activity. Again, the goal for a person with high individual interest is focused on learning and skill development, which is also known as a mastery goal (e.g., Barron & Harackiewicz, 2001; Harackiewicz et al., 2008; Pintrich, Ryan, & Patrick, 1998; Wolters, 1998).

This goal is likely to keep those with high individual interest focused on the content that is available in the environment. For them, the activity offers an opportunity to explore content, manipulate ideas, and add to their existing knowledge (Hidi & Renninger, 2006). For instance, the student who has an individual interest in history might choose to take an optional elective course on Native American history primarily because it will offer her an opportunity to grow her domain knowledge.

In contrast, those engaged in the activity without an individual interest in the domain may engage for some reason besides their own personal desire to master the content. They may be engaged in the activity for any number of reasons (Hidi & Harackiewicz, 2000). These individuals may engage for an achievement purpose (e.g., complete course requirements for graduation, to outperform a roommate) or for a purpose that is not related to achievement (e.g., to meet new people). In this case, what is critical is that the content of the activity is not central to the purpose of task engagement. Therefore, whereas the person with high individual interest is focused on the content itself, the person with lower individual interest may or may not be focused on the content. For example, the student who is uninterested in history might choose to take an optional elective course on Native American history because it fits nicely into her schedule and fulfills her elective requirement.

Target Goals Target goals are the other type of goal put forth in the theoretical model (Harackiewicz & Sansone, 1991). Target goals specify how an individual plans to accomplish the purpose goal. Similar to purpose goals, target goals would likely vary depending on the level of individual interest and reflect specific strategies that can be used while interacting with content in order to learn and develop skills. Overall, the target goals for those with high individual interest would be expected to focus on strategies for both exploration and careful study of the content. Consistent with this, intrinsic value and mastery goals have been associated with deep learning strategies, effort, and persistence (e.g., Pintrich & De Groot, 1990; Wolters, 1998; 2004; Zimmerman, 1990).

In addition, the prior knowledge and experience that accompanies individual interest may provide an additional resource to support learning (Hidi, 1990). Specifically, mastery goals do not always predict performance (see Harackiewicz, Barron, & Elliot, 1998 for a review), which may be related to lack of specificity (cf. Grant & Dweck, 2003). Consistent with research on goal setting more generally (Locke & Latham, 1985), specific mastery goals predict performance better than general mastery goals (Senko & Harackiewicz, 2005). The knowledge that those with high individual interest bring to the task may help them set specific target goals, which can foster learning. Consistent with this, research examining grit, which involves a combination of deep interest and single-minded commitment to a goal, is associated with deliberate practice, which promotes performance (Duckworth, Kirby, Tsukayama, Berstein, & Ericsson, 2011). Deliberate practice involves attending to and putting effort toward specific aspects of an activity that are not yet mastered. People with high individual interest have prior knowledge and experience, which may help them identify specific features of task engagement that might facilitate skill development. Moreover, their value for the domain is also likely to help them persist through difficulty and maintain effort (Fulmer & Frijters, 2011).

In contrast, the target goals of those with low individual interest may vary quite a bit depending on the purpose goal and the situation. Among these individuals, those who do not adopt an achievement goal are unlikely to adopt a target goal that is relevant to the content. For example, if the purpose of task engagement is to meet new people, then the target goal might be to join different work groups when opportunities arise. Given that this purpose goal is not focused on the content, the target goals would not be expected to be relevant to the content either. If these individuals are to become involved in the content, it will be due to other aspects of the task or situation (Hidi & Harackiewicz, 2000). That said, some individuals with low individual interest may adopt achievement-related target goals, and these goals could match the purpose goal. If a person with low individual interest is engaging in an activity for the purpose of outperforming a roommate, then the target goals would be related to the standard set by the roommate. Given that inherent value for the activity is not present for those with low individual interest, these other goals may support positive achievement striving in the absence of individual interest (Hidi & Harackiewicz, 2000).

In sum, individuals who have varying levels of individual interest in a domain will begin task engagement with different goals. For those with individual interest, the purpose and target goals are matched toward the same end, which is hypothesized to facilitate goal pursuit (Harackiewicz & Sansone, 1991). Moreover, the purpose goals for those with high individual interest emanate from views of the self and are likely coherent with each other. These features of goal hierarchies tend to have motivational benefits (Sheldon & Kasser, 1995).

Individual Interest and Process Measures Related to Situational Interest

When those with individual interest approach a task in their domain of interest, their mastery goal is focused on learning content. However, the mastery goal does not automatically facilitate the experience of situational interest. The situation needs to afford opportunities relevant to the goal and the individual needs to be open to those opportunities. Three process variables that can emerge during task engagement were posited as the mechanisms through which goals can translate into the experience of situational interest (Harackiewicz & Sansone, 1991). These are competence valuation, perceived competence, and task engagement. Competence valuation refers to the extent to which individuals personally care about doing well on the task. Perceived competence refers to how successful at the task a person feels while doing the task. Finally, task involvement refers to absorption and immersion in the task.

Importantly, these processes do not always lead to the experience of situational interest for all individuals, or in all contexts (Harackiewicz & Sansone, 1991). Consequently, the processes can provide windows into the phenomenological aspects of task engagement that are more relevant for certain individuals or in certain situations (Durik, Hulleman, & Harackiewicz, 2015a). To help illuminate the nature of task engagement for those with varying levels of individual interest, a distinction should be made involving the role of the self. The self is fairly central to theoretical accounts of individual interest (Hidi & Renninger, 2006; Krapp 2002; Schiefele, 1999); however, researchers have yet to clarify how beliefs about the self unfold in the moment of task engagement. Most of the empirical approaches to considering how the self fits into situational interest have been related to self-concept of ability and efficacy beliefs, which are critical to the experience of situational interest (Bandura, 1986; Csikszentmihalyi, 1990; Deci & Ryan, 1985; Pajares, 1996). However, we would like to expand the discussion of the self to consider how the self manifests during task engagement more broadly. The available evidence with regard to the process variables that are hypothesized to predict situational interest can provide a window into how the self is relevant during task engagement and how the role of the self may be different for those with low versus high individual interest in the domain content.

Two assumptions are important to the following analysis. First, we contend that the self is inherent to two of the process measures (competence valuation and perceived competence) and not the other (task involvement). Second, we assume that individuals with high individual interest in the domain have a positive possible self that is consistent with developing knowledge and skills within the domain. As such, during task engagement, the self may be a resource for those with high individual interest but a source of vulnerability for those with low individual interest. This distinction may translate into differences in how those along the whole continuum of individual interest experience the process variables and whether the process variables support or undermine situational interest.

Competence Valuation Although competence valuation can change across a task, it has often been measured prior to task engagement to assess the extent to which individuals are willing to invest themselves in the activity prior to doing it. Not surprisingly, those with high individual interest evidence higher competence valuation than those with lower individual interest (Durik & Harackiewicz, 2007). In other words, those with individual interest are more willing to invest themselves in their task performance than those with low individual interest. There may be two reasons for this: self-concept of ability and possible selves.

First, those with high individual interest have a secure self-concept of ability with the domain, reflected in high correlations between individual interest and domain self-concept of ability (see Wigfield & Cambria, 2010 for review). Therefore, those with high individual interest may be willing to care more about doing well because they have high expectancies for their future performance. This is consistent with experimental evidence suggesting that the provision of positive feedback contributed to individuals' willingness to value competence in an activity (Elliot et al.,

2000). In contrast, those with lower individual interest may be in the opposite situation. They tend not to have a secure self-concept of ability in the domain and may recoil from caring about performing well for self-protective reasons (O'Keefe, 2013). As such, students who have individual interest in history are likely to invest themselves in their history project because they believe they can perform well, which makes caring about their performance safe. Contrarily, students who lack individual interest in history may be reluctant to invest themselves in their history project in order to protect themselves from the possibility that they will not perform well. Because it is less painful to fail at something one does not care about than to fail at something that one cares deeply about, when a learner perceives that failure is likely (i.e., insecure self-concept of ability), not caring may be a way to protect the self.

Second, the presence of an unrealized positive possible self may help those with high individual interest care about doing well. Indeed, if possible selves clarify a higher level of knowledge or skill than what individuals currently have, then the possible selves may prompt individuals to care about doing well. This essentially converts the possible self into a goal that is related to achievement in the context of task engagement. Consistent with this, in a laboratory experiment, participants who were told about how the experimental task could be personally useful to them showed higher competence valuation than those who were not told about the personal utility of the task (Durik & Harackiewicz, 2007). One interpretation is that the statement of personal utility helped participants imagine a possible self to which they could aspire. For those with high individual interest, this possible self landed on fertile ground and provided clarity about what the situation could offer. Those with lower individual interest also cared more about competence after receiving information about personal utility, but this may have been meaningless (or even threatening) without having an available possible self with which to connect it. For instance, the student from our opening example who is uninterested in history might be threatened by information communicating how useful it is to know history. Indeed, if individuals perceive that they are likely to do poorly in the course (i.e., low interest and an insecure self-concept of ability), then telling them about the usefulness and importance of the content may make failure scarier.

Competence valuation, by definition, involves the self. Consequently, competence valuation at relatively high levels may serve as a resource for individuals with high individual interest. Competence valuation, as observed among those with high individual interest, may be associated with higher-level values associated with the domain and the relation of that domain to the self. Therefore, in the context of task engagement, these individuals' concern for competence may reflect a high level of construal and a sense of purpose in what they are doing. These processes may be more complex for those with low individual interest. It is likely important for these individuals to care about competence at a minimal level so that they attend to the task, but caring about competence at a very high level may be deleterious. These individuals have an insecure self-concept of ability within the domain. If they care too much about competence without it being backed by stored knowledge and stored value, then they might experience high pressure to perform well that could undermine situational interest.

Perceived Competence Given the link between individual interest and self-concept of ability at the domain level, it is not surprising that those with higher individual interest also report higher perceived competence in tasks that are related to their domain of interest (Bong, 2001; Durik et al., 2015a; Hulleman, Godes, Hendricks, & Harackiewicz, 2010; Linnenbrink-Garcia et al., 2013; Patall, 2013; Pintrich & De Groot, 1990). Moreover, there is a long history of theory and research showing that people report higher interest in tasks that provide them with a sense of competence (Csikszentmihalyi, 1990; Deci & Ryan, 1985; Vallerand & Reid, 1984).

Those with higher individual interest may report higher perceived competence in a domain-relevant task in part because they are likely to have had prior experiences of success and practice in the domain (Alexander et al. 1995; Hidi & Renninger, 2006; Marsh et al., 2005). Their stored knowledge and skills also serve as a resource for them during task engagement. These individuals have multiple strategies at their disposal, and prior experience provides evidence that they may need to switch strategies because there are situations in which some strategies work better than others (Linnenbrink-Garcia et al., 2013; Tobias, 1994; Wolters, 1998). In other words, for those with high individual interest, their level of perceived competence should remain relatively high and stable throughout task engagement. Consistent with this, those with individual interest have been shown to persist and maintain effort even in very difficult tasks (Fulmer & Frijters, 2011; O'Keefe & Linnenbrink-Garcia, 2014).

In contrast, those with low individual interest may be especially vulnerable to feeling low perceived competence, which can undermine their situational interest. Situations that allow those with low individual interest to establish a minimal amount of perceived competence, but in a way that downplays the importance of competence, might be optimal for them. Again, these individuals have relatively nonexistent positive possible selves related to the domain (and they might even have feared selves related to demonstrating incompetence). They may need assistance developing those possible selves, but this assistance should be provided within the limits of their fragile sense of self-concept of ability. Prior research shows that those with low self-concept of ability reported more situational interest when they were prompted to generate how material they were engaged in was useful or personally relevant to them (Hulleman & Harackiewicz, 2009; Hulleman et al., 2010). Moreover, the process of generating utility contributed to these individuals' perceived competence (Canning & Harackiewicz, 2015). Given that those with low self-concept of ability also tend to be those with low individual interest, it is likely that these individuals needed to derive for themselves any personal significance of the task and to do so within their comfort zone of perceived competence (Durik, et al., 2015a). Consistent with this notion, those with low individual interest reported lower perceived competence when they were told by an experimenter about how a task could be useful, but not when the information was communicated to them from peers (Gaspard et al., 2015).

In general, those with high individual interest will experience relatively stable and high perceived competence in the face of challenging or changing task demands (Fulmer & Frijters, 2011). These same challenges or changes in the task may threaten those with low individual interest. In general, contexts that help those with low individual interest to feel secure in their current level of perceived competence will likely promote their situational interest. For example, contexts that downplay the cost of low performance (Eccles et al., 1983) while also validating the promise of effort (Dweck & Leggett, 1988) are likely to support perceived competence and situational interest for those with low individual interest. For example, the history student with low interest may benefit from having many small assignments in a course that can help build skills and foster a sense of mastery over time rather than have one assignment that might highlight evaluation rather than growth.

Task Involvement Task involvement is the deep absorption with an activity that occurs when an individual is actively focused and energetically responsive to task demands. In contrast to the other two process variables presented in the model, task involvement is related more directly to the experience of psychological flow (Csikszentmihalyi, 1990). Psychological flow is the pinnacle of the experience of intrinsic motivation (Deci & Ryan, 1985). This state of deep immersion in an activity occurs when individuals' skills match the challenges of the environment and is accompanied by the experience of enjoyment and the desire to keep doing the activity.

It is not surprising that those with higher individual interest report higher task involvement in domain-relevant activities than those with lower individual interest (Durik & Harackiewicz, 2007; Durik, Shechter, Noh, Rozek, & Harackiewicz, 2015b). Those with individual interest have greater stored knowledge and skills that can help them to navigate various kinds of challenges and to adjust strategies based on situational demands. Their stored knowledge in the domain plays a particular role. Those with high individual interest are able to not only solve problems and manage challenges during task engagement as they emerge, but they are also able to recognize and create new challenges for themselves (Azevedo, 2011; Barron, 2006). For example, those with high individual interest may have the desire and knowledge to identify new questions for themselves and to pursue answers to those questions during task engagement (Barron, 2006; Renninger, 1990). Their own curiosity about the domain and prior knowledge allows them to go beyond the boundaries of either their current knowledge or the explicit task that is presented. They are on their own mission when interacting with domain content, which will facilitate their task involvement.

Those with high individual interest become deeply concentrated on domain-relevant tasks, and as they face, overcome, and create new challenges, they likely experience efficacy and positive emotion that facilitate their continued task engagement (Ainley et al., 2002; Bandura, 1986; Csikszentmihalyi, 1990; Deci & Ryan, 1985). This positive affect may also help keep their goals activated. Overall, affect serves as a cue regarding the desirability of goals, with positive affect indicating a very desirable goal and negative affect indicating an undesirable goal (Carver &

Scheier, 1981; Pervin, 1989). When goals were experimentally manipulated to be associated with positive affect, the goals were perceived as especially desirable and were more likely to be pursued (Custers & Aarts, 2007).

In contrast, when people are engaged in an activity for which they do not have an individual interest, task involvement is likely to be low. Given that these individuals' interest, by definition, is not in the domain, they will be prone to distractions if the task allows them time to reflect. For example, because their skills are less developed, challenges are likely to cause them to question their (already low) perceived competence. Moreover, once engagement stops, they might consider why they are even doing the task and have difficulty convincing themselves to get started again. In sum, task involvement is a primary challenge for those with low individual interest. Not only are these individuals' attention not on the task, but their attention is likely to be focused somewhere else instead. Experimental studies have been conducted to examine the effects of involving task characteristics on situational interest for those with varying levels of individual interest (Durik & Harackiewicz, 2007; Durik & Matarazzo, 2009; Sadoski, Goetz, & Fritz, 1993). When those with low individual interest engaged in materials that had bright colors and varied fonts, they reported more interest in the task (Durik & Harackiewicz, 2007). Importantly, this was mediated by task involvement, such that the task features helped those with low individual interest become involved in the activity and to find it interesting.

Those with low individual interest tend to experience low competence valuation, low perceived competence, and low task involvement. However, task involvement may have a secret advantage over the other process variables that make it a good target for intervention. Unlike the other process variables, task involvement does not require (and may even exclude) the experience of self-awareness. Self-awareness during task engagement may be a vulnerability for those with low individual interest. Research on self-awareness suggests that when individuals think about themselves, discrepancies between their current state and standards of where they could or should be become salient (Duval & Wicklund, 1972). In other words, the state of self-awareness can make individuals aware of ways in which they are not currently meeting standards and cause negative affect (Mor & Winquist, 2002).

In contrast, the state of psychological flow, which includes deep task involvement, has been associated with a state of reduced self-awareness (Csikszentmihalyi, 1990; Dietrich, 2004). If the involvement aspect of flow is responsible for the reduced experience of self-awareness, then task involvement may help those with low individual interest experience situational interest. When these individuals' attention is focused on the environment, attention is not focused on the self. This reduced self-focus may provide a respite from feelings of incompetence and low task value. Features of tasks that support task involvement might help those with otherwise low individual interest to experience situational interest (Durik & Harackiewicz, 2007). Task involvement may be a primary target of intervention for those with low individual interest. Consistent with this, when participants who completed a boring task were asked how to make it more interesting, the modal response was to change how they did the activity. The specific behavioral manifestation of this may have been to create variability in experience in order to increase involvement (Sansone, Weir, Harpster, & Morgan, 1992).

When Engagement Is Over

After task engagement, in addition to any skills and knowledge that they acquired, individuals are left with their memory for the event. For those with high individual interest, it is likely that they reflect positively on the activity and conclude that it was valuable and contributed to their developing possible selves. They may also be satisfied with the progress that they made. In addition, given that the activity was important to them, the progress that they perceive may contribute to their return to the activity in the future and their continued goal pursuit (Koo & Fishbach, 2008). That said, even though progress may have been made, it is unlikely that a single activity would lead to the development of a satisfying and complete possible self. This aspect of the unachieved goal will likely move them toward making choices that will lead to further growth in the future.

A question remains regarding what individuals actually take away from an instance of task engagement. It is clear from prior discussion in this chapter that memory plays a role in choosing to engage in a task, via stored value, as well as actually engaging in the task, via the working memory enabled by stored knowledge. For example, memories of positive experiences involving learning a foreign language in school predicted adults' motivation to learn a foreign language later in life (Gorges & Kandler, 2012). Sometimes individual interest owes to an accumulation of several indistinct experiences, but sometimes a single outstanding task experience illuminates certain values that stand out to individuals, which subsequently revolutionizes the way they think about domain content (Pugh, 2011).

Those with low individual interest are in a very different situation when it comes to what they take away from task engagement. Left on their own, they will likely attribute their engagement to an external source. Moreover, given that the domain is not perceived as important, they are likely to abandon the current domain and switch to other pursuits if they perceive they have made sufficient progress (Koo & Fishbach, 2008). Finally, although these individuals may have acquired experience in the domain, they may not feel like they did well and, therefore, will not care about doing well. All of this said, memories are malleable and this feature allows for some provocative possibilities. For example, over time, difficulty might be interpreted as an opportunity to grow and learn (Dweck, 1999; Dweck & Leggett, 1988). A student in a particularly challenging history course might come to reinterpret the unpleasantly difficult class as being one of the most important classes ever taken because of how much was learned.

Summary: Keeping Them on Track

Once individual interest for a domain is developed, there are still points at which external supports can help promote engagement with the domain.

One area in which external supports may be helpful is to facilitate the development of stored value and domain-relevant desired possible selves. For example, parents may be able to help their children develop possible selves in certain careers that may facilitate their decisions to take optional courses in these disciplines (Harackiewicz, Rozek, Hulleman, & Hyde, 2012). In a related fashion, expert role models may foster the development of individual interest by encouraging those with developing interest to ask questions and to consider what they know from different perspectives (Hidi & Renninger, 2006; Renninger, 2009). Indeed, a person might acquire stored knowledge for a domain, but may not take the extra step of considering what else they could possibly learn and, therefore, fail to recognize an opportunity to grow. Without recognizing the opportunity, the person is unlikely to form a desired possible self. For those with high individual interest, highlighting a potential discrepancy might spark a student's curiosity and lead them to consider a desired possible self.

External supports may also be beneficial for engagement when individuals have a desired possible self but have not taken steps to adopt the goal to pursue knowledge in the domain. Therefore, it may be beneficial at this point to support the individuals' self-concept of ability and to help them focus on their potential for growth (Renninger, 2009). Educators might support their students' self-concept of ability by prompting students to consider the amount of knowledge that has been acquired over time and by pointing out specific times that they have overcome difficulties through hard work (Dweck & Leggett, 1988). Messages that focus on the importance of growth are best for promoting a secure self-concept of ability, as well as continued engagement with a domain (Dweck, 2007).

Once a mastery goal to acquire knowledge in the domain has been set, the individual is likely to self-regulate toward domain content and will ultimately choose to engage. Consistent with this, learning environments that focus students on learning and skill development help students set mastery goals, which can foster their continued interest (O'Keefe, Ben-Eliyahu, & Linnenbrink-Garcia, 2013). That said, those with individual interest need a certain amount of freedom to engage with domain-relevant content. It is critical that, once individuals have begun to engage in the task, they have access to content and can make their own choices (Patall, 2013). Along these lines, parents and teachers can make enrichment opportunities known to the individuals, and once the opportunities are known, allow individuals to identify and pursue their own goals (Renninger, 2009).

References

Ainley, M., & Ainley, J. (2011). A cultural perspective on the structure of student interest in science. *International Journal of Science Education, 33*, 51–71.

Ainley, M., Hidi, S., & Berndorff, D. (2002). Interest, learning, and the psychological processes that mediate their relationship. *Journal of Educational Psychology, 94*, 545–561.

Alexander, P. A. (1997). Mapping the multidimensional nature of domain learning: The interplay of cognitive, motivational, and strategic forces. *Advances in Motivation and Achievement, 10*, 213–250.

Alexander, P. A., Jetton, T. L., & Kulikowich, J. M. (1995). The interrelationship of knowledge, interest, and recall: Assessing a model of domain learning. *Journal of Educational Psychology, 87*, 559–575.

Alexander, P. A., Murphy, P. K., Woods, B. S., Duhon, K. E., & Parker, D. (1997). College instruction and concomitant changes in students' knowledge, interest, and strategy use: A study of domain learning. *Contemporary Educational Psychology, 22*, 125–146.

Azevedo, F. S. (2011). Lines of practice: A practice-centered theory of interest relationships. *Cognition and Instruction, 29*, 147–184.

Bandura, A. (1986). *Social foundations of thought and action: A social cognitive theory.* Englewood Cliffs, NJ: Prentice-Hall.

Barron, B. (2006). Interest and self-sustained learning as catalysts of development: A learning ecology perspective. *Human Development, 49*, 193–224.

Barron, K. E., & Harackiewicz, J. M. (2001). Achievement goals and optimal motivation: Testing multiple goal models. *Journal of Personality and Social Psychology, 80*, 706–722. doi:10.1037//0022-3514.80.5.706.

Bong, M. (2001). Role of self-efficacy and task-value in predicting college students' course performance and future enrollment intentions. *Contemporary Educational Psychology, 26*, 553–570. http://dx.doi.org/10.1006/ceps.2000.1048.

Canning, E. A., & Harackiewicz, J. M. (2015). Teach it, don't preach it: The differential effects of directly-communicated and self-generated utility–value information. *Motivation Science, 1*, 47–71. http://dx.doi.org/10.1037/mot0000015.

Carver, C. S., & Scheier, M. F. (1981). *Attention and self-regulation: A control-theory approach to human behavior.* New York: Springer.

Chi, M. T. H., Glaser, R., & Rees, E. (1982). Expertise in problem solving. In R. J. Sternberg (Ed.), *Advances in the psychology of human intelligence* (Vol. 1, pp. 7–75). Hillsdale, NJ: Erlbaum.

Cohen, G. L., Garcia, J., Apfel, N., & Master, A. (2006). Reducing the racial achievement gap: A social-psychological intervention. *Science, 313*, 1307–1310. doi:10.1126/science.1128317.

Csikszentmihalyi, M. (1990). *Flow: The psychology of optimal experience.* New York: Harper & Row.

Custers, R., & Aarts, H. (2007). Positive affect as implicit motivator: On the nonconscious operation of behavioral goals. *Journal of Personality and Social Psychology, 89*, 129–142. doi:10.1037/0022-3514.89.2.129.

Deci, E. L. (1992). The relation of interest to the motivation of behavior: A self-determination theory perspective. In K. A. Renninger, S. Hidi, & A. Krapp (Eds.), *The role of interest in learning and development* (pp. 43–70). Hillsdale, NJ: Lawrence Erlbaum.

Deci, E. L., & Ryan, R. M. (1985). *Intrinsic motivation and self-determination in human behavior.* New York, NY: Plenum. http://dx.doi.org/10.1007/978-1-4899-2271-7.

DeVolder, M. L., & Lens, W. W. (1982). Academic achievement and future time perspective as a cognitive–motivational concept. *Journal of Personality and Social Psychology, 42*, 566–571. doi:10.1037/0022-3514.42.3.566.

Dietrich, A. (2004). Neurocognitive mechanisms underlying the experience of flow. *Consciousness and Cognition, 13*, 746–761. doi:10.1016/j.concog.2004.07.002.

Duckworth, A. L., Kirby, T., Tsukayama, E., Berstein, H., & Ericsson, K. A. (2011). Deliberate practice spells success: Why grittier competitors triumph at the National Spelling Bee. *Social Psychological & Personality Science, 2*, 174–181.

Durik, A. M., & Harackiewicz, J. M. (2007). Different strokes for different folks: How individual interest moderates the effects of situational factors on task interest. *Journal of Educational Psychology, 99*, 597–610. http://dx.doi.org/10.1037/0022-0663.99.3.597.

Durik, A. M., Hulleman, C. S., & Harackiewicz, J. M. (2015a). One size fits some: Instructional enhancements to promote interest. In K. A. Renninger & M. Nieswandt (Eds.), *Interest, the self, and K-16 mathematics and science learning*. Washington, DC: American Educational Research Association.

Durik, A. M., & Matarazzo, K. L. (2009). Revved up or turned off? How domain knowledge changes the relationship between perceived task complexity and task interest. *Learning and Individual Differences, 19*, 155–159.

Durik, A. M., Shechter, O. G., Noh, M., Rozek, C. S., & Harackiewicz, J. M. (2015b). What if I can't? Success expectancies moderate the effects of utility value information on situational interest and performance. *Motivation and Emotion, 39*, 104–118. http://dx.doi.org/10.1007/s11031-014-9419-0.

Duval, S., & Wicklund, R. (1972). *A theory of objective self-awareness*. New York, NY: Academic.

Dweck, C. S. (1999). *Self-theories: Their role in motivation, personality, and development*. Philadelphia, PA: Psychology Press.

Dweck, C. S. (2007). Boosting achievement with messages that motivate. *Education Canada, 47*, 6–10.

Dweck, C. S., & Leggett, E. L. (1988). A social-cognitive approach to motivation and personality. *Psychological Review, 95*, 256–273.

Eccles, J. (2009). Who am I and what am I going to do with my life? Personal and collective identitiesasmotivatorsofaction.*EducationalPsychologist,44*,78–89.doi:10.1080/00461520902832368.

Eccles, J., Adler, T. F., Futterman, R., Goff, S. B., Kaczala, C. M., Meece, J. L., et al. (1983). Expectancies, values, and academic behaviors. In J. T. Spence (Ed.), *Achievement and achievement motives: Psychological and sociological approaches* (pp. 75–146). San Francisco: Freeman.

Eccles, J. S., & Wigfield, A. (1995). In the mind of the actor: The structure of adolescents' achievement task values and expectancy-related beliefs. *Personality and Social Psychology Bulletin, 21*, 215–220. doi:10.1177/0146167295213003.

Elliot, A. J., Faler, J., McGregor, H. A., Campbell, W. K., Sedikides, C., & Harackiewicz, J. M. (2000). Competence valuation as a strategic intrinsic motivation process. *Personality and Social Psychology Bulletin, 26*, 780–794.

Ericsson, K. A., & Kintsch, W. (1995). Long term working memory. *Psychological Review, 102*, 211–245.

Feather, N. T. (1988). Values, valences, and course enrollment: Testing the role of personal values within an expectancy-value framework. *Journal of Educational Psychology, 80*, 381–391.

Ferguson, M. J., & Bargh, J. A. (2004). Liking is for doing: The effects of goal pursuit on automatic evaluation. *Journal of Personality and Social Psychology, 87*, 557–572. doi:10.1037/0022-3514.87.5.557.

Fishbach, A., & Shah, J. Y. (2006). Self-control in action: Implicit dispositions toward goals and away from temptations. *Journal of Personality and Social Psychology, 90*, 820–832. doi:10.1037/0022-3514.90.5.820.

Freitas, A. L., Gollwitzer, P., & Trope, Y. (2004). The influence of abstract and concrete mindsets on anticipating and guiding others' self-regulatory efforts. *Journal of Experimental Social Psychology, 40*, 739–752.

Fujita, K., Eyal, T., Chaiken, S., Trope, Y., & Liberman, N. (2008). Influencing attitudes toward near and distant objects. *Journal of Experimental Social Psychology, 44*, 562–572.

Fulmer, S. M., & Frijters, J. C. (2011). Motivation during an excessively challenging reading task: The buffering role of relative topic interest. *The Journal of Experimental Education, 79*, 185–208.

Gaspard, H., Dicke, A. L., Flunger, B., Brisson, B. M., Hafner, I., Nagengast, B., & Trautwein, U. (2015). Fostering adolescents' value beliefs for mathematics with a relevance intervention in the classroom. *Developmental Psychology, 51*, 1226–1240.

Gorges, J., & Kandler, C. (2012). Adults' learning motivation: Expectancy of success, value, and the role of affective memories. *Learning and Individual Differences, 22*, 610–617. doi:10.1016/j.lindif.2011.09.016.

Grant, H., & Dweck, C. S. (2003). Clarifying achievement goals and their impact. *Journal of Personality and Social Psychology, 85*, 541–553.

Harackiewicz, J. M., Barron, K. E., & Elliot, A. J. (1998). Rethinking achievement goals: When are they adaptive for college students and why? *Educational Psychologist, 33*, 1–21.

Harackiewicz, J. M., Durik, A. M., Barron, K. E., Linnenbrink-Garcia, L., & Tauer, J. M. (2008). The role of achievement goals in the development of interest: Reciprocal relations between achievement goals, interest and performance. *Journal of Educational Psychology, 100*(1), 105–122.

Harackiewicz, J. M., Rozek, C. R., Hulleman, C. S., & Hyde, J. S. (2012). Helping parents motivate adolescents in mathematics and science: An experimental test. *Psychological Science, 43*, 899–906. doi:10.1177/0956797611435530.

Harackiewicz, J. M., & Sansone, C. (1991). Goals and intrinsic motivation: You can get there from here. *Advances in Motivation and Achievement, 7*, 21–49.

Harackiewicz, J. M., Tibbetts, Y., Canning, E., & Hyde, J. S. (2014). Harnessing values to promote motivation in education. In S. A. Karabenick & T. C. Urdan (Eds.), *Motivational interventions, Advances in motivation and achievement* (Vol. 18, pp. 71–105). Bingley: Emerald Group Publishing Limited.

Hidi, S. (1990). Interest and its contribution as a mental resource for learning. *Review of Educational Research, 60*, 549–571. http://dx.doi.org/10.3102/00346543060004549.

Hidi, S., & Harackiewicz, J. M. (2000). Motivating the academically unmotivated: A critical issue for the 21st century. *Review of Educational Research, 70*, 151–179.

Hidi, S., & Renninger, K. A. (2006). The four-phase model of interest development. *Educational Psychologist, 41*(2), 111–127.

Hulleman, C. S., Godes, O., Hendricks, B. L., & Harackiewicz, J. M. (2010). Enhancing interest and performance with a utility value intervention. *Journal of Educational Psychology, 102*, 880–885. http://dx.doi.org/10.1037/a0019506.

Hulleman, C. S., & Harackiewicz, J. M. (2009). Promoting interest and performance in high school science classes. *Science, 326*, 1410–1412. http://dx.doi.org/10.1126/science.1177067.

Husman, J., & Lens, W. (1999). The role of the future in student motivation. *Educational Psychologist, 34*, 113–125. doi:10.1207/s15326985ep3402_4.

Koller, O., Baumert, J., & Schnabel, K. (2001). Does interest matter? The relationship between academic interest and achievement in mathematics. *Journal for Research in Mathematics Education, 32*, 448–470.

Koo, M., & Fishbach, A. (2008). Dynamics of self-regulation: How (un)accomplished goal actions affect motivation. *Journal of Personality and Social Psychology, 94*, 183–195. doi:10.1037/0022-3514.94.2.183.

Krapp, A. (2000). Interest and human development during adolescence: An educational-psychological approach. In J. Heckhausen (Ed.), *Motivational psychology of human development* (pp. 109–128). London: Elsevier.

Krapp, A. (2002). An educational-psychological theory of interest and its relation to SDT. In E. L. Deci & R. M. Ryan (Eds.), *Handbook of self-determination research* (pp. 405–427). Rochester, NY: University of Rochester Press.

Kruglanski, A. W., & Kopetz, C. (2009). What is so special (and nonspecial) about goals? A view from the cognitive perspective. In G. B. Moskowitz & G. Heidi (Eds.), *The psychology of goals* (pp. 27–55). New York, NY: Guildford Press.

Linnenbrink-Garcia, L., Patall, E. A., & Messersmith, E. E. (2013). Antecedents and consequences of situational interest. *British Journal of Educational Psychology, 83*, 591–614.

Litman, J., Hutchins, T., & Russon, R. (2005). Epistemic curiosity, feeling-of-knowing, and exploratory behaviour. *Cognition & Emotion, 19*, 559–582.

Locke, E. A., & Latham, G. P. (1985). The application of goal setting to sports. *Journal of Sport Psychology, 7*(3), 205–222.

Lockwood, P., & Kunda, Z. (1997). Superstars and me: Predicting the impact of role models on the self. *Journal of Personality and Social Psychology, 73*, 91–103.

Loewenstein, G. (1994). The psychology of curiosity: A review and reinterpretation. *Psychological Bulletin, 116*, 75–98.

Markus, H., & Nurius, P. (1986). Possible selves. *American Psychologist, 41*, 954–969.

Markus, H., & Ruvolo, A. (1989). Possible selves: Personalized representations of goals. In L. A. Pervin (Ed.), *Goal concepts in personality and social psychology* (pp. 211–242). Hillsdale, NJ: Erlbaum.

Marsh, H. W., Trautwein, U., Ludtke, O., Koller, O., & Baumert, J. (2005). Academic self-concept, interest, grades, and standardized test scores: Reciprocal effects models of causal ordering. *Child Development, 76*, 397–416.

Miyake, A., Kost-Smith, L. E., Finkelstein, N. D., Pollock, S. J., Cohen, G. L., & Ito, T. A. (2010). Reducing the gender achievement gap in college science: A classroom study of values affirmation. *Science, 330*, 1234–1237. doi:10.1126/science.1195996.

Mor, N., & Winquist, J. (2002). Self-focused attention and negative affect: A meta-analysis. *Psychological Bulletin, 128*, 638–662. http://dx.doi.org/10.1037/0033-2909.128.4.638.

Nicholls, J. G. (1984). Achievement motivation: Conceptions of ability, subjective experience, task choice, and performance. *Psychological Review, 91*, 328–346.

Oyserman, D., Bybee, D., & Terry, K. (2006). Possible selves and academic outcomes: How and when possible selves impel action. *Journal of Personality and Social Psychology, 91*, 188–204.

O'Keefe, P. A. (2013). Mindsets and self-evaluation: How beliefs about intelligence can create a preference for growth over defensiveness. In S. B. Kaufman (Ed.), *The complexity of greatness: Beyond talent or practice* (pp. 119–134). Oxford: Oxford University Press. doi:10.1093/acprof:oso/9780199794003.003.0008.

O'Keefe, P. A., Ben-Eliyahu, A., & Linnenbrink-Garcia, L. (2013). Shaping achievement goal orientations in a mastery-structured environment and concomitant changes in related contingencies of self-worth. *Motivation and Emotion, 37*(1), 50–64. doi:10.1007/s11031-012-9293-6.

O'Keefe, P. A., & Linnenbrink-Garcia, L. (2014). The role of interest in optimizing performance and self-regulation. *Journal of Experimental Social Psychology, 53*, 70–78. doi:10.1016/j.jesp.2014.02.004.

Pajares, F. (1996). Self-efficacy beliefs in academic settings. *Review of Educational Research, 66*, 543–578. doi:10.2307/1170653.

Patall, E. A. (2013). Constructing motivation through choice, interest, and interestingness. *Journal of Educational Psychology, 105*(2), 522–534.

Pervin, L. A. (1989). Goal concepts: Themes, issues, and questions. In L. A. Pervin (Ed.), *Goal concepts in personality and social psychology* (pp. 473–479). Hillsdale, NJ: Erlbaum.

Pintrich, P. R. (2000). Multiple goals, multiple pathways: The role of goal orientation in learning and achievement. *Journal of Educational Psychology, 92*, 544–555.

Pintrich, P. R., & De Groot, E. V. (1990). Motivational and self-regulated learning components of classroom academic performance. *Journal of Educational Psychology, 82*, 33–40.

Pintrich, P. R., Ryan, A. M., & Patrick, H. (1998). The differential impact of task value and mastery orientation on males' and females' self-regulated learning. In L. Hoffmann, A. Krapp, A. K. Renninger, & J. Baumert (Eds.), *Interest and learning: Proceedings of the Seeon Conference on interest and gender* (pp. 337–353). Kiel: International Press Network.

Prenzel, M. (1992). The selective persistence of interest. In K. A. Renninger, S. Hidi, & A. Krapp (Eds.), *The role of interest in learning and development* (pp. 71–98). Hillsdale, NJ: Erlbaum.

Pugh, K. J. (2011). Transformative experience: An integrative construct in the spirit of Deweyan pragmatism. *Educational Psychologist, 46*, 107–121. doi:10.1080/00461520.2011.558817.

Renninger, K. A. (1990). Children's play interests, representation, and activity. In R. Fivush & K. Hudson (Eds.), *Knowing and remembering in young children* (pp. 127–165). New York: Cambridge University Press.

Renninger, K. A. (2009). Interest and identity development in instruction: An inductive model. *Educational Psychologist, 44*, 105–118. doi:10.1080/00461520902832392.

Renninger, K. A., & Hidi, S. (2011). Revisiting the conceptualization, measurement, and generation of interest. *Educational Psychologist, 46*, 168–184. doi:10.1080/00461520.2011.587723.

Renninger, K. A., Hidi, S., & Krapp, A. (1992). *The role of interest in learning and development*. Hillsdale, NJ: Erlbaum.

Sadoski, M., Goetz, E. T., & Fritz, J. B. (1993). Impact of concreteness on comprehensibility, interest, and memory for text: Implications for dual coding theory and text design. *Journal of Educational Psychology, 85*, 291–304. doi:10.1037/0022-0663.85.2.291.

Sansone, C., & Harackiewicz, J. M. (1996). I don't feel like it: The function of interest in self-regulation. In L. Martin & A. Tesser (Eds.), *Striving and feeling: The interaction of goals and affect*. Hillsdale, NJ: Erlbaum.

Sansone, C., & Thoman, D. B. (2005). Interest as the missing motivator in self-regulation. *European Psychologist, 10*, 175–186. (special section on "Motivation and Affect in the Self-Regulation of Behavior."). Published, 2005.

Sansone, C., Weir, C., Harpster, L., & Morgan, C. (1992). Once a boring task always a boring tas? Interest as a self-regulatory mechanism. *Journal of Personality and Social Psychology, 63*, 379–390.

Schiefele, U. (1991). Interest, learning, and motivation. *Educational Psychologist, 26*, 299–323.

Schiefele, U. (1999). Interest and learning from text. *Scientific Studies of Reading, 3*, 257–279.

Schwartz, S. H. (1992). Universals in the content and structure of values: Theoretical advances and empirical tests in 20 countries. In M. P. Zanna (Ed.), *Advances in experimental social psychology* (Vol. 25, pp. 1–65). San Diego: Academic.

Senko, C., & Harackiewicz, J. M. (2005). Achievement goals, task performance, and interest: Why perceived goal difficulty matters. *Personality and Social Psychology Bulletin, 31*, 1739–1753. doi:10.1177/0146167205281128.

Shah, J. Y., Friedman, R., & Kruglanski, A. W. (2002). Forgetting all else: On the antecedents and consequences of goal shielding. *Journal of Personality and Social Psychology, 83*, 1261–1280. doi:10.1037//0022-3514.83.6.1261.

Shah, J. Y., & Kruglanski, A. W. (2003). When opportunity knocks: Bottom-up priming of goals and its effects on self-regulation. *Journal of Personality and Social Psychology, 84*, 1109–1122. doi:10.1037/0022-3514.84.6.1109.

Sheldon, K. M., & Elliot, A. J. (1999). Goal striving, need satisfaction, and longitudinal well-being: The self-concordance model. *Journal of Personality and Social Psychology, 76*, 482–497.

Sheldon, K. M., & Kasser, T. (1995). Coherence and congruence: two aspects of personality integration. *Journal of Personality and Social Psychology, 68*, 531–543.

Silvia, P. J. (2006). *Exploring the psychology of interest*. New York: Oxford University Press.

Simons, J., Dewitte, S., & Lens, W. (2000). Wanting to have versus wanting to be: The effect of perceived instrumentality on goal orientation. *British Journal of Psychology, 91*, 335–351.

Simpkins, S. D., Davis-Kean, P. E., & Eccles, J. S. (2006). Math and science motivation: A longitudinal examination of the links between choices and beliefs. *Developmental Psychology, 42*, 70–83.

Smith, G. C., & Oyserman, D. (2015). Just not worth my time? Experienced difficulty and time investment. *Social Cognition, 33*, 85–103.

Tobias, S. (1994). Interest, Prior Knowledge, and Learning. *Review of Educational Research, 64*(1), 37–54.

Trope, Y., & Liberman, N. (2000). Temporal construal and time-dependent changes in preference. *Journal of Personality and Social Psychology, 79*, 876–889.

Trope, Y., & Liberman, N. (2010). Construal-level theory of psychological distance. *Psychological Review, 117*, 440–442.

Vallerand, R. J., & Reid, G. (1984). On the causal effects of perceived competence on intrinsic motivation: A test of cognitive evaluation theory. *Journal of Sport Psychology, 6*, 94–102.

Wigfield, A., & Eccles, J. S. (2000). Expectancy-Value Theory of Achievement Motivation. *Contemporary Educational Psychology, 24*, 68–81. doi:10.1006/ceps.1999.1015.

Wigfield, A., & Cambria, J. (2010). Students' achievement values, goal orientations, and interest: Definitions, development, and relations to achievement outcomes. *Developmental Review, 30*, 1–35. doi:10.1016/j.dr.2009.12.001.

Wolters, C. A. (1998). Self-regulated learning and college students' regulation of motivation. *Journal of Educational Psychology, 90*, 224–235.

Wolters, C. A. (2004). Advancing Achievement Goal Theory: Using Goal Structures and Goal Orientations to Predict Students' Motivation, Cognition, and Achievement. *Journal of Educational Psychology, 96*(2), 236–250.

Zimmerman, B. J. (1990). Self-regulated learning and academic achievement: An overview. *Educational Psychologist, 25*, 3–17.

Chapter 8
On the Two Faces of Passion: The Harmonious and the Obsessive

Robert J. Vallerand

I wonder when my interest for basketball turned into a passion

Bill Bradley, Former Professional basketball player for the NBA New York Knicks and former US Senator of the State of New Jersey

The above quote is fascinating as it raises at least two issues. First, it underscores the fact that interest and passion are not identical. As one may intuitively believe, passion implies having more than a passing interest in the activity or object of one's passion; it implies finding the activity meaningful, spending lots of time on it, and seeing the activity as an extension of one's self, as part of our identity. Having a passion for an activity is thus something special. One may have several interests but only one or two passions. Thus, in line with Bill Bradley's perception, interest and passion would appear to be different constructs. The second point raised by Bill Bradley deals with the actual development of passion. How did such a passion develop? Further, once developed, how is passion maintained or modified over time? In other terms, what are the processes through which passion for an activity or object first develops and then evolves? Further, are all passions the same, or do different passions exist? And if so, what are their effects on optimal functioning. These two issues are discussed in this chapter.

Vallerand, R.J. (in press). Chapter to appear in Paul A. O'Keefe and Judith M. Harackiewicz (Eds.). *The Science of Interest*. Springer

R.J. Vallerand, PhD (✉)
Laboratoire de Recherche sur le Comportement Social, Département de Psychologie,
Université du Québec à Montréal, 8888, Station "Ctr-ville", Montreal, QC H3C 3P8, Canada

Institute for Positive Psychology and Education, Australian Catholic University,
Banyo, QLD, Australia
e-mail: Vallerand.bob@gmail.com

The construct of interest has enjoyed a rich history, dating at least back to Greek philosophers. As we will see, the construct of passion also dates back the early times of philosophers, although it has been largely neglected in contemporary psychology until recently. I hope to convince the reader that this need not be the case. Indeed, passion matters as it reflects a reality for a majority of individuals in a variety of cultures ranging from North America to Europe to China and Russia and leads to important life outcomes (see Vallerand, 2015). As such, it deserves our scientific attention. In this chapter, I address a number of issues. First, I discuss the nature of passion and in so doing introduce the Dualistic Model of Passion that my colleagues and I have developed. I also present a brief history of the passion concept and compare it to interest and highlight differences between the two constructs. Second, I review initial research on passion followed by research on the development of passion distinguishing between the factors involved in the initial and the ongoing development of passion. I then review research on the effects of passion. Finally, I end the chapter with some concluding thoughts and some suggestions for future research.

On the Nature of Passion

On the History of Passion

Passion has generated a lot of attention from philosophers. Indeed, centuries of scholarship have been devoted to it. Three positions have emerged (see Vallerand, 2015, Chap. 2). The first posits that passion entails a loss of reason and control (see Plato, 429–347 BC and Spinoza, 1632–1677). In line with the etymology of the word passion (from the latin *passio* for suffering) people who have a passion are seen as experiencing some suffering. They are slaves to their passion as it comes to control them. The second perspective portrays passion in a more positive light. The Romantics were important proponents of this second perspective. Hegel (1770–1831), for instance, argues that passions are necessary to reach the highest levels of achievement and Kierkegaard (1813–1855) even writes that "To exist, if we do not mean by that only a pseudo existence, cannot take place without passion." Thus, this second view of passion posits that passion can lead to some positive outcomes. Taken together, these two positions highlight the duality of passion.

A third perspective of passion, however, emerged at the turn of the twentieth century, at the junction of philosophy and psychology. This third position suggests that some passions are "good" and others are "bad." For instance, basing himself on the work of Descartes (1596–1650), Kant (1724–1804), and Ribot (1907), Joussain (1928) proposed that there were two broad types of passion: the "noble" passions oriented toward the well-being or benefit of others or society, and the "selfish" passions that sought personal satisfaction. Of additional interest, Joussain further suggested that passions could interact among themselves in at least two ways. First, some passions can conflict with other passions and in fact crowd out other passions and try to extinguish them. Second, other passions can peacefully coexist with others. In fact, Joussain proposed that "virtue is to be obtained through the *equilibrium* that we establish among our passions and the multiple consequences that they create for us and others, keeping in mind the knowledge that we have of the world and ourselves" (p. 103; the translation from French and italics are mine). Inherent in such a statement is that all passions are not equivalent and that they may play different roles in the outcomes that we experience. As we shall see, this is clearly one of the themes of this chapter. Unfortunately, Joussain did not conduct research on passion and to the best of my knowledge no scholarship or research has followed his work.

After a period of relative neglect, empirical work in psychology began and focused on passionate love (e.g., Hatfield & Walster, 1978). Although such research is important, it does not deal with passion for activities. More recently, psychologists have started to focus on this very issue. For instance, some authors have proposed that people will spend large amounts of time and effort in order to reach their passionate goals (see Frijda, Mesquita, Sonemans, & Van Goozen, 1991). Others have devoted attention to passion for work where passion is defined as love for work (Baum & Locke, 2004). Finally, Vallerand et al. (2003) proposed the Dualistic Model of Passion to explain the nature, determinants, and consequences of passion while incorporating the duality inherent in passion underscored by philosophers and early psychologists.

The Dualistic Model of Passion

The Dualistic Model of Passion (DMP; Vallerand, 2010, 2012a, 2015) defines passion as a strong inclination toward a self-defining activity that one loves, finds important and meaningful, and in which one invests time and energy. Such an activity comes to be so self-defining that it represents a central feature of one's identity. For instance, the teenager who has a passion for hockey is not simply playing hockey, she sees herself as a "hockey player," and the student who has developed a passion for playing the guitar perceives himself as a "guitarist" or as a "musician."

The DMP further posits that there are two types of passion. The DMP postulates that activities that people like (or even love) will be internalized in the person's identity and self to the extent that these are highly valued and meaningful for the person (Aron, Aron, & Smollan, 1992; Csikszentmihalyi, Rathunde, & Whalen, 1993). Furthermore, it is proposed that there are two types of passion, obsessive and harmonious, that can be distinguished in terms of how the passionate activity has been internalized. Harmonious passion results from an autonomous internalization of the activity into the person's identity and self. In line with self-determination theory (Deci & Ryan, 2000; Ryan & Deci, 2000), such internalization occurs when individuals have freely accepted the activity as important for them without any contingencies attached to it, such as feelings of social acceptance or self-esteem (e.g., Lafrenière, Bélanger, Sedikides, & Vallerand, 2011; Mageau, Carpentier, &

Vallerand, 2011). This type of internalization emanates from the intrinsic and integrative tendencies of the self (Deci & Ryan, 2000; Ryan & Deci, 2003) and produces a motivational force to engage in the activity willingly and engenders a sense of volition and personal endorsement about pursuing the activity. When harmonious passion is at play, individuals freely choose to engage in the beloved activity. With this type of passion, the activity occupies a significant but not overpowering space in the person's identity and is in harmony with other aspects of the person's life. In other words, with harmonious passion, the authentic integrating self (Deci & Ryan, 2000) is at play allowing the person to fully partake in the passionate activity with mindfulness (Brown & Ryan, 2003; St-Louis, Verner-Filion, Bergeron, & Vallerand, 2016) and an openness that is conducive to positive experiences (Hodgins & Knee, 2002). Consequently, with harmonious passion, people are able to fully focus on the task at hand and experience positive outcomes both during task engagement (e.g., positive affect, concentration, flow) and after task engagement (general positive affect, satisfaction, etc.). Thus, there should be little or no conflict between the person's passionate activity and his or her other life activities. Furthermore, when prevented from engaging in their passionate activity, people with a harmonious passion should be able to adapt well to the situation and focus their attention and energy on other tasks that need to be done.

Finally, with harmonious passion, the person is in control of the activity and can decide when to and when not to engage in the activity. Thus, when confronted with the possibility of playing basketball with his friends or preparing a new class lecture to be delivered the next day, the teacher with a harmonious passion for playing basketball can readily tell his friends that he will take a rain check and proceed to be fully immersed in the preparation of the lecture without thinking about the missed opportunity to play basketball. With harmonious passion, people are able to decide to forego activity engagement on a given day if needed or even to eventually terminate the relationship with the activity if they decide it has become a permanent negative factor in their life. Thus, behavioral engagement in the passionate activity can be seen as flexible.

Conversely, obsessive passion, results from a controlled internalization of the activity into one's identity. In line with self-determination theory (Deci & Ryan, 2000; Ryan & Deci, 2000), such an internalization process leads to values and regulations associated with the activity to be at best partially internalized in the self, and at worse to be internalized in the person's identity but completely outside the integrating self (Deci & Ryan, 2000), in line with the ego-invested self (Hodgins & Knee, 2002). A controlled internalization originates from intra and/or interpersonal pressure typically because certain contingencies are attached to the activity (Lafrenière et al., 2011; Mageau et al., 2011), or because the sense of excitement derived from activity engagement is uncontrollable. People with an obsessive passion can thus find themselves in the position of experiencing an uncontrollable urge to partake in the activity they view as important and enjoyable. They cannot help but to engage in the passionate activity. Consequently, they risk experiencing conflicts and other negative affective, cognitive, and behavioral consequences during and after activity engagement. For example, when confronted with the possibility of playing basketball with his friends or prepare the unfinished class lecture for the next day, a teacher with an obsessive passion for basketball may not be able to resist the invitation and will go and scrimmage with his friends instead of preparing the lecture. During the pickup, he might feel upset with himself for playing instead of working on the lecture. He might therefore have difficulties focusing on the task at hand (i.e., basketball) and may not experience as much positive affect and flow as he would while playing.

It is thus proposed that with obsessive passion, individuals come to display a rigid persistence toward the activity, as oftentimes they cannot help but to engage in the passionate activity that they love. This is so because ego-invested rather than integrative self-processes (Hodgins & Knee, 2002) are at play with obsessive passion leading the person to eventually becoming dependent on the activity. While such persistence may lead to some benefits in the long term (e.g., improved performance at the activity), it may also come at a cost for the individual, potentially leading to less than optimal functioning within the confines of the passionate activity because of the lack of flexibility that it entails. Furthermore, such a rigid persistence may lead the person to experience conflict with other aspects of his or her life when engaging in the passionate activity (when one should be doing something else, for instance), as well as to frustration and ruminations about the activity when prevented from engaging in it. Thus, if the teacher has an obsessive passion for basketball but nevertheless manages to say no to his friends and basketball, he still may end up suffering because of the difficulties of concentrating on the lecture preparation due to ruminations about the lost opportunity to play basketball.

The above presentation allows us to highlight some similarities and distinctions between the concepts of passion and interest. Before delving into this analysis, it is important to underscore that interest is a concept that encapsulates different meanings (see Chap. 1, this volume; Renninger & Hidi, 2011 for reviews). For instance, Hidi and Renninger (2006) present a developmental model of interest wherein interest is initially conceived as a short-term reaction to environmental stimuli ("triggered situational interest"; see Chap. 6, this volume for a review) that becomes progressively more personal in nature over time leading to a final stage of a "well-developed individual interest" (see Chap. 7, this volume for a review). Thus, clearly, passion differs from the first stage of "situational interest" as passion is not fleeting or short lived but long lasting in nature (see Vallerand, 2015, Chap. 2). However, it is possible and even likely that situational interest represents a precursor of passion.

The concepts of "well-developed individual interest" and passion seem relatively similar. For instance, both entail positive feelings for a specific object or activity that becomes meaningful, engaged in regularly, and eventually part of identity. Still, some important distinctions can be seen between the two concepts. First, with passion the activity becomes a central part of identity whereas it is not clear if it is the case with interest even at this later stage. Second, the high value of the activity coupled with its centrality in identity is likely to lead to more "fuel" (or emotional activation) associated with passionate activity engagement. Third, the process through which the activity becomes part of identity does not seem to represent a major focus of interest theories whereas it is central in the Dualistic Model of Passion. In fact, two different types of internalization processes (autonomous vs. controlled) are proposed and hypothesized to lead to the two types of passion, namely, the harmonious and obsessive passions. Fourth, related to the above, the duality of passion exemplified in these two types of passion is a crucial dimension of the Passion Model that helps explain why passion may lead to either adaptive or maladaptive outcomes. Conversely, no theory addresses the possibility of having adaptive and maladaptive forms of interest. Finally, whereas interest researchers have looked at the impact of interest on outcomes mostly in one area (e.g., education), passion research as we will see below has looked at outcomes both within the purview of the activity one is passionate about and other areas in the person's life. In sum, although related, the two concepts of passion and interest would appear different. As such, considering the construct of passion may lead to novel areas unexplored by interest researchers.

Initial Research on the Concept of Passion and the DMP

Initial contemporary research on the construct of passion for activities (Vallerand et al., 2003) focused on three goals: (1) to determine the prevalence of passion for an activity in people's lives and the nature of activities that passionate people are engaged in, (2) to develop the Passion Scale, and (3) to test the validity of some of the elements of the passion constructs. In the initial study, Vallerand et al. (2003, Study 1) had over 500 college students complete the Passion Scale with respect to an activity that they loved, that they valued, and in which they invested time and energy (i.e., the main passion definition criteria), as well as other scales allowing them to test predictions derived from the DMP. Of importance regarding the first purpose of this research, 84% of participants indicated that they had at least a moderate level of passion for a given activity in their lives (they scored at least 4 out of 7 on a question asking them if their favorite activity was a "passion" for them). A subsequent study (Philippe, Vallerand, & Lavigne, 2009, Study 1) with over 750 participants ranging in age from 18 to 90 years and using a more stringent criterion of having a mean of 5 out of 7 on 4 criteria of passion (loving the activity, activity valuation, activity engagement, and perceiving the activity as a passion) revealed that 75% of participants had a high level of passion for an activity in their life. These findings have been obtained in other countries as well (see Lecoq & Rimé, 2009; Liu, Chen, & Yao, 2011; Stenseng, 2008). Overall, these results reveal that the prevalence of passion is rather high and is not limited to simply a few individuals. Passion pervades people's lives!

It should be noted that a diversity of passionate activities were reported. In fact, participants indicated having a passion for one of over a hundred different activities ranging from physical activity and individual and team sports to watching movies, playing a musical instrument, and reading. Participants also reported engaging in one specific passionate activity for an average of 8.5 h per week and had been engaging in that activity for almost 6 years. Thus, clearly passionate activities are meaningful to people and are long lasting in nature.

A second goal of the initial passion research dealt with the development of the Passion Scale. Vallerand et al. (2003, Study 1) conducted exploratory and confirmatory factor analyses supporting the presence of two factors corresponding to the two types of passion. These findings on the factor validity of the Passion Scale have been replicated in at least 20 studies in a variety of settings and activities (see Vallerand, 2015, Chap. 4 for a review). Further, more recently, Marsh, Vallerand, and colleagues (2013) have provided support not only for the bifactorial nature of the Passion Scale but also for its invariance as a function of gender, language (French and English), and several types of activities. The Scale has also been validated in a number of languages, including Spanish (Chamaro et al., 2015) and Chinese (Zhao, St-Louis, & Vallerand, 2015). The Passion Scale consists of two subscales of six items each reflecting Obsessive (e.g., "I almost have an obsessive feeling toward this activity") and Harmonious Passion (e.g., "This activity is in harmony with other activities in my life"). Furthermore, internal consistency analyses have shown that both subscales are reliable (typically 0.75 and above). Finally, test-retest correlations over periods ranging from 4 to 6 weeks revealed moderately high stability values (in the 0.80s, Rousseau, Vallerand, Ratelle, Mageau, & Provencher, 2002), thereby supporting the factorial validity and reliability of the scale.

With respect to the third purpose of the initial passion research of Vallerand et al. (2003, Study 1), a series of critical findings with partial correlations (controlling for the correlation between the two types of passion) revealed that both harmonious and obsessive passions were positively associated with all passion criteria thereby providing support for the definition of passion. In addition, both types of passion were found to relate to one's identity, and obsessive passion was found to more strongly relate to a measure of conflict with other life activities than harmonious passion. These findings support the view that both harmonious and obsessive passions are indeed a "passion" as each one reflects the definition of the passion construct (see also Marsh et al., 2013, for additional support on the construct validity of the passion concept). Finally, other studies in this initial research (Vallerand et al., 2003) have also shown that obsessive (but not harmonious) passion correlated to rigid persistence in ill-advised activities (Vallerand et al., 2003, Studies 3 and 4). Overall, these results provide important support for the conceptual validity of the two types of passion and their divergent effects on various outcomes.

Since the 2003 Vallerand et al. initial publication, approximately 200 studies have been conducted on the construct of passion, looking at both the development of passion and its role in a host of cognitive, affective, behavioral, relational, and performance outcomes experienced within the realms of hundreds of passionate activities. Such research has been conducted in both our own and other laboratories. Further, most of these studies have used the DMP as a theoretical framework, have employed a variety of methodological designs (e.g., cross-sectional, longitudinal, diary study, and even experimental), and have been conducted in a variety of countries. Some of this research is presented in the next few sections, starting with those on the development of passion.

On the Development of Passion

The DMP proposes that people engage in various activities throughout life. After a period of trial and error that would appear to start in early adolescence (Erikson, 1968), most people eventually start to show preference for some activities, especially those that are perceived as particularly enjoyable and important, and that have some resonance with how they see themselves. These activities have the potential to become passionate activities. Back to Bill Bradley's question regarding the transformation of interest into passion, the DMP (Vallerand, 2008, 2010, 2012a, 2015; Vallerand & Verner-Filion, 2013; Vallerand et al., 2003) posits that there are at least three processes involved in such a transformation: activity valuation, identification with the activity, and internalization of the activity in one's identity. These three processes are discussed in turn.

Activity valuation refers to the importance one gives to an activity. In line with past research (Aron et al., 1992; Deci, Eghrari, Patrick, & Leone, 1994), an activity is likely to be internalized when it is highly valued and meaningful. Consequently, activity valuation should facilitate the internalization of the activity into one's identity, and by the same token should facilitate the development of passion. Parents, teachers, and coaches all play an important role in children's or students' valuation of a given activity (e.g., Eccles & Wigfield, 2002). For instance, adults can underscore the value of an activity either by being themselves passionate about it, by spending time with children in the context of the activity, or by encouraging specialization in the activity at the expense of other activities.

Identification with the activity is a second important process in the development of passion (Schlenker, 1985). When an enjoyable activity becomes so central that it contributes to one's identity or has the potential to do so in the future, individuals are more likely to become passionate about this particular activity. Indeed, enjoying science and having the perception that one may become a scientist later on (a possible self, Markus & Nurius, 1986) should make this potential identity element salient and thereby facilitating its internalization in identity (Houser-Marko & Sheldon, 2006), and the subsequent development of passion for science.

Finally, the type of passion (i.e., harmonious vs. obsessive) that will develop depends on the type of internalization that takes place. As seen above, in line with self-determination theory (Ryan & Deci, 2000), two types of internalization can take place: autonomous and controlled. Further, two important variables can determine the type of internalization process that will occur: the social environment and one's individual differences. To the extent that one's social environment (e.g., parents, teachers, coaches, principals) is autonomy-supportive, an autonomous internalization is likely to take place (e.g., Vallerand, 1997; Vallerand, Fortier, & Guay, 1997), leading to harmonious passion. An autonomy-supportive environment provides the person with choice and autonomy in engaging in activities that one wishes to pursue and in the way that he or she wants to do so (see Ryan & Deci, 2000). Conversely, to the extent that one's social environment is controlling, a controlled internalization will take place leading to obsessive passion. A controlling environment is one where the person feels coerced in engaging in a given activity or in a way that differs from the one he or she would prefer (see Ryan & Deci, 2000). Thus, an autonomy-supportive music teacher would allow students to select one musical piece out of several to focus on and master, whereas a controlling teacher would force students to engage in the musical piece that he or she has selected. Similarly, individual differences that trigger autonomous internalization process should lead to harmonious passion, whereas those that facilitate the controlled internalization process should lead to the development of obsessive passion.

The DMP posits that there are two types of passion development that need our attention. First, the initial development of passion for a novel activity and, second, continuous, ongoing development that takes place once a passion for a given activity has initially developed. In this section, we look at some of the factors involved in the two types of development.

Initial Development of Passion

In a first series of studies, Mageau et al. (2009) tested the role of the social environment in the initial development of passion from time zero. In Study 3 of this article, first-year high school students who had *never* played a musical instrument before and who were taking their first compulsory music class completed a series of questionnaires early in the term assessing activity selection and valuation (perceived parental activity valuation and perceived parental and child activity specialization), autonomy support from parents and music teachers, as well as identity processes. The main idea was to see who would develop a passion for music by the end of the semester, and which type they would display (i.e., harmonious or obsessive passion). Results from discriminant analyses revealed that the students who ended up being passionate for music (only 36% of the sample) at the end of the term had, earlier in the term, reported higher levels of activity valuation and specialization, identity processes, and parental and teacher autonomy support than those students who did not develop a passion. Furthermore, among the students who ended up being passionate, those with high-perceived autonomy support from close adults (parents and music teachers) and (children's) valuation for music led to the development of harmonious passion. High levels of parental perceived valuation for music and *lack of* autonomy support (i.e., controlling behavior) were found to predict the development of obsessive passion. Results of two other studies involving students interacting in sports and music settings revealed that both perceived parental autonomy support (Mageau et al., 2009, Study 1) and *actual* autonomy support (as reported by the parents themselves; Mageau et al., 2009, Study 2) were conducive to harmonious passion and the lack of such support to obsessive passion. In sum, the results of the Mageau et al. (2009) studies demonstrate the role of activity valuation, identity processes, and autonomy support from significant adults in the development of a passion in general, and harmonious and obsessive passion in particular.

The role of individual differences in passion development was assessed in a second series of studies conducted by Vallerand, Rousseau, Grouzet, Dumais, and Grenier (2006, Studies 1 and 3). These authors tested the role of personal orientations and activity valuation in the occurrence of the two types of passion among student athletes. In the first study (Vallerand et al., 2006, Study 1), results from a path analysis revealed that activity valuation coupled with an autonomous internalization style (as assessed by the Global Motivation Scale; Guay, Mageau, & Vallerand, 2003) predicted harmonious passion. Obsessive passion was predicted by activity valuation coupled with a controlled internalization style. These findings were replicated in a second study (Vallerand et al., 2006, Study 3) using a short longitudinal design. Thus, individual differences also play a role in the development of both types of passion.

The Ongoing Development of Passion

The studies discussed so far pertained to activities where participants had been engaging in the activity for only a few months or years. Thus, these studies pertained more to the *initial* development of passion. However, once developed, passion can also undergo an ongoing development as it is affected by a variety of social and personal variables (Vallerand, 2010, 2015). For instance, in a study with students with an average of over 7 years of musical experience and enrolled in a college music program, Bonneville-Roussy, Vallerand, and Bouffard (2013) tested an integrated model on the development of passion. Results from a path analysis revealed that a musical identity coupled with autonomy support from one's music teachers predicted harmonious passion toward music, while obsessive passion was predicted by a musical identity coupled with controlling behavior from one's music teachers. Thus, to the extent that an activity is already internalized in identity, autonomy support from teachers facilitates the development of harmonious passion whereas controlling behavior leads to obsessive passion.

Other research has looked at task factors as determinants of passion. In studies with novice teachers, Fernet, Lavigne, and Vallerand (2014, Study 1) found that experiencing some levels of autonomy as to how to perform one's teaching positively predicted harmonious passion but negatively predicted obsessive passion for teaching. These findings were replicated and extended in a second study (Fernet et al., 2014, Study 2) with teachers using a cross-lagged panel design over a 12-month period. Of major importance, results from structural equation modeling showed that task autonomy predicted an *increase* in harmonious passion for teaching and a decrease in obsessive passion over time. On the other hand, the two types of passion did not predict changes in task autonomy, suggesting that the direction of causality is from task autonomy to passion and not the other way around.

Another task element of importance deals with the task demands and resources at our disposal (Bakker & Demerouti, 2007). Trépanier, Fernet, Austin, Forest, and Vallerand (2014) conducted research on their role as determinants of passion. Task demands refer to task imposed pressure or restrictions that one has to cope with while engaging in the activity. Because task demands should be experienced as controlling in nature, they should connect with elements that have been internalized in a controlled fashion and therefore facilitate obsessive passion. Thus, the more one experiences pressure to perform a demanding activity, the more one is to mobilize and use obsessive passion to get the job done. In addition, experiencing pressure to get the job done could even undermine harmonious passion as such pressure may disrupt harmony among one's various life domains. Conversely, task resources can be seen as support that one has access to in order to better perform one's task (e.g., having access to a nursing aide when overloaded). Task resources can be seen as affordances to efficiently perform the task as one chooses to do so. Thus, they should trigger elements that have been internalized in an autonomous fashion, including harmonious passion.

In sum, task resources should facilitate harmonious passion while task demands should facilitate obsessive passion. Trépanier et al. (2014) conducted a large-scale study with over 1000 nurses and tested a model that posited that task resources were expected to positively predict harmonious passion while task demands were hypothesized to positively predict obsessive passion. Furthermore, task demands were hypothesized to undermine harmonious passion. Results confirmed the hypothesized model.

The role of personal factors in the ongoing development of passion has also been empirically scrutinized. Individuals passionate about a given activity not only care a great deal about the activity but also typically want to do very well at it. Thus, a relevant personal determinant of passion should be perfectionism. Perfectionism refers to holding excessively high standards of achievement. Hewitt and Flett (2002) have proposed the existence of three major types of perfectionism with two being of interest here. Self-oriented perfectionism (i.e., holding excessively high standards for self and not for others) is under the person's control and involves standards that may be changed by the person in a proactive manner. This type of perfectionism typically leads to some positive outcomes (see Miquelon, Vallerand, Grouzet, & Cardinal, 2005). The second type of perfectionism is socially prescribed perfectionism (i.e., high standards imposed by others) and it generally leads to negative outcomes. Because the first type of perfectionism takes origin in the integrated self, one would suggest that it should primarily predict having a harmonious passion toward an activity that we highly value. On the other hand, because the second type of perfectionism (i.e., socially prescribed perfectionism) is rooted in the ego-invested self, one would predict that it should primarily lead to obsessive passion.

Verner-Filion and Vallerand (2016) recently tested some of these hypotheses in two studies. In Study 1, university students completed the Passion Scale for their studies and the Multidimensional Perfectionism Scale (Cox, Enns, & Clara, 2002). Results from structural equation modeling analyses revealed that self-oriented perfectionism positively predicted harmonious passion, but also obsessive passion to a lesser degree. In contrast, socially prescribed perfectionism only predicted obsessive passion. These findings underscore the fact that harmonious passion results from the more adaptive form of perfectionism whereas obsessive passion is predicted by both the adaptive and less adaptive forms of perfectionism. These findings were basically replicated in a second study (Verner-Filion & Vallerand, 2016, Study 2).

Another individual difference of importance is our signature strengths (Peterson & Seligman, 2004). Research has shown that focusing on what we do best (our signature strengths) such as using our social skills or our sense of humor has a positive impact on a variety of outcomes. In a recent study, Forest et al. (2012) tested and found support for the hypothesis that using our signature strengths facilitates harmonious passion for the passionate activity. Thus, encouraging people to use their strengths within the activity that they are passionate about nurtures their harmonious passion and facilitates the experience of positive outcomes such as one's psychological well-being. Dubreuil, Forest, and Courcy (2014) also replicated these findings.

In sum, the research reviewed in this section shows that both the social environment and personal orientations are important factors in the initial and ongoing development of passion. We now turn our attention to the role of passion in outcomes.

Passion and Outcomes

Passion research has typically looked at the consequences of passion while distinguishing these on two counts: those that take place within the purview of the activity one is passionate about and those that take place in other areas or in the person's life in general. Below, we address these two issues.

Passion and Outcomes Within the Purview of the Activity

As mentioned previously, the position of the DMP is that harmonious passion leads to adaptive outcomes and optimal functioning both within the area of one's passion and in the rest of the person's life. This is because harmonious passion triggers adaptive self-processes. Adaptive self-processes (e.g., a growth mindset; Dweck, 2006) refer to operations of the self that allow full engagement with little or no limitation. Conversely, the effects of obsessive passion are much less adaptive because it entails outcomes and processes associated with an ego-invested self and processes of lower psychological quality than harmonious passion (e.g., a fixed mindset; Dweck, 2006). Although some adaptive functioning may take place with obsessive passion, it should be mainly limited to the area of one's passion and much less in other areas of one's life.

Cognitions Research on passion and outcomes has looked at a number of on-task cognitive outcomes. Such research reveals that harmonious passion leads to positive cognitions such as attention, concentration, task absorption, and flow during task engagement (e.g., Forest et al., 2012; Vallerand et al., 2003, Study 1). For instance, in a study with adult workers, Ho, Wong, and Lee (2011) found that harmonious passion predicts better attention on the job. Similarly, much research reveals that harmonious passion (but not obsessive passion) leads to experiencing higher levels of flow in a variety of contexts that include sports (e.g., Philippe et al., 2009) and work (e.g., Forest et al., 2012). Using a cross-lagged panel design, Lavigne, Forest, and Crevier-Braud (2012) showed that harmonious passion had a strong effect on increases of flow experienced at work over a 3-month period but that flow did not predict increases in passion. Further, obsessive passion had a small but positive effect on flow as well.

Research also reveals that obsessive passion is either negatively or unrelated to positive forms of cognitions such as concentration (see Curran, Hill, Appleton, Vallerand, & Standage, 2015). Furthermore, it should be noted that obsessive passions not only typically yields less adaptive cognitions than harmonious passion but also leads to some maladaptive ones. For instance, research reveals that obsessive passion positively predicts ruminations about the activity (e.g., Vallerand et al., 2003, Study 1; Vallerand, Paquet, Philippe, & Charest, 2010, Studies 1–2) and cognitive conflict between the passionate activity and other activities in the person's life (e.g., Caudroit, Boiché, Stephan, Le Scanff, & Trouilloud, 2011).

Affect A lot of research has focused on affective outcomes such as positive and negative affect and task satisfaction with harmonious passion leading to more positive affect and typically less negative affect than obsessive passion (see Curran et al., 2015 for a meta-analysis of such effects). For instance, in a study with basketball players, Vallerand et al. (2006, Study 2) showed that harmonious passion positively predicted positive, but negatively predicted negative affect following a game. Conversely, obsessive passion positively predicts negative affect and is either unrelated or negatively related to negative affect. These findings have been replicated in a number of studies conducted in a variety of settings such as sports, work, and school (e.g., Carbonneau, Vallerand, & Massicotte, 2010; Philippe, Vallerand, Houlfort, Lavigne, & Donahue, 2010; see Curran et al., 2015; Vallerand, 2015, Chap. 7, for reviews).

Sustained Activity Engagement and Performance Passion has also been found to predict behavioral engagement. In this case both harmonious passion and obsessive passion have been typically found to positively predict sustained engagement in the passionate activity. For instance, in a study with Greek exercisers, Parastatidou, Doganis, Theodorakis, and Vlachopoulos (2012) showed that both types of passion for exercise led one to engage in exercise several hours weekly and to do so for years. In addition, both harmonious passion and obsessive passion have been found to positively predict engagement in highly demanding task activities (i.e., deliberate practice) aimed at improving on the activity (e.g., Vallerand et al., 2007, 2008). It is through such regular engagement in deliberate practice activities that long-term improvement in performance takes place (see Bonneville-Roussy, Lavigne, & Vallerand, 2011; Vallerand et al., 2007, Studies 1 and 2; Vallerand, Mageau et al., 2008, Studies 1 and 2). Thus, because both the harmonious and obsessive passions lead one to engage in deliberate practice to a similar extent, they both facilitate long-term performance. Although the long-term performance effects of the two types of passion may be similar, the process would appear to be quite different. Specifically, because harmonious passion also facilitates the experience of more adaptive on-task cognitive and affective as well as life outcomes (see below), the harmonious road to excellence would appear to be much more adaptive than the obsessive road that is devoid of such a positive process and may include emotional suffering along the way (Vallerand, 2015).

Finally, passion also affects short-term performance. Thus, although obsessive passion can also bolster performance in the short term, especially when the self is being threatened (e.g., Bélanger, Lafrenière, Vallerand, & Kruglanski, 2013a), it is typically harmonious passion that facilitates objective performance through its positive effects on various cognitive mediators such as concentration and absorption (e.g., Ho, Wong, & Lee, 2011). Research on creativity at work has led to similar findings with respect to both subjective reports (Luh & Lu, 2012; St-Louis & Vallerand, 2015) and employee supervisor reports of creativity (Liu Chen, & Yao, 2011, Studies 1 and 2; Shi, 2012).

Relationships Research has also assessed the link between passion and interpersonal outcomes. It is often assumed that passionate people are charismatic and should make more friends within the purview of the activity. Research reveals that it is indeed true, but only for harmonious passion (e.g., Philippe et al., 2010). For instance, in a short longitudinal study, Philippe et al. (2010, Study 3) showed that over the course of a 1-week basketball camp, harmonious passion for basketball predicted making more new friends over the course of the week. Such was not the case for obsessive passion. Further, once developed, friendships are maintained much more with harmonious passion than with obsessive passion (Philippe et al., 2010). Of interest is the major finding of the Philippe et al. (2010) series of studies that showed that the respective positive and negative effects of harmonious and obsessive passion on relationships were due to the mediating role of positive and negative emotions. Of additional interest, several studies also collected the perceptions of informants (or third-party assessment) of the quality of relationships (e.g., Philippe et al., 2010, Studies 2 and 4). These studies yielded the same findings as those reported by the participants themselves. Finally, other research reveals that the same processes operate in one-up relationships such as with supervisors and subordinates (Jowett, Lafrenière, & Vallerand, 2013; Lafrenière, Jowett, Vallerand, Donahue, & Lorimer, 2008).

Recent research has also ventured into romantic passion (Carbonneau & Vallerand, 2013, 2016; Ratelle, Carbonneau, & Vallerand, 2013). Here the passion is for the loved one within a relationship. Further, there is a nice twist as both partners can be passionate (and of different types), and thus can influence each other. Thus, one's passion can affect not only oneself but also the romantic partner on both personal and relational outcomes experienced within the romantic realm. The more harmonious the romantic passion, the more positive outcomes within the romantic sphere will be experienced. Conversely, obsessive passion can lead to some negative outcomes such as personal suffering, lower levels of relational satisfaction, and relationship breakups. For instance, Ratelle et al. (2013) found that harmonious passion led to relational satisfaction (Study 1) and predicted remaining in the relationship 3 months later (Study 3) whereas obsessive passion was either negatively related or weakly associated with dimensions of relationship satisfaction and predicted breakups. Furthermore, other research (Carbonneau & Vallerand, 2013) revealed that these differential outcomes may result from conflict behaviors triggered by one's obsessive passion, whereas harmonious passion facilitates repair behaviors both during and after romantic conflict. For a more complete review, see Vallerand and Carbonneau (2016).

Finally, other studies have looked at when interpersonal behavior becomes negative. For instance, research reveals that obsessive passion leads to negative intergroup behavior such as verbally provoking others (Vallerand, Ntoumanis et al., 2008, Study 2) and being ready to physically hurt other people (e.g., Donahue, Rip, & Vallerand, 2009; Gousse-Lessard, Vallerand, Carbonneau, & Lafrenière, 2013; Vallerand et al., 2008, Study 2) who do not share our beliefs or worse, who dare provoke us (Rip, Vallerand, & Lafrenière, 2012, Study 2). Such is not the case with harmonious passion. Once more, processes experienced while engaging in the passionate activity have been identified as a mediator of the effects of passion. Specifically, experiencing hatred toward others who attack one's faith mediates the impact of obsessive passion on intended violent behavior toward these other individuals (Rip et al., 2012, Study 2).

In sum, research on outcomes and experiences that are experienced during task engagement reveals that harmonious passion leads to positive advantages relative to obsessive passion, except for sustained engagement in the activity that is experienced with both types of passion. Because such outcomes are experienced in a recurrent fashion, they are conducive to optimal functioning, and much more so for harmonious passion than obsessive passion.

Passion and Outcomes in Other Spheres of the Person's Life

The research briefly mentioned in the previous section is important in that it underscores the fact that passion matters with respect to optimal functioning within the realm of the passionate activity. Furthermore, as seen above, the quality of such outcomes differs as a function of the type of passion involved, with harmonious passion leading to more adaptive outcomes than obsessive passion. The DMP makes a second assumption: passion can also affect outcomes that take place in other areas of one's life and such outcomes should differ as a function of the type of passion at play. Below, I briefly review research that supports this claim both at the intra and the interpersonal levels.

Cognitions Research has looked at the role of passion in cognitions experienced outside the realm of the passionate activity (see Curran et al., 2015). Such research reveals strong advantages of harmonious passion over obsessive passion. For instance, research reveals that harmonious passion for one's favorite activity (e.g., playing the guitar) positively contributes to experiencing flow in a second activity (e.g., when studying), whereas such is not the case with obsessive passion (Carpentier, Mageau, & Vallerand, 2012). In fact, with obsessive passion, ruminations about the passionate activity conflict with the second activity and prevent flow from being experienced when studying! A series of studies by Belanger and colleagues went one step further. In this research, Bélanger, Lafrenière, Vallerand, and Kruglanski (2013b) showed that being led to unconsciously think about the passionate activity when engaging in a nonpassionate activity leads to conflict with the activity that one is currently doing, thereby preventing smooth performance on this other activity. In the long run, adaptive functioning in these other activities will be curtailed by the conflict induced by obsessive passion about the passionate activity. However, it should be underscored that this "goal-shielding" effect only takes place with obsessive passion. With harmonious passion, no conflict takes place and the person can think about the passionate activity and still be efficient on whatever the person is doing. Thus, one can be passionate about a given activity and still thrive in other areas in one's life.

Affect We have seen in the previous section that harmonious passion leads to experiencing more positive, and obsessive passion to more negative, affect during task engagement. Furthermore, research has also shown that these effects influence what people experience after task engagement as well as later on that evening in other areas of their lives. Of interest is a diary study conducted by Mageau and Vallerand (2007) that revealed that over a 2-week period, each day that one engaged in the passionate activity, harmonious passion led to an increase of positive affect over baseline level, whereas failing to engage in the passionate activity led obsessive passion to predict a decrease in positive affect over baseline days. These findings were basically replicated in a 2-week diary study with women passionate about physical exercise (Guérin, Fortier, & Williams, 2013).

Vallerand et al. (2003, Study 2) went further and followed collegiate football players over the course of an entire football season. They found that harmonious passion and obsessive passion predicted increases in general positive and negative affect, respectively, that took place over the course of an entire football season. Furthermore, these findings were obtained while controlling for intrinsic and extrinsic motivation toward football. Thus, passion can trigger affect that can be long lasting and that generalizes to one's life in general. However, with harmonious passion, it is positive affect that spreads to other dimensions of one's life and not negative emotions as is the case with obsessive passion.

Psychological Well-Being Other research has looked at the role of passion in psychological well-being. Once more, research reveals that having harmonious passion for an activity has some positive effects on one's psychological well-being (e.g., Burke, Sabiston, & Vallerand, 2012; Houlfort, Philippe, Vallerand, & Ménard, 2014, 2015; Houlfort, Vallerand, & Laframboise, 2015; Lafrenière, St-Louis, Vallerand, & Donahue, 2012; Lafrenière, Vallerand, & Sedikides, 2013; Lavigne et al., 2012;

Przybylski, Weinstein, Ryan, & Rigby, 2009; Rousseau & Vallerand, 2003, 2008; St-Louis, Carbonneau, & Vallerand, 2016). No such benefits take place with obsessive passion. In fact, research reveals that obsessive passion can predict various forms of psychological ill-being such as generalized anxiety and depression (Rousseau & Vallerand, 2003).

It should be noted that longitudinal research also reveals that obsessive passion for work can predict several years down the road being unable to psychologically adjust following retirement whereas harmonious passion protects from such psychological problems and leads to a highly fulfilling state of retirement (Houlfort, Vallerand et al., 2015). Research has also shed light on some of the mediating processes of such effects and reveals that on-task experiences mediate some of the observed effects of passion on well- and ill-being. For instance, positive affect experienced during exercise (Rousseau & Vallerand, 2008) mediate the positive and preventive effects of harmonious passion on life satisfaction and burnout, respectively.

Finally, it should be underscored that the adaptive outcomes engendered by harmonious passion are experienced on a recurrent basis because people engage in the activity that they are passionate about several hours weekly. For instance, harmonious passion leads to an increase of psychological well-being, and obsessive passion to a decrease of well-being, over a 1-year period (Philippe et al., 2009, Study 2). Thus, contrary to the belief that gains in outcomes are not sustained and that people return to baseline after a while (the so-called treadmill effect), the positive effects due to harmonious passion are indeed "sustainable" and long lasting (see Vallerand, 2012b, 2015). Once more, this is not the case with obsessive passion where minimal gains and in fact some losses in adaptive outcomes are experienced.

Relationships Passion for an activity can also have important effects on interpersonal outcomes outside the passionate activity. For instance, research reveals that having a harmonious passion for the Internet and Facebook can promote friendships outside the passionate activity, whereas obsessive passion does not (Utz, Jonas, & Tonkens, 2012). In fact, contrary to harmonious passion, with obsessive passion there is a risk of losing one's friends due to over engagement in Facebook or other activities that they do not engage with us. Research has also shown that having an obsessive passion for an activity can conflict with other aspects of one's life and lead to negative relationship outcomes in other dimensions of one's life. For instance, in a study with soccer fans from the UK, Vallerand et al. (2008, Study 3) have demonstrated that having an obsessive passion for soccer leads to conflict between soccer and one's romantic relationship that, in turn, undermines the quality of the relationship.

In sum, with obsessive passion, people seem to lose twice: adaptive functioning at the task level is limited at best and it contributes to further curtailing optimal functioning in other areas of the person's life. Thus, with obsessive passion, functioning and development are not optimal but rather limited in scope. However, with harmonious passion, a recurrent series of micro-moments of adaptive outcomes and functioning take place where those positive moments experienced in the passionate activity contributes to adaptive outcomes with respect to the passionate activity as well as outside of it, and so on. Passion does matter!

Conclusions and Research Directions

The purpose of this chapter was to introduce the concept of passion and show how it matters with respect to a number of important outcomes. I have presented the Dualistic Model of Passion (e.g., Vallerand, 2010, 2015; Vallerand et al., 2003; Vallerand & Houlfort, 2003) and subsequently have focused on the determinants and outcomes. The research reviewed in this chapter leads to four major conclusions. First, there is an overwhelming support for the DMP. The model defines passion as a strong inclination toward a self-defining activity that one loves, finds important, and devotes significant amount of time and energy to. Furthermore, two types of passion are proposed depending on how the activity representation has been internalized in one's identity. While harmonious passion entails control of the activity and a harmonious coexistence of the passionate activity with other activities of the person's life, obsessive passion entails the relative lack of control over the passionate activity, rigid persistence, and conflict with other life activities. Research reviewed provided strong support for the existence of the two types of passion as well as for the processes that the DMP posits that they entail.

The second major conclusion is that although a number of determinants of passion have been identified, additional research is clearly necessary. We have seen that such research can be divided into the initial and the ongoing development of passion. We have seen that both social and personal factors are involved in the two types of development. Additional research may want to focus on the role of personality variables (such as the Big Five) in the initial development of the two types of passion. Although, such research (e.g., Lecoq & Rimé, 2009) has shown that personality types have meager effects on the two types of passion, the facets were not assessed in their study. Furthermore, Lecoq and Rimé only looked at the prediction of the two types of passion without considering the types of activities involved. It is possible that personality predicts which type of activities is selected and eventually turns into a passion. For instance, extraverted individuals may develop a passion for social activities (such as team sports) whereas introverted individuals may turn toward individual sports or even more solitary activities such as reading. Research on vocational interest (e.g., Harrington & Long, 2013) and the Holland categorization of activities may provide a blueprint as to how to best proceed here. The ongoing development of passion also deserves attention. One area in particular that would benefit from such research is how best to diminish obsessive passion and increase harmonious passion. Research reveals that activity engagement out of obsessive passion may come in part from one's intention to avoid negativity or to escape problems that take place in other areas of one's life (Fuster, Chamaro, Carbonell, & Vallerand, 2014; Lalande et al., 2016). These findings suggest that alleviating such problems (e.g., improving relationship with one's spouse) may diminish obsessive passion for one's favorite activity and increase harmonious passion. Future research on this issue appears promising.

A third conclusion is that passion clearly matters with respect to outcomes. Clearly, being passionate for a given activity leads to adaptive outcomes, especially if the passion is harmonious in nature. Whereas obsessive passion may lead to some positive outcomes, the effects are much less positive than those produced by harmonious passion. Past research on interest has typically assumed that interest only leads to positive outcomes. Conversely, the DMP posits that passion can lead to both adaptive and maladaptive outcomes depending on the type of passion at play. The present position would therefore appear to lead to an interesting glimpse into human nature: Loving something can sometimes go awry and yield maladaptive effects. Furthermore, such a conclusion applies across the life span. Indeed, research has found the same findings with participants ranging in age from 8 to 90 years (Philippe et al., 2009; Vallerand, 2015). In other words, passion, and especially harmonious passion, contributes to optimal functioning across the life span. Such a perspective on the duality of passion may be worth considering for future research on the construct of interest.

A fourth and final conclusion is that passion matters with respect to two types of outcomes: those within the realm of the activity one is passionate about and those outside of it. Past research on interest has typically focused only on those outcomes taking place within the realm of the activity (e.g., educational or vocational interest). However, we have seen that there is evidence that harmonious passion leads to adaptive outcomes that takes place both *outside* the realm of the activity and in other areas of the person's life. Conversely, obsessive passion can trigger less positive, and at times deleterious, effects both inside and outside the realm of the passionate activity. Although a number of outcomes have been studied so far, an array of consequences still deserves empirical scrutiny. One recent approach suggests looking at optimal functioning from a multidimensional perspective. For instance, according to Vallerand (2013; Vallerand & Carbonneau, 2013), to be optimally functioning in society, people should score high on five elements: psychological, physical, and relational well-being; high performance in one's main field of endeavor (e.g., work or education); and contributing to one's immediate community or society at large. The DMP posits that harmonious passion should promote full optimal functioning, while obsessive passion should only partially contribute to it by contributing to some elements (most notably performance and contributions to society) while undermining or not facilitating others. Future research on this issue would appear important.

Caveats and Limitations

The findings reviewed in this chapter provide strong support for the DMP. One limitation, however, is that most studies used correlational designs. This raises the causality issue. Research using cross-lagged panel designs in which both outcomes and the two types of passion are measured at two points in time, however, reveals that passion leads to outcomes and not the other way around (e.g., Carbonneau, Vallerand, Fernet, & Guay, 2008; Lavigne et al., 2012). Furthermore, some research in which the experimental induction of the two types of passion (and random assignment to conditions) was used has led to the same findings as those using the Passion Scale (e.g., Bélanger et al., 2013b; Lafrenière et al., 2013, Study 2). Specifically, inducing harmonious passion led to increases in outcomes relative to the induction of obsessive passion or that of a control group. Furthermore, a recent meta-analysis involving more than 94 studies and over 1300 independent effect sizes coming from a number of different laboratories provide strong support for the differentiated role of harmonious and obsessive passion in outcomes (see Curran et al., 2015). Overall, there is a strong support for the validity of the findings reported in this chapter.

In sum, although interest has enjoyed a longer tradition in psychology than passion, the latter offers the promise to take the issue of high involvement for activity in unchartered territories and to provide a new understanding of human nature focusing on both optimal functioning and human foibles.

References

Aron, A., Aron, E. N., & Smollan, D. (1992). Inclusion of other in the self scale and the structure of interpersonal closeness. *Journal of Personality and Social Psychology, 63*, 596–612.

Bakker, A. B., & Demerouti, E. (2007). The job demands-resources model: State of the art. *Journal of Managerial Psychology, 22*, 309–328.

Baum, J. R., & Locke, E. A. (2004). The relationship of entrepreneurial traits, skill, and motivation to subsequent venture growth. *Journal of Applied Psychology, 89*, 587–598.

Bélanger, J. J., Lafrenière, M.-A. K., Vallerand, R. J., & Kruglanski, A. W. (2013a). When passion makes the heart grow colder: The role of passion in alternative goal suppression. *Journal of Personality and Social Psychology, 104*, 126–147.

Bélanger, J. J., Lafrenière, M.-A. K., Vallerand, R. J., & Kruglanski, A. W. (2013b). Driven by fear: The effect of success and failure information on passionate individuals' performance. *Journal of Personality and Social Psychology, 104*(1), 180–195.

Bonneville-Roussy, A., Lavigne, G. L., & Vallerand, R. J. (2011). When passion leads to excellence : The case of musicians. *Psychology of Music, 39*, 123–138.

Bonneville-Roussy, A., Vallerand, R. J., & Bouffard, T. (2013). The roles of autonomy support and harmonious and obsessive passions in educational persistence. *Learning and Individual Differences, 24*, 22–31.

Brown, K. W., & Ryan, R. M. (2003). The benefits of being present: Mindfulness and its role in psychological well-being. *Journal of Personality and Social Psychology, 84*, 822–848.

Burke, S. M., Sabiston, C. M., & Vallerand, R. J. (2012). Passion in breast cancer survivors: Examining links to emotional well-being. *Journal of Health Psychology, 17*(8), 1161–1175.

Carbonneau, N., & Vallerand, R. J. (2013). On the role of harmonious and obsessive passion in conflict behavior. *Motivation and Emotion, 37*, 743–757.

Carbonneau, N., & Vallerand, R. J. (2016). "I'm not the same person since I met you": The role of romantic passion in how people change when they get involved in a romantic relationship. *Motivation and Emotion, 40*, 101–117.

Carbonneau, N., Vallerand, R. J., Fernet, C., & Guay, F. (2008). The role of passion for teaching in intra and interpersonal outcomes. *Journal of Educational Psychology, 100*, 977–988.

Carbonneau, N., Vallerand, R. J., & Massicotte, S. (2010). Is the practice of yoga associated with positive outcomes? The role of passion. *The Journal of Positive Psychology, 5*, 452–465.

Carpentier, J., Mageau, G. A., & Vallerand, R. J. (2012). Ruminations and flow: Why do people with a more harmonious passion experience higher well-being? *Journal of Happiness Studies, 13*, 501–518.

Caudroit, J., Boiché, J., Stephan, Y., Le Scanff, C., & Trouilloud, D. (2011). Predictors of work/family interference and leisure-time physical activity among teachers: The role of passion towards work. *European Journal of Work and Organizational Psychology, 20*(3), 326–344.

Chamaro, A., Penelo, E., Fornieles, A., Oberst, U., Vallerand, R. J., & Fernández-Castro, J. (2015). Evidence on the validity and measurement invariance of the Spanish version of the passion scale. *Psicothema, 27*, 402–409.

Cox, B. J., Enns, M. W., & Clara, I. P. (2002). The multidimensional structure of perfectionism in clinically distressed and college student samples. *Psychological Assessment, 14*(3), 365–373.

Csikszentmihalyi, M., Rathunde, K., & Whalen, S. (1993). *Talented teenagers: The roots of success and failure*. New York: Cambridge University Press.

Curran, T., Hill, A. P., Appleton, P. R., Vallerand, R. J., & Standage, M. (2015). The psychology of passion: A meta-analytical review of a decade of research on intrapersonal outcomes. *Motivation and Emotion, 39*, 631–655.

Deci, E. L., Eghrari, H., Patrick, B. C., & Leone, D. R. (1994). Facilitating internalization: The self-determination perspective. *Journal of Personality, 62*, 119–142.

Deci, E. L., & Ryan, R. M. (2000). The "what" and "why" of goal pursuits: Human needs and the self-determination of behavior. *Psychological Inquiry, 11*, 227–268.

Donahue, E. G., Rip, B., & Vallerand, R. J. (2009). When winning is everything: On passion, identity, and aggression in sport. *Psychology of Sport and Exercise, 10*, 526–534.

Dubreuil, P., Forest, J., & Courcy, F. (2014). From strengths use to work performance: The role of harmonious passion, subjective vitality, and concentration. *The Journal of Positive Psychology, 9*, 335–349.

Dweck, C. S. (2006). *Mindset: The new psychology of success*. New York: Random House.

Eccles, J. S., & Wigfield, A. (2002). Motivational beliefs, values, and goals. *Annual Review of Psychology, 53*, 109–132.

Erikson, E. H. (1968). *Identity: Youth and crisis*. New York: W.W. Norton.

Fernet, C., Lavigne, G., & Vallerand, R. J. (2014). Fired up with passion: The role of harmonious and obsessive passion in burnout in novice teachers. *Work and Stress, 28*, 270–288.

Forest, J., Mageau, G. A., Crevier-Braud, L., Bergeron, É., Dubreuil, P., & Lavigne, G. L. (2012). Harmonious passion as an explanation of the relation between signature strengths' use and well-being at work: Test of an intervention program. *Human Relations, 65*(9), 1233–1252.

Frijda, N. H., Mesquita, B., Sonnemans, J., & Van Goozen, S. (1991). The duration of affective phenomena or emotions, sentiments and passions. In K. T. Strongman (Ed.), *International review of studies on emotion* (Vol. 1, pp. 187–225). New York: Wiley.

Fuster, H., Chamaro, A., Carbonell, X., & Vallerand, R. J. (2014). Relationship between passion and motivation for gaming in massively multiplayer online role-playing games. *Cyberpsychology, Behavior, and Social Networking, 17*, 292–297.

Gousse-Lessard, A.-S., Vallerand, R. J., Carbonneau, N., & Lafrenière, M.-A. K. (2013). The role of passion in mainstream and radical Behaviors: A look at environmental activism. *Journal of Environmental Psychology, 35*, 18–29.

Guay, F., Mageau, G. A., & Vallerand, R. J. (2003). On the hierarchical structure of self-determined motivation: A test of top-down, bottom-up, reciprocal, and horizontal effects. *Personality and Social Psychology Bulletin, 29*, 992–1004.

Guérin, E., Fortier, M., & Williams, T. (2013). Because I need to move: Examining women's passion for physical activity and its relationship with daily affect and vitality. *Psychology of Well-Being: Theory, Research, and Practice, 3*, 1–24.

Harrington, T., & Long, J. (2013). The history of interest inventories and career assessments in career counseling. *The Career Development Quarterly, 61*, 83–92.

Hatfield, E., & Walster, G. W. (1978). *A new look at love*. Reading, MA: Addison-Wesley.
Hewitt, P. L., & Flett, G. L. (2002). Perfectionism and stress enhancement, perpetuation, anticipation, and generation in psychopathology. In G. L. Flett & P. L. Hewitt (Eds.), *Perfectionism: Theory, research, and treatment* (pp. 742–775). Washington, DC: American Psychological Association.
Hidi, S., & Renninger, K. A. (2006). The four-phase model of interest development. *Educational Psychologist, 41*(2), 111–127.
Hodgins, H. S., & Knee, R. (2002). The integrating self and conscious experience. In E. L. Deci & R. M. Ryan (Eds.), *Handbook on self-determination research: Theoretical and applied issues* (pp. 87–100). Rochester, NY: University of Rochester Press.
Houlfort, N., Philippe, F., Vallerand, R. J., & Ménard, J. (2014). On passion as heavy work investment and its consequences. *Journal of Managerial Psychology, 29*, 25–45.
Houlfort, N., Vallerand, R. J., & Laframboise, A. (2015). Heavy work investment: The role of passion. In I. Harpaz & R. Snir (Eds.), *Heavy work investment: Its nature, sources, outcomes, and future directions* (pp. 47–67). New York: Routledge.
Houser-Marko, L., & Sheldon, K. M. (2006). Motivating behavioral persistence: The self-as-doer construct. *Personality and Social Psychology Bulletin, 32*, 1037–1049.
Joussain, A. (1928). *Les passions humaines* [The human passions]. Paris: Ernest Flammarion.
Jowett, S., Lafrenière, M.-A. K., & Vallerand, R. J. (2013). Passion for activities and relationship quality: A dyadic approach. *Journal of Social and Personal Relationship, 30*, 734–749.
Lafrenière, M.-A., Jowett, S., Vallerand, R. J., Donahue, E. G., & Lorimer, R. (2008). Passion in sport: On the quality of the coach-player relationship. *Journal of Sport and Exercise Psychology, 30*, 541–560.
Lafrenière, M.-A. K., Bélanger, J. J., Sedikides, C., & Vallerand, R. J. (2011). Self-esteem and passion for activities. *Personality and Individual Differences, 51*, 541–544.
Lafrenière, M.-A. K., St-Louis, A. C., Vallerand, R. J., & Donahue, E. G. (2012). On the relation between performance and life satisfaction: The moderating role of passion. *Self and Identity, 11*, 516–530.
Lafrenière, M.-A. K., Vallerand, R. J., & Sedikides, C. (2013). On the relation between self-enhancement and life satisfaction: The moderating role of passion. *Self and Identity, 12*, 516–530.
Lalande, D., Vallerand, R.J., Lafrenière, M-A.K., Verner-Filion, J., Laurent, F-A., Forest, J., & Paquet, Y. (2016). Obsessive passion: A compensatory response to unsatisfied needs. *Journal of Personality*.
Lavigne, G. L., Forest, J., & Crevier-Braud, L. (2012). Passion at work and burnout: A two-study test of the mediating role of flow experiences. *European Journal of Work and Organizational Psychology, 21*(4), 518–546.
Lecoq, J., & Rimé, B. (2009). Les passions: aspects émotionnels et sociaux. *Revue Européenne de Psychologie Appliquée/European Review of Applied Psychology, 59*, 197–209.
Liu, D., Chen, X.-P., & Yao, X. (2011). From autonomy to creativity: A multilevel investigation of the mediating role of harmonious passion. *Journal of Applied Psychology, 96*, 295–309.
Luh, D.-B., & Lu, C.-C. (2012). From cognitive style to creativity achievement: The mediating role of passion. *Psychology of Aesthetics, Creativity, and the Arts, 6*(3), 282–288.
Mageau, G., Carpentier, J., & Vallerand, R. J. (2011). The role of self-esteem contingencies in the distinction between obsessive and harmonious passion. *European Journal of Social Psychology, 6*, 720–729.
Mageau, G., & Vallerand, R. J. (2007). The moderating effect of passion on the relation between activity engagement and positive affect. *Motivation and Emotion, 31*, 312–321.
Mageau, G. A., Vallerand, R. J., Charest, J., Salvy, S.-J., Lacaille, N., Bouffard, T., & Koestner, R. (2009). On the development of harmonious and obsessive passion: The role of autonomy support, activity valuation, and identity processes. *Journal of Personality, 77*, 601–645.
Markus, H., & Nurius, P. (1986). Possible selves. *American Psychologist, 41*(9), 954–969.

Marsh, H. W., Vallerand, R. J., Lafreniere, M. A. K., Parker, P., Morin, A. J. S., Carbonneau, N., ... Paquet, Y. (2013). Passion: Does one scale fit all? Construct validity of two-factor passion scale and psychometric invariance over different activities and languages. *Psychological Assessment, 25,* 796–809.

Miquelon, P., Vallerand, R. J., Grouzet, F., & Cardinal, G. (2005). Perfectionism, academic motivation, and personal adjustment: An integrative model. *Personality and Social Psychology Bulletin, 31,* 913–924.

Parastatidou, I. S., Doganis, G., Theodorakis, Y., & Vlachopoulos, S. P. (2012). Exercising with passion: Initial validation of the passion scale in exercise. *Measurement in Physical Education and Exercise Science, 16,* 119–134.

Peterson, C., & Seligman, M. E. P. (2004). Vitality [zest, enthusiasm, vigor, energy]. In C. Peterson & M. E. P. Seligman (Eds.), *Character strengths and virtues: A handbook and classification* (pp. 273–289). Washington, DC: American Psychological Association.

Philippe, F., Vallerand, R. J., & Lavigne, G. (2009). Passion does make a difference in people's lives: A look at well-being in passionate and non-passionate individuals. *Applied Psychology: Health and Well-Being, 1,* 3–22.

Philippe, F. L., Vallerand, R. J., Houlfort, N., Lavigne, G., & Donahue, E. G. (2010). Passion for an activity and quality of interpersonal relationships: The mediating role of positive and negative emotions. *Journal of Personality and Social Psychology, 98,* 917–932.

Przybylski, A. K., Weinstein, N., Ryan, R. M., & Rigby, C. S. (2009). Having to versus wanting to play: Background and consequences of harmonious versus obsessive engagement in video games. *Cyberpsychology & Behavior, 12,* 485–492.

Ratelle, C. F., Carbonneau, N., Vallerand, R. J., & Mageau, G. (2013). Passion in the romantic sphere: A look at relational outcomes. *Motivation and Emotion, 37,* 106–120.

Renninger, K. A., & Hidi, S. (2011). Revisiting the conceptualization, measurement, and generation of interest. *Educational Psychologist, 46,* 168–184.

Ribot, T. (1907). *Essai sur les passions.* Paris: Alcan.

Rip, B., Vallerand, R. J., & Lafrenière, M.-A. K. (2012). Passion for a cause, passion for a creed: On ideological passion, identity threat, and extremism. *Journal of Personality, 80*(3), 573–602.

Rousseau, F. L., & Vallerand, R. J. (2003). Le rôle de la passion dans le bien-être subjectif des aînés [The role of passion in the subjective well-being of the elderly]. *Revue Québécoise de Psychologie, 24,* 197–211.

Rousseau, F. L., & Vallerand, R. J. (2008). An examination of the relationship between passion and subjective well-being in older adults. *International Journal of Aging and Human Development, 66,* 195–211.

Rousseau, F. L., Vallerand, R. J., Ratelle, C. F., Mageau, G. A., & Provencher, P. (2002). Passion and gambling: On the validation of the Gambling Passion Scale (GPS). *Journal of Gambling Studies, 18,* 45–66.

Ryan, R. M., & Deci, E. L. (2000). Self-determination and the facilitation of intrinsic motivation, social development, and well-being. *American Psychologist, 55,* 68–78.

Ryan, R. M., & Deci, E. L. (2003). On assimilating identities of the self: A self-determination theory perspective on internalization and integrity within cultures. In M. R. Leary & J. P. Tangney (Eds.), *Handbook of self and identity* (pp. 253–272). New York: Guilford.

Schlenker, B. R. (1985). Identity and self-identification. In B. R. Schlenker (Ed.), *The self and social life* (pp. 65–99). New York: McGraw-Hill.

Shi, J. (2012). Influence of passion on innovative behavior: An empirical examination in Peoples Republic of China. *African Journal of Business Management, 6*(30), 8889–8896.

Stenseng, F. (2008). The two faces of leisure activity engagement: Harmonious and obsessive passion in relation to intrapersonal conflict and life domain outcomes. *Leisure Sciences, 30,* 465–481.

St-Louis, A., Verner-Filion, J., Bergeron, C., & Vallerand, R.J. (2016). *The role of passion in facilitating adaptive self-processes: The case of mindfulness.* Manuscript submitted for publication.

St-Louis, A. C., Carbonneau, N., & Vallerand, R. J. (2016). Passion for a cause: How it affects health and well-being. *Journal of Personality, 84,* 263–276.

St-Louis, A. C., & Vallerand, R. J. (2015). A successful creative process: The role of passion and emotion. *Creativity Research Journal, 27,* 1–13.

Trépanier, S.-G., Fernet, C., Austin, S., Forest, J., & Vallerand, R. J. (2014). Linking job demands and resources to burnout and work engagement: Does passion underlie these differential relationships? *Motivation and Emotion, 38,* 353–366.

Utz, S., Jonas, K. J., & Tonkens, E. (2012). Effects of passion for massively multiplayer online role-playing games on interpersonal relationships. *Journal of Media Psychology: Theories, Methods, and Applications, 24,* 77.

Vallerand, R. J. (1997). Toward a hierarchical model of intrinsic and extrinsic motivation. *Advances in Experimental and Social Psychology, 29,* 271–360.

Vallerand, R. J. (2008). On the psychology of passion: In search of what makes people's lives most worth living. *Canadian Psychology, 49,* 1–13.

Vallerand, R. J. (2010). On passion for life activities: The dualistic model of passion. In M. P. Zanna (Ed.), *Advances in experimental social psychology* (Vol. 42, pp. 97–193). New York: Academic Press.

Vallerand, R. J. (2012a). From motivation to passion: In search of the motivational processes involved in a meaningful life. *Canadian Psychology, 53,* 42–52.

Vallerand, R. J. (2012b). The role of passion in sustainable psychological well-being. *Psychological Well-Being: Theory, Research, and Practice, 2,* 1–21.

Vallerand, R. J. (2013). Passion and optimal functioning in society: A eudaimonic perspective. In A. S. Waterman (Ed.), *The best within us: Positive psychology perspectives on eudaimonic functioning* (pp. 183–206). Washington, DC: APA Books.

Vallerand, R. J. (2015). *The psychology of passion.* New York: Oxford University Press.

Vallerand, R. J., Blanchard, C. M., Mageau, G. A., Koestner, R., Ratelle, C. F., et al. (2003). Les passions de l'âme: On obsessive and harmonious passion. *Journal of Personality and Social Psychology, 85,* 756–767.

Vallerand, R. J., & Carbonneau, N. (2013). The role of passion in optimal functioning in society. In D. McInerney, H. W. Marsh, R. Craven, & F. Guay (Eds.), *Theory driving research: New wave perspectives on self-processes and human development.* Greenwich, CT: Information Age Publishing.

Vallerand, R. J., & Carbonneau, N. (2016). Passion and optimal relationships. In R. C. Knee & H. Reiss (Eds.), *Positive approaches to optimal relationship development.* New York: Cambridge.

Vallerand, R. J., Fortier, M. S., & Guay, F. (1997). Self-determination and persistence in a real-life setting: Toward a motivational model of high school dropout. *Journal of Personality and Social Psychology, 72,* 1161–1176.

Vallerand, R. J., & Houlfort, N. (2003). Passion at work: Toward a new conceptualization. In S. W. Gilliland, D. D. Steiner, & D. P. Skarlicki (Eds.), *Emerging perspectives on values in organizations* (pp. 175–204). Greenwich, CT: Information Age Publishing.

Vallerand, R. J., Mageau, G. A., Elliot, A., Dumais, A., Demers, M.-A., & Rousseau, F. L. (2008). Passion and performance attainment in sport. *Psychology of Sport & Exercise, 9,* 373–392.

Vallerand, R. J., Ntoumanis, N., Philippe, F., Lavigne, G. L., Carbonneau, C., Bonneville, A., Lagacé-Labonté, C., & Maliha, G. (2008). On passion and sports fans: A look at football. *Journal of Sports Sciences, 26,* 1279–1293.

Vallerand, R. J., Paquet, Y., Philippe, F. L., & Charest, J. (2010). On the role of passion in burnout: A process model. *Journal of Personality, 78,* 289–312.

Vallerand, R. J., Rousseau, F. L., Grouzet, F. M. E., Dumais, A., & Grenier, S. (2006). Passion in sport: A look at determinants and affective experiences. *Journal of Sport & Exercise Psychology, 28*, 454–478.

Vallerand, R. J., Salvy, S. J., Mageau, G. A., Elliot, A. J., Denis, P., Grouzet, F. M. E., & Blanchard, C. B. (2007). On the role of passion in performance. *Journal of Personality, 75*, 505–534.

Vallerand, R.J., & Verner-Filion, J. (2013). Passion and positive psychology: On making life worth living for. *Terapia Psicológica* (Special Issue on positive psychology)*, 31*, 5–9.

Verner-Filion, J., & Vallerand, R.J. (2016). *On the differential relationships involving perfectionism and academic adjustment: The mediating role of passion and affect.* Manuscript submitted for publication.

Zhao, Y., St-Louis, A., & Vallerand, R. J. (2015). On the validation of the passion scale in Chinese. *The Psychology of Well-Being: Theory, Research, and Practice, 5*, 1–11.

Chapter 9
Creative Geniuses, Polymaths, Child Prodigies, and Autistic Savants: The Ambivalent Function of Interests and Obsessions

Dean Keith Simonton

Consider the following three real people.

Person A devoted virtually his whole life to a single interest: music. He began as a child prodigy, both as a virtuoso keyboardist and as a composer, already making a mark on the contemporary music scene as a preteenager. By the time he passed away, he was widely considered among the greatest contemporary composers. Yet beyond his obsession with music, his interests were rather narrow. His letters contain very little discussion beyond family affairs, job searches, and current compositions and performances. At his death he was found to possess only two books.

Person B also made a name for herself as a composer, her works still getting performed and recorded several centuries after her death. Yet her interests were much broader than those of Person A. Besides music, she wrote extensively on theology, philosophy, medicine, and science. She even composed poetry as well as a drama that is considered the oldest surviving morality play. Besides all this, she was a religious leader and mystic who was posthumously canonized. Now she is recognized as a polymath—a person whose expertise spans several distinct domains.

Person C was born with severe brain damage and other disabilities. Having had his eyes surgically removed as an infant, he at first could not eat his own food, nor could he stand until he was 12 nor walk until 15. But at age 16, he discovered an intense passion for music, learned to play the piano, and within a short time was performing a variety of pieces, including classical and ragtime. Although he eventually would give concerts and appeared on various television shows, he never composed his own creative work, unlike Persons A and B.

These three individuals all manifested a lifelong interest in music, an interest that developed into an expertise sufficient to attract attention from others. Although only the first two can be said to have attained the level of musical genius, they did so in

D.K. Simonton (✉)
Department of Psychology, University of California, Davis, Davis, CA, USA
e-mail: dksimonton@ucdavis.edu

© Springer International Publishing AG 2017
P.A. O'Keefe, J.M. Harackiewicz (eds.), *The Science of Interest*,
DOI 10.1007/978-3-319-55509-6_9

entirely different ways. Where Person A was far more obsessed with music, Person B viewed music as an integral part of a much wider range of interests.

Who are these people? Person A = Wolfgang Amadeus Mozart (1756–1791), one of the most famous classical composers who ever lived, Person B = Hildegard of Bingen (1098–1179), a medieval abbess, and Person C = Leslie Lemke (1952–), an often discussed autistic savant. Collectively they illustrate the kinds of people who are the subject of this chapter: creative geniuses, polymaths, child prodigies, and savants. Despite their differences, such individuals start with an interest—even obsession—that motivates the acquisition of an exceptional domain-specific expertise, in their case music.

Creative Geniuses

Mozart's life and career illustrates an important developmental reality: Talent alone cannot guarantee genius, but rather the person must first master the requisite domain-specific expertise. This necessity takes us to what has been called the *10-year rule* (Ericsson, 1996). According to this supposed rule, a person cannot even begin to make world-class contributions to a given domain of creativity without first engaging in "deliberate practice" (Ericsson, 2014). This practice involves an extensive commitment to the acquisition of the requisite knowledge and skill. For example, Mozart could not compose anything more than juvenilia and apprentice pieces until he had attained complete competence in all of the complexities of harmony, counterpoint, instrumentation, and a host of other aspects of the Western classical music tradition (Kozbelt, 2014). For this reason, even though Mozart started his music training at an exceptionally young age—his father Leopold was a composer and instructor of note—it took him at least a decade before he had sufficient expertise to create his first masterpieces (Hayes, 1989). In this respect, Mozart was somewhat atypical. On average, the greatest classical composers require somewhat less time to master the domain relative to their less prominent colleagues (Simonton, 2016). Could boy Mozart's busy concert schedule have slowed his expertise acquisition?

In any event, what explains the general tendency for the most eminent creative geniuses to take the least time in mastering the needed knowledge and skills? One obvious explanation is that the greatest creators enjoy a special talent, an innate capacity that enables them to accelerate the acquisition process (Simonton, 2008, 2014). The talented just get better faster. Yet another interpretation is possible, namely, that the gift actually entails an unusual fascination with the domain that enables the youth to devote more hours per day and to concentrate better each hour of the day. A truly strong obsession would better help the individual to filter out all of the distractions that might otherwise pull the person away from study and practice. Such extraneous interference in talent development can become especially potent in teenagers (Csikszentmihalyi, Rathunde, & Whalen, 1993). Fortunately, those youths who possess sufficient preoccupation with their chosen domain will persevere in expertise acquisition come what may.

In fact, the continuity of interests will persist all the way through adulthood. This persistence is illustrated in the lives of highly creative scientists. In their early years, these individuals would get involved in hobbies and interests that were obviously connected with their later achievements, such as electronics for future physical scientists or natural history for future biological scientists (Roe, 1953; Segal, Busse, & Mansfeld, 1980). This involvement does not go away once the youths develop into adult researchers. Indeed, illustrious scientists commonly devote 8–10 h per day for 80–90% of the year on their investigations (Simon, 1974). Yet this effort is not drudgery because eminent scientists derive much more satisfaction from their research than do their less notable colleagues (Chambers, 1964). According to Roe (1952), elite scientists display a "driving absorption in their work" (p. 25) in that each "works hard and devotedly at his laboratory, often seven days a week. He says his work is his life, and has few recreations" (p. 22). "They have worked long hours for many years, frequently with no vacations to speak of, because they would rather be doing their work than anything else" (p. 25). Sounds like an obsession rather than a fleeting interest?

Of course, I have not really addressed where these interests might have come from. No doubt environmental influences play a role, both at home and at school. Yet given that behavioral genetics has established substantial heritabilities for personality, interests, and values (Bouchard, 2004), nature has a place alongside nurture. In that case, a portion of talent may entail not abilities per se but rather interests. These interests not only help accelerate expertise acquisition but also support creative productivity throughout the course of a career. In fact, strong interests could even underlie "more bang for the buck" effects in which creative performance outstrips the objective level of domain-specific expertise (Simonton, 2014). Albert Einstein's contributions to theoretical physics exceeded his actual knowledge and skill in both physics and mathematics. He just would not give up on problems. As an example, his special theory of relativity was the long-sought solution to a problem that he had conceived as a 16 year old!

Whatever the contributions of nature and nurture, the foregoing analysis suggests that creative geniuses should have very narrow interests—interests that are so highly domain-specific that we might even call them obsessions. They would seem like monomaniacs. Yet a very important empirical finding is diametrically opposed to this view: The personality trait that correlates most highly with creative achievement is Openness to Experience, one of the dimensions of the Big Five Factor Model (McCrae & Greenberg, 2014). By and large, creative geniuses exhibit far broader interests than colleagues who fail to attain that degree of eminence. For example, the former are better informed on a wider range of topics and engage in diverse hobbies far removed from their domain of creative expertise. This openness can even be seen in the sciences, where the more eminent the scientist the greater the engagement in artistic avocations (Root-Bernstein et al., 2008; Root-Bernstein, Bernstein, & Garnier, 1995). For instance, Galileo's discovery of the lunar mountains, a discovery that other astronomers missed, was facilitated by his conspicuous interests in the visual arts (Simonton, 2012). Openness is correlated not only with creative achievement but also with other variables associated with the creative process, such as divergent thinking and cognitive disinhibition (Carson, 2014). Hence, the association is not incidental but rather integral to creativity.

This paradox then leads to a critical question: If interests can motivate the acquisition of domain-specific expertise, then can sufficiently diverse interests motivate the acquisition of expertise in multiple domains? If so, can openness drive creative versatility? That issue leads us to the next group under discussion.

Polymaths

Hildegard of Bingen was by no means the only polymath in the world. Table 9.1 provides a longer list, and even that list is highly selective. To be sure, not every creative genius is a polymath, and many will be far narrower in the scope of their creative achievements, whatever the breadth of their interests might be. To get a better idea of the phenomenon, we can turn to an empirical study of 2102 creative geniuses (Cassandro, 1998). All creators were assessed on their versatility, which was defined by achieving eminence in more than one domain or subdomain (see also Simonton, 1976; White, 1931). Although 61% did not demonstrate versatility according to this definition, 15% attained eminence in more than one subdomain within a domain (e.g., poetry and drama within literature; such as William

Table 9.1 Some representative polymaths in world history

Aristotle (Greek, 384–322 B.C.E.): metaphysics, logic, biology, psychology, political science, ethics, asthetics
Al-Kindi (Arab, 801–873): astronomy, geography, mathematics, meteorology, music, philosophy, medicine, physics, political science
Abhinavagupta (Indian, fl. c. 975–1025): philosophy, esthetics, criticism, poetry, drama, music, theology, logic, dance
Shen Kuo (Chinese, 1031–1095): mathematics, astronomy, geology, meteorology, zoology, botany, pharmacology, ethnography, poetry, technology, engineering, politics, government, administration, war
Omar Khayyám (Persian, 1048–1131): poetry, astronomy, mathematics, philosophy
Hildegard of Bingen (German, 1098–1179): music composition, drama, natural history, philosophy, medicine, poetry, religion
Leonardo da Vinci (Italian, 1452–1519): painting, sculpture, architecture, engineering, invention, mathematics, anatomy, geology, botany, music
Blaise Pascal (French, 1623–1662): mathematics, physics, literary prose, philosophy, religion
Mikhail Lomonosov (Russian, 1711–1765): physics, chemistry, poetry, geology, linguistics, education
Thomas Jefferson (American, 1743–1826): political leadership, political philosophy, horticulture, architecture, archeology, paleontology, technology, education
Thomas Young (British, 1773–1829): optics, physics, physiology, mathematics, medicine, Egyptology, linguistics, music

Shakespeare), and fully 24% achieved eminence in more than one domain (e.g., literature and science; such as Johann Wolfgang Goethe). Thus, more than one-third exhibited creative versatility to some degree. Furthermore, creative versatility appears to be positively correlated with achieved eminence (Simonton, 1976; Sulloway, 1996). The double- or triple-threat creator tends to become more eminent than the specialist creator. Accordingly, we cannot dismiss the connection by saying that these versatile creators have their expertise diluted to the level of mere dilettantes.

Note that the very existence of highly versatile creators—and especially the polymaths—introduces a very serious problem with the 10-year rule. If a decade is needed to acquire the domain-specific expertise necessary for exceptional creativity, then how is creative versatility even possible in a single human lifespan? Consider Herbert Simon (1916–2001), psychology's own polymath, who attained distinction not just in cognitive psychology but also in computer science, economics, political science, sociology, the philosophy of science, and statistics. Given that he won major awards in multiple disciplines—including a Nobel in economics!—his breadth represented versatile creativity, not just openness. So presumably, it should have taken him at least half of his life to obtain the expertise for achievement in each domain—which would have left him insufficient time to author the approximately 1000 publications on his curriculum vita!

At this point, we are far from a complete resolution of this seeming contradiction. The best we can do is cite a couple of empirical findings that might shed a little light on the problem.

First, for some creative domains, such as literature and the visual arts, versatile creativity is positively associated with life span (Cassandro, 1998). Thus, the creators do indeed have more opportunity to develop some of their diverse interests into full-fledged expertise. However, scientific genius is an exception, the highly versatile tending to have shorter life expectancies! That said, Herbert Simon lived until he was 84 years old.

Second, versatility is positively correlated with general intelligence, a correlation that may facilitate the accelerated acquisition of more than one domain-specific expertise (Simonton, 1976). Samuel Johnson (1781), the lexicographer who assembled the first English language dictionary, once observed that "the true Genius is a mind of large general powers, accidentally determined to some particular direction" (p. 5). Given sufficiently large "general powers," genius might be accidentally channeled into the development of more than one interest, thus yielding a versatile creator if not outright polymath.

One reason why so little is known about polymaths is that they are so very rare. As seen in Table 9.1, the listed exemplars span two millennia and about a dozen nationalities. If the sample had to be restricted to a given nation at a single point in time—such as active polymaths currently living in the United States—the list would become much shorter, probably even shorter than a list of contemporary child prodigies. It is that better researched group to which we now turn.

Child Prodigies

Mozart was not only an undisputable child prodigy, but he also became the very first such prodigy to serve as the subject of scientific research! During a concert tour in London, his prodigal musicianship was directly investigated by a Fellow of the Royal Society. The investigator objectively scrutinized the child's impressive skills at the keyboard, such as sight reading previously unknown scores and improvising music on given themes (e.g., a "Song of Anger"). It was manifest that the youth's proficiency at both performance and composition was already comparable to, if not exceeding, adult professionals. The results were reported in the *Philosophical Transactions of the Royal Society of London*, the oldest scientific journal in the English language (Barrington, 1770). The researcher also took care to verify Mozart's age using public records available back in Bavaria, and then reinforced the official age with observations regarding the prodigy's age-appropriate immaturity involving anything nonmusical—such as taking a break from the harpsichord by hopping around the room with a stick between his legs as a hobby horse! Mozart's age was, in fact, 8 years and 5 months. Because the report was not published until Mozart was around 14 years old—publication pressures were apparently less intense back then!—the researcher was able to add some further observations about the talent's subsequent career on the European continent. In what now seems an understatement, but would probably appear as an exaggeration at the time, the author speculated that Mozart may eventually equal George Frideric Handel in musical greatness.

Subsequent research on more contemporary child prodigies indicates that Mozart was fairly typical (Radford, 1990; Winner, 2014). For example, Mozart received exceptional familial support in the development of his talent—his father, mother, and older sister were all directly involved. If he ever experienced any flagging of interest in music, it would have been quickly revived. Besides direct instruction and encouragement from his father, Mozart did concert tours with his musically gifted sister, and his mother would provide the adult chaperon when the father was unable to do so. Nor was all of this familial support purely altruistic. After all, the young Mozart was expected to help contribute to the household income.

But even more telling was Mozart's asymmetrical development, another characteristic of child prodigies (Winner, 2014). On the one hand, his musical growth was truly prodigious. In less than 8 years—for his keyboard lessons started at age 3—Mozart had already attained a domain-specific expertise of top professionals. When the young Mozart performed a duet with his father in a sight-reading task, it was his father who made the mistakes and who received a disapproving glare from his son (Barrington, 1770). On the other hand, Mozart's development outside of music was not accelerated at all. When a cat strayed into the room during the examination, the 8-year old did what most kids his age would have done—drop everything to play with the adorable intruder! His extra-musical interests were more or less age typical.

Of course, the asymmetry extends from social development to cognitive development (Winner, 2014). Like most child prodigies, Mozart did not develop a breadth of intellectual interests, as noted earlier. Although his IQ has been estimated to fall between 150s and 160s, that estimate is based solely on his musical precocity (Cox, 1926). Except perhaps in acquiring sufficient proficiency in Italian and Latin (beyond his native German) to competently set texts in three different languages to music, there was little else to place Mozart apart from other children and teenagers of his time. In short, he was not intellectually gifted in any general sense.

All of these congruencies notwithstanding, in one significant manner Mozart is unrepresentative of most child prodigies: He actually grew up to become an adult genius! Very few prodigies manage to do so (Winner, 2014). One of the more outstanding examples is William James Sidis (1898–1944), a mathematical prodigy who at age 11 became the youngest person to enroll at Harvard University, and shortly after delivered a lecture on a topic in advanced mathematics before the Harvard Mathematical Club. Yet by early adulthood, he had lost all interest in mathematics, becoming instead an eccentric who wrote on a diversity of odd subjects that left no impression on any creative domain whatsoever (Montour, 1977). If an intense interest in a particular domain dissipates, and nothing else replaces it as a powerful incentive for expertise acquisition, then the onetime prodigy can reduce to adulthood mediocrity (Winner, 2014). The humorist Will Rogers had something like this in mind when he quipped: "I was not a Child Prodigy, because a Child Prodigy is a child who knows as much when it is a Child as it does when it grows up" (Day, 1949, p. 4).

The fact that child prodigies most often end up no different than the rest of us may be considered yet another puzzle. You would think that having a head start must increase the odds of getting to the finish line first. Yet that can sometimes lead to early burnout. And what may be fascinating to a child may not carry over to adulthood.

Autistic Savants

We now come to the final and perhaps the most mysterious group, the autistic savants (Miller, 1999). Superficially, savants might appear like a more extreme form of child prodigies. Both are most likely to appear in the same domains, such as mathematics, music, and art, and exhibit an intense and rather narrow interest in their chosen domain. In both groups, that exclusive interest translates into rapid acquisition of domain-specific expertise. Both are prone to display levels of performance that matches or exceeds adult levels. Indeed, in the case of certain savants, such as calendrical calculators who can rapidly determine the day of the week for any given date, adult performance levels are not meaningfully defined.

Yet the differences are profound as well. The asymmetrical development seen in the child prodigy becomes far more accentuated in the savant. Whereas the social development of the child prodigy may not keep pace with their talent development, they can still grow up to become well-adjusted, mature adults. Mozart had normal relationships with his family, maintained close friendships, negotiated with potential patrons, got married, and fathered children (six all told, with two surviving infancy, both becoming musicians). In contrast, the savant, as indicated by the frequent adjective "autistic," will have their social development so impaired as to become nonexistent—with the notable exception of those with "high-functioning" autism. Very often such individuals require live-in caretakers such as parents (Treffert, 2010).

Furthermore, even talent development will differ between the two groups. Whereas the child prodigy will normally master the full range of knowledge and skills associated with their creative domain, the savant will tend to acquire a narrow sliver of that domain—such as arithmetic calculation in mathematics, instrumental performance in music, and specific imagery and media in art. As a consequence, it is even rarer for savants to become creative geniuses, albeit a few can exhibit some degree of creativity (Miller, 1999). An extraordinary example in music is Hikari Ōe (1963–), who learned to communicate his feelings through composition, recordings of his music having sold more than a million copies. An illustration of the realm of art is Alonzo Clemons (1958–) who creates and sells extremely realistic clay sculptures of animals. In fact, the domains in which savants might demonstrate the most genuine creativity appear to be music and art (cf. Treffert, 2010). The prominence of these two domains among creative savants is suggestive because musical and artistic genius tends to display the lowest level of creative versatility relative to other domains of creative genius (White, 1931). So broad interests are again not always necessary for creative success.

All in all, autistic savants not only illustrate the most extreme case of domain-specific obsessions but also show how such intense interests seldom convert into creativity, and even fewer transform into creative genius (Treffert, 2010; Winner, 2014).

Discussion

I have just provided an overview of how interests or obsessions function in four closely related phenomena: creative geniuses, polymaths, child prodigies, and autistic savants. Taken singly and together, these groups illustrate some of the ambiguities involved in the connections between interests and creativity. In the case of creative geniuses, intense engagement in a specific domain may accelerate the acquisition of the relevant expertise, the narrower the focus the greater the acceleration—and thereby shorten the apprentice period to a length less than specified by the 10-year rule. Nevertheless, actual performance as a creative adult is positively associated with Openness to Experience, including an impressive breadth of interests. How one attains the right balance between these two effects is not obvious. Naturally, one might argue that the individual could just start with narrow interests in youth and then switch to broad interests as an adult, but this solution seems implausible. Not only does Openness have a strong genetic component (Bouchard, 2004), but additionally Openness is more likely to decrease rather than increase in the adult years (McCrae & Greenberg, 2014). So something's amiss.

The polymaths somewhat resolve the above problem because breadth of interests is translated directly into breadth of expertise. Yet this introduces another problem, namely, how creative development can manage to accelerate the acquisition of domain-specific expertise in multiple domains and still have time left over to make contributions to the separate domains. According to the 10-year rule, the most amazing polymaths would require a whole lifetime just to become sufficiently competent to contribute to all of the creative domains in which they achieved distinction. I only offered the speculation that the most impressive polymaths may take advantage of exceptional general intelligence to accelerate talent development across the board. Another possibility applicable in some instances is to select domains that overlap sufficiently so that the individual can enjoy considerable positive transfer of knowledge and expertise. For instance, all of the domains may involve words as the main means of conceiving and communicating creative ideas. This interpretation then helps us understand why musical and artistic geniuses are less versatile than the rest: Both domains involve forms of expertise that would feature minimal positive transfer to other domains involving words, such as philosophy or literature.

The child prodigies offer a very different picture of interests from what is seen in the previous two groups. Their expertise acquisition not only tends to start much earlier but also tends to accelerate much faster. Still, both of these developmental anomalies are aided by the more narrow focus of their interests. Child prodigies typically concentrate on a single domain, such as music or mathematics. Even so, that concentration may have a cost if that obsession cannot be maintained into maturity. That is one reason why prodigies seldom become creative geniuses. If the youths had started with broader interests, expertise acquisition might be prolonged, but they would also leave open the option of switching domains. Even though autistic savants display the same narrow interests—indeed, even narrower—they face more severe obstacles than do the child prodigies. Except in the case of high-functioning autism, the savant's domain-specific obsessions offer little or no help in overcoming the liabilities in social development. Although some autistic savants can exhibit creativity, much fewer can claim to have become creative geniuses.

One final issue should be addressed: late bloomers. These are persons who do not discover a creative domain in which they attain the greatest eminence until much later in life. In a sense, they represent the opposite of the child prodigy. A frequently cited example is Grandma Moses (1860–1961) who was in her late 70s when she became a serious painter. Although she had expressed artistic interests much earlier, it was channeled into folk crafts, such as quilts and embroidery, activities that become impossible when arthritis set in when she was in her mid-70s. When a relative suggested that she take up painting as an alternative, she turned to the creative domain that would make her famous. The precipitating event can be styled a "crystallizing experience," a moment in which a person finds their true calling (Walters & Gardner, 1986). Of course, Grandma Moses was able to largely bypass the 10-year rule because her craft skills contributed directly to her painting expertise.

Yet one must wonder if this conversion would have ever happened had her fingers not become disabled. She thus illustrates the precarious relation between interests and creativity.

Although late bloomers offer eternal hope to those of us who have yet to discover a burning interest that we can turn into overt creative achievements, that fantasy must be tempered by the fact that late bloomers must be relatively rare. Besides the inertia that keeps us going along the same path, confronting the exigencies of expertise acquisition is not easy when one is past the prime of life. The latter obstacle is especially difficult in those domains that require abstract skills, such as mathematics. Worse yet, even if we succeed in launching a second career in some creative domain, our prospects for success will seldom match those who got a head start. Nonetheless, I do not want to discourage anyone who thinks that they have a great idea that needs to be presented before the world. Frank McCourt (1930–2009) was 66 when he published his first and last major work, the memoir *Angela's Ashes*. Not only did it win a Pulitzer Prize, but it was made into a movie, and the book sold so well that he became a millionaire!

References

Barrington, D. (1770). Account of a very remarkable musician. *Philosophical Transactions of the Royal Society of London, 60*, 54–64.

Bouchard Jr., T. J. (2004). Genetic influence on human psychological traits: A survey. *Current Directions in Psychological Science, 13*, 148–151.

Carson, S. H. (2014). Cognitive disinhibition, creativity, and psychopathology. In D. K. Simonton (Ed.), *The Wiley handbook of genius* (pp. 198–221). Oxford, UK: Wiley.

Cassandro, V. J. (1998). Explaining premature mortality across fields of creative endeavor. *Journal of Personality, 66*, 805–833.

Chambers, J. A. (1964). Relating personality and biographical factors to scientific creativity. *Psychological Monographs: General and Applied, 78* (7, Whole No. 584).

Cox, C. (1926). *The early mental traits of three hundred geniuses*. Stanford, CA: Stanford University Press.

Csikszentmihalyi, M., Rathunde, K., & Whalen, S. (1993). *Talented teenagers: The roots of success and failure*. Cambridge, England: Cambridge University Press.

Day, D. (Ed.). (1949). *The autobiography of Will Rogers*. Boston: Houghton Mifflin.

Ericsson, K. A. (1996). The acquisition of expert performance: An introduction to some of the issues. In K. A. Ericsson (Ed.), *The road to expert performance: Empirical evidence from the arts and sciences, sports, and games* (pp. 1–50). Mahwah, NJ: Erlbaum.

Ericsson, K. A. (2014). Creative genius: A view from the expert-performance approach. In D. K. Simonton (Ed.), *The Wiley handbook of genius* (pp. 321–349). Oxford, UK: Wiley.

Hayes, J. R. (1989). *The complete problem solver* (2nd ed.). Hillsdale, NJ: Erlbaum.

Johnson, S. (1781). *The lives of the most eminent English poets* (Vol. 1). London: Bathurst et al.

Kozbelt, A. (2014). Musical creativity over the lifespan. In D. K. Simonton (Ed.), *The Wiley handbook of genius* (pp. 451–472). Oxford, UK: Wiley.

McCrae, R. R., & Greenberg, D. M. (2014). Openness to experience. In D. K. Simonton (Ed.), *The Wiley handbook of genius* (pp. 222–243). Oxford, UK: Wiley.

Miller, L. K. (1999). The savant syndrome: Intellectual impairment and exceptional skill. *Psychological Bulletin, 125*, 31–46.

Montour, K. (1977). William James Sidis, the broken twig. *American Psychologist, 32*, 265–279.

Radford, J. (1990). *Child prodigies and exceptional early achievers*. New York: Basic Books.

Roe, A. (1952, November). A psychologist examines 64 eminent scientists. *Scientific American, 187*(5), 21–25.

Roe, A. (1953). *The making of a scientist*. New York: Dodd, Mead.

Root-Bernstein, R. S., Bernstein, M., & Garnier, H. (1995). Correlations between avocations, scientific style, work habits, and professional impact of scientists. *Creativity Research Journal, 8*, 115–137.

Root-Bernstein, R., Allen, L., Beach, L., Bhadula, R., Fast, J., Hosey, C., Kremkow, B., Lapp, J., Lonc, K., Pawelec, K., Podufaly, A., Russ, C., Tennant, L., Vrtis, E., & Weinlander, S. (2008). Arts foster scientific success: Avocations of Nobel, National Academy, Royal Society, and Sigma Xi members. *Journal of the Psychology of Science and Technology, 1*, 51–63.

Segal, S. M., Busse, T. V., & Mansfield, R. S. (1980). The relationship of scientific creativity in the biological sciences to predoctoral accomplishments and experiences. *American Educational Research Journal, 17*, 491–502.

Simon, R. J. (1974). The work habits of eminent scientists. *Sociology of Work and Occupations, 1*, 327–335.

Simonton, D. K. (1976). Biographical determinants of achieved eminence: A multivariate approach to the Cox data. *Journal of Personality and Social Psychology, 33*, 218–226.

Simonton, D. K. (2008). Scientific talent, training, and performance: Intellect, personality, and genetic endowment. *Review of General Psychology, 12*, 28–46.

Simonton, D. K. (2012). Foresight, insight, oversight, and hindsight in scientific discovery: How sighted were Galileo's telescopic sightings? *Psychology of Aesthetics, Creativity, and the Arts, 6*, 243–254.

Simonton, D. K. (2014). Creative performance, expertise acquisition, individual-differences, and developmental antecedents: An integrative research agenda. *Intelligence, 45*, 66–73.

Simonton, D. K. (2016). Early and late bloomers among classical composers: Were the greatest geniuses also prodigies? In G. McPherson (Ed.), *Musical prodigies: Interpretations from psychology, music education, musicology and ethnomusicology* (pp. 185–197). New York: Oxford University Press.

Sulloway, F. J. (1996). *Born to rebel: Birth order, family dynamics, and creative lives*. New York: Pantheon.

Treffert, D. A. (2010). *Islands of genius: The bountiful mind of the autistic, acquired, and sudden savant*. London: Jessica Kingsley.

Walters, J., & Gardner, H. (1986). The crystallizing experience: Discovering an intellectual gift. In R. J. Sternberg & J. E. Davidson (Eds.), *Conceptions of giftedness* (pp. 306–331). New York: Cambridge University Press.

White, R. K. (1931). The versatility of genius. *Journal of Social Psychology, 2*, 460–489.

Winner, E. (2014). Child prodigies and adult genius: A weak link. In D. K. Simonton (Ed.), *The Wiley handbook of genius* (pp. 297–320). Oxford, UK: Wiley.

Chapter 10
The Promotion and Development of Interest: The Importance of Perceived Values

Chris S. Hulleman, Dustin B. Thoman, Anna-Lena Dicke, and Judith M. Harackiewicz

Why would Marcus, a high school volleyball player, spend countless hours practicing his serve in his backyard, until his arms were so tired that he could hardly move? Does the value he sees in practicing help him overcome his fatigue and maintain his passion toward volleyball? Why would Erica, a high school student, spend her weekends attending math competitions, often travelling many hours each way? Why does she enjoy math and see the importance of math to her future when so many other students do not? In the parlance of interest research, these two individuals exhibit well-developed interests in volleyball and math, respectively. In this chapter we consider how finding value and meaning in activities and topics leads to the development of interest. We also highlight a program of research that we have pursued over the last decade designed to promote interest development. Finally, we discuss how other people in our lives influence value, both directly and indirectly, and as a result, the development of interest.

Author Note:
Please direct correspondence to Chris Hulleman, Center for Advanced Study of Teaching and Learning, University of Virginia, PO Box 400877, Charlottesville, VA, 22904, chris.hulleman@virginia.edu. This research was supported by NSF (DRL 1252463 and 1534835) Grants to the first author, NSF (DRL 1420271) and NIH (1R01GM098462). Grants to the second author, and NIH Grant R01GM102703 to the last author.

C.S. Hulleman (✉)
University of Virginia, Charlottesville, VA, USA
e-mail: chris.hulleman@virginia.edu

D.B. Thoman
San Diego State University, San Diego, CA, USA

A.-L. Dicke
University of California, Irvine, CA, USA

J.M. Harackiewicz
Department of Psychology, University of Wisconsin, Madison, WI, USA

© Springer International Publishing AG 2017
P.A. O'Keefe, J.M. Harackiewicz (eds.), *The Science of Interest*,
DOI 10.1007/978-3-319-55509-6_10

The Role of Value in the Development of Interest

The word "interest" is often used in everyday conversation, such as when talking to friends about an interesting television program or when we say we are interested in taking an exercise class. These more momentary types of interest can often give way to more enduring interests, such as being interested in the well-being of our children. As often as interest is used in everyday parlance, it is no surprise that interest has captured the attention of researchers who have quite particular ways of defining interest. John Dewey defined interest as being engaged or engrossed with an activity, object or topic (Dewey, 1913, p. 17). This more fleeting version of interest described by Dewey has more recently been called *situational interest*, whereas more enduring interest that transcends particular times and places has been called *individual interest* (Hidi & Baird, 1988; Renninger, 2000). *Situational interest* can be understood as a focused attention triggered by particular content, activities or events within a particular moment. In contrast, *individual interest* is often conceptualized as a relatively enduring predisposition to actively reengage with particular contents, activities or events over time resulting in an enriched sense of value and knowledge for these contents, activities or events (Renninger & Su, 2012). Having our attention drawn to a humorous video clip is an example of situational interest, whereas Marcus and Erica's long-term interest and engagement with volleyball and math, respectively, are examples of individual interest.

Previous research suggests that both situational and individual interest can play a powerful role in predicting future choices and career paths (Harackiewicz & Knogler, 2017). Research with both laboratory and academic tasks reveals that situational and individual interest are both associated with persistence, attention, and effort (e.g., Ainley, Hidi, & Berndorff, 2002; Schiefele, 1991; Knogler, Harackiewicz, Gegenfutner, & Lewalter, 2015; O'Keefe & Linnenbrink-Garcia, 2014). A meta-analysis of over 150 studies tested the relationship between interest and performance (Schiefele, Krapp, & Winteler, 1992). The findings revealed that interest was correlated with performance in both naturalistic ($r = 0.31$) and laboratory settings ($r = 0.27$). In several longitudinal studies, Harackiewicz and colleagues followed college students throughout a semester of an introductory course (Harackiewicz, Barron, Carter, Lehto, & Elliot, 1997; Harackiewicz, Barron, Tauer, Carter, & Elliot, 2000), and in other studies, followed students from the first semester of their freshman year through graduation (Harackiewicz, Barron, Tauer, & Elliot, 2002; Harackiewicz, Durik, Barron, Linnenbrink, & Tauer, 2008). In these studies, Harackiewicz et al. found that the situational interest that students reported during and at the end of their first semester of introductory psychology predicted the number of additional psychology courses taken over the course of their academic career, as well as whether or not they decided to major in psychology. Other researchers have found similar results with middle and high school students (Meece, Wigfield, & Eccles, 1990; Updegraff, Eccles, Barber, & O'Brien, 1996; Wigfield, 1994; Xiang, Chen, & Bruene, 2005). Thus, interest in a topic or activity can have a powerful influence on people's lives, by influencing their academic performance, course-taking and major selections, how they choose to spend their free time, and post-education career pathways (Harackiewicz, Smith, & Priniski, 2016).

How does situational interest, such as that sparked in introductory courses or by an interesting television program on space flight, develop into a more enduring interest in a topic, such as majoring in psychology, or a deep interest in aerospace engineering? (Hidi & Renninger, 2006; Renninger & Hidi, 2011, 2016) have outlined a model of interest development specifying the conditions under which situational interest can develop into individual interest. In their model, it is the interaction between the person and the topic or activity that determines the extent of interest development. This interaction idea is not new, and is in fact foundational to many classic theories in social psychology, such as Lewin's field theory (1935) in which he argued that behavior is a function of both the person and the situation.

In their model, Renninger and Hidi outline four factors that contribute to interest development: knowledge and confidence, positive affect, personal value, and contextual support. As individuals learn more about a topic, they become more skilled, knowledgeable, and confident in their abilities. An increase in knowledge can bring about positive affect as individuals feel more competent and skilled through task engagement. In addition, as they spend more time with the activity, they may find personal meaning and relevance in the activity, such as when a high school student discovers that an understanding of chemistry can help him pursue his dream of becoming a pharmacist. The contextual support that students experience when engaging in an activity has the potential to enhance, or undermine, the development of interest. For example, Marcus's volleyball coach might provide additional time for him to practice his serve in the gym in the morning before school, thereby affording him the opportunity to develop his skills in a much deeper way. This additional practice might lead to increased feelings of confidence and excitement about competing in matches against challenging opponents. In contrast, if Erica's mother was overly critical of even the slightest mistake when doing her math homework, this could create negative affect, an unwillingness to take on challenge, and reduce her enthusiasm—thereby decreasing the likelihood that she takes advantage of the opportunity to participate in weekend math competitions. In both Marcus's and Erica's situations, the contextual supports offered by a coach and a parent, respectively, serve to either promote or undermine their on-going interests.

In our research, we have focused on the role of perceived value for a topic or activity in the development of interest (Harackiewicz & Hulleman, 2010). As social psychologists, we noted the overlap in the classic expectancy-value models of achievement motivation (e.g., Atkinson, 1957; Eccles et al., 1983) and interest theory. Expectancy-value models of motivation posit that an individual will be motivated to engage in a task to the extent that they feel they can be successful at it (expectancy) and perceive the task as being important to them in some way (value). In this model, tasks are important because they are fun and enjoyable (intrinsic value), are useful and relevant to important goals (utility value), and are important to the person's sense of self (attainment value). In this work we focused on intrinsic and utility value because they are the most malleable in educational contexts, due to their close connection with specific academic tasks (Hulleman, Durik, Schweigert & Harackiewicz, 2008).

Research utilizing the Eccles et al. (1983) perspective indicates that perceived task values tend to be associated with achievement choices, such as course enrollment decisions, free-time activities, and intentions, whereas expectancies for success tend to be associated with performance (e.g., Jacobs, Lanza, Osgood, Eccles, & Wigfield, 2002). In addition, longitudinal research has revealed that task values play an important role in the development of interest (Durik & Harackiewicz, 2007; Hulleman et al., 2008). For example, Hulleman et al. (2008) assessed perceived intrinsic and utility value in two contexts: an introductory psychology course for undergraduates and a summer football camp for high school athletes. Task values were measured at the mid-point of a 15-week semester and a 4-day summer football camp. Interest in psychology was assessed at the end of the semester, and interest in football was assessed at the end of camp. The results indicated that students' and athletes' perceptions of intrinsic and utility value for their course topic and sport, respectively, were associated with their interest at the end of the semester and the summer camp. Other researchers have also found that utility value is related to both interest and performance (e.g., Bong, 2001; Cole, Bergin, & Whitaker, 2008; Durik, Vida, & Eccles, 2006; Gaspard, Dicke, Flunger, Schreier et al., 2015; Mac Iver, Stipek, & Daniels, 1991; Simons, Dewitte, & Lens, 2004). Thus the perception of value can be critically important in the development and deepening of interest.

Interventions that Promote Value and Interest

These correlational findings indicate the critical role of value perceptions in interest development, but also raise questions of causality. Can we influence students' perceptions of value and thus promote interest? In a foundational series of laboratory experiments, Durik and colleagues (Durik & Harackiewicz, 2007; Durik, Schechter, Noh, Rozek, & Harackiewicz, 2015; Schechter, Durik, Miyamoto, & Harackiewicz, 2011) manipulated the availability of information about task value while teaching participants a novel mental math technique, and examined the effects of this intervention on subsequent task interest. During this learning session, participants in the utility value condition were instructed how the new math technique could be useful in everyday life, using examples such as calculating tips at restaurants and when shopping. Participants in the control condition did not receive this information. Following the learning session, participants solved as many multiplication problems as they could in 5 min. After they completed the problems, they were asked to indicate how interested they were in the new technique. The results indicated that directly communicating the utility value of math enhanced interest for those with initially high levels of math confidence compared to the control condition, whereas the intervention did not increase interest for those with lower levels of confidence, and even seemed to undermine interest in some studies.

These findings raised questions about other ways to promote the perception of value, and led to a new utility value experimental paradigm, in which participants were encouraged to make personalized connections to the material for themselves, instead of being told how the material was valuable in general (Hulleman, Godes, Hendricks, & Harackiewicz, 2010, Study 1). The experiment was conducted in the laboratory with the same basic procedures as in the Durik and Harackiewicz (2007) study in which participants learned a new mental math technique and then performed a set of multiplication problems. The difference was in how utility value was manipulated. In the first of these studies (Hulleman et al., 2010), participants were asked to write about how they could apply the mental math technique to their own lives after they had learned the technique (i.e., self-generated utility value, instead of being told about the usefulness of the math task, as in the Durik study). Participants in the control group wrote an essay that was unrelated to the mental math technique. The results indicated that the self-generated utility value intervention increased interest in the math technique compared to the control group for all participants, on average, regardless of how competent participants thought they were at math. However, further analyses showed that the intervention was particularly beneficial for participants who did not expect to do well in math. In fact, participants with low success expectancies were as interested in the technique as the participants with high success expectancies in either the control group or the utility value group. The participants who reported the least amount of interest in the math technique were control group participants with low success expectancies. The results from this study suggest that the self-generated utility value manipulation was particularly successful for students who lacked confidence in their math ability (for reviews, see Durik, Hulleman, & Harackiewicz, 2015; Harackiewicz, Tibbetts, Canning, & Hyde, 2014).

The results from these two different types of utility value manipulations (directly communicated, self-generated) seemed to indicate that individuals respond differently to manipulations of utility value based on their levels of confidence. Canning and Harackiewicz (2015) conducted a series of studies that examined the effects of both directly communicated and self-generated utility value interventions within the same study. Using similar procedures, Canning and Harackiewicz (Study 1) found that the self-generated utility value manipulation raised interest for less confident students and had no effect for more confident students, whereas the directly communicated intervention undermined interest for the less confident students but increased interest for the more confident students. In addition, Canning and Harackiewicz found that the negative effects of directly communicated utility value for less confident students were ameliorated when students were also asked to generate their own utility value examples (i.e., students were first given information about the utility value of the math task and then prompted to write an essay about how the math task related to their own lives; Study 2), or when the directly communicated utility value information contained references to daily lives (as opposed to careers and school, Study 3). These results clarify previous findings, and suggest that the positive effects of the self-generated utility value manipulation for less confident students may result from the opportunity to generate their own sense of utility value and engage within their own comfort zone, instead of being presented with utility value information that might be perceived as threatening (Durik, Schechter et al., 2015). This could also explain why directly communicated utility value was more effective for less confident students when it referred to daily life instead of career and schools. Everyday life examples are less consequential for students than future educational and career pathways, and this may reduce the anxiety aroused by the prospect of not doing well on an academic task, and thereby open students up to experience value and interest with the activity.

Overall, the results of these laboratory experiments suggest that we can help students develop interest by highlighting the utility value of the material. Although the experimental laboratory method allows us to determine causality and refine our experimental manipulations so that they can be as effective as possible, laboratory studies have limited generalizability to real-world contexts (Harackiewicz & Barron, 2004; Hulleman & Barron, 2016). In contrast, the randomized field experiment combines the ability to make causal inference based on the experimental method with the naturalistic setting inherent to observational studies. The power of this approach is that it can generate information that furthers theoretical understanding and also provides practical information for practitioners who work in the real world (Cook, 2002).

Thus, a series of randomized field experiments were conducted to test the self-generated utility value intervention in educational settings (Harackiewicz, Canning et al., 2016; Hulleman et al., 2010, Study 2; Hulleman, Hendricks, & Harackiewicz, 2007; Hulleman & Harackiewicz, 2009; Hulleman, Kosovich, Barron, & Daniel, 2017). In the first field experiment, utility value was manipulated in several college high school classes using the self-generated utility value intervention developed in the earlier laboratory research (Hulleman et al., 2010, Study 1), and effects on self-reports of utility value and interest were examined. In the first two college studies, introductory psychology ($N = 237$; Hulleman et al., 2010) and statistics students ($N = 44$; Hulleman et al., 2007) received an essay assignment to complete within 3 weeks following their first course exam. In a third college study, general psychology students ($N = 357$; Hulleman et al., 2017) received an online essay prompt to complete as part of their regular course assignments immediately following the first and second course exams. In a fourth college study, biology students received an essay assignment via email in each of the three sections of the course, approximately 2 weeks before midterm exams ($N = 1040$; Harackiewicz, Canning et al., 2016).

In all of these RCT studies, all students selected a topic that they had studied previously. In the utility value conditions, students then wrote about how this topic applied to their lives in some way, whereas students in the control condition wrote a summary of what they had learned about the topic. At the end of the semester, students' interest in classroom activities, the content being learned, intentions to take additional courses in the subject, and careers related to the subject were assessed via an in-class or online survey. Based on prior research, we examined whether the utility value intervention worked better for student low in either initial course performance (e.g., exam grades) or their initial success expectancies from the beginning of the year. The results replicated our laboratory findings (Hulleman et al., 2010, Study 1). Students with low exam scores or low success expectancies reported higher levels of interest in psychology (or science, or greater inclination to take more statistics courses) in the utility value condition than the control condition. Students with high exam scores or high success expectancies reported equally high amounts of interest at the end of the semester regardless of experimental condition. Thus, we were able to promote interest development in college and high school classes with a simple utility value intervention. Furthermore, our mediation analyses revealed that the intervention worked, at least in part, by promoting students' perceptions of utility value (Hulleman et al., 2010; Hulleman & Harackiewicz, 2009).

The results from these randomized trials corroborate the laboratory findings and confirm the predictive power of value in the promotion of interest. The self-generated utility value intervention tested in our laboratory and randomized field studies was shown to increase students' perception of value for the learning material, and was particularly beneficial for students who had low success expectancies and/or low performance in the course (Durik, Hulleman et al., 2015; Harackiewicz, Smith et al., 2014). In other words, this intervention was most effective in promoting interest for students who most need help—those who are struggling academically or lack confidence in their skills. This type of intervention has also been effective in promoting performance for underrepresented students in science classes (Harackiewicz et al., 2016, Tibbetts, Harackiewicz, Priniski, & Canning, 2016), underperforming students in college psychology (Hulleman et al., 2017), and low confidence students in high school science classes (Hulleman & Harackiewicz, 2009). In addition, the directly communicated utility value intervention was shown to promote interest for students high in confidence, and for all students when combined with self-generated utility value (Canning & Harackiewicz, 2015).

In a study inspired by these utility value interventions, Gaspard and colleagues developed a classroom intervention aimed to foster students' utility value beliefs in mathematics within a high school context (Gaspard, Dicke, Flunger, Brisson et al., 2015). Importantly, the intervention contained both directly communicated and self-generated utility value, which was shown to promote interest for all students (Canning & Harackiewicz, 2015). Conducted in Germany, students in the math classrooms were randomly assigned to one of two utility value conditions or a control condition. Students in the intervention conditions took part in a 90-min researcher-led intervention session, and students in the control condition were put on a waitlist to receive the intervention at a later time. The intervention session consisted of two parts. In the first part, information about the utility of mathematics in daily life and for future careers was directly communicated to students in both intervention conditions. In the second part, students in the *essay* condition wrote about how mathematics applied to their lives in some way. Students in the *quotations* condition read quotations about the utility of mathematics articulated by young adults. The results indicated that both intervention conditions successfully fostered students' perceptions of utility value up to 5 months after the intervention compared to the control condition (Gaspard, Dicke, Flunger, Brisson et al., 2015). In contrast to previous findings, the intervention was equally effective for students with high and low success expectancies.

Researchers have also focused on correlational and experimental investigations on the role of specific types of utility values that seem important to promote broader interest in scientific fields and science research. Scientific fields are stereotypically viewed as providing a wealth of opportunities to fulfill intrinsic values, such as curiosity and passion for scientific discovery. But these fields are also seen as lacking opportunities to fulfill communal, or prosocial, values of working with or helping others, or giving back to society, more broadly (e.g., Diekman et al., 2010; Morgan, Isaac, & Sansone, 2001). In correlational studies with undergraduate students, researchers found that those who perceived science as providing more opportunities to fulfill their communal values reported greater interest in science careers (Brown, Thoman, Smith, & Diekman, 2015). In complementary experimental research, researchers provided students with descriptions of scientific research that included connections to communal values (versus other important values or control conditions that just described the research). Students randomly assigned to read the research descriptions with communal values connections rated that research as more important, felt greater interest in that research, and expressed greater motivation to pursue research careers (Brown, Smith, Thoman, Allen, & Muragishi, 2015). Several studies have found that making communal or prosocial value connections in science is particularly important for women, underrepresented minorities, and first-generation college students (Allen, Muragishi, Smith, Thoman, & Brown, 2015; Diekman et al., 2010; Harackiewicz et al., 2015; Jackson, Galvez, Landa, Buonora, & Thoman, 2016; Smith, Cech, Metz, Huntoon, & Moyer, 2014; Thoman, Brown, Mason, Harmsen, & Smith, 2015).

In sum, the utility value interventions reviewed here contained two of the four main factors identified as critical in the development of interest (Renninger & Hidi, 2011): perceived value and contextual support. The interventions, delivered in educational contexts, served as contextual support that facilitated the discovery of value, which provided the opportunity for students to develop interest. Furthermore, these interventions were designed to directly influence students' perceptions of value by prompting them to generate written reflections and/or to read examples making connections between the topics and their lives. These types of direct, explicit interventions are only one type of situational influence on value and interest. In the next section, we review several additional situational factors that have the potential to influence perceived values and interest development.

Value and Interest in the Social Context

The intervention research described above demonstrates that structured activities within specific learning contexts can be utilized to successfully promote interest by enhancing value. Outside of specific learning contexts that are rich with scaffolds to promote value perception and interest development, however, individuals often look to others as a source of value. For example, our interactions with others in the social context, either directly or indirectly, have the potential to play a significant role in the development of interest (McCaslin, 2009). Although interest is experienced at the individual level, the social contexts in which a person's interest develops can shape that development (for better or worse) through multiple social psychological processes.

Values can be transmitted intentionally and directly (e.g., most parents have the conscious goal of sharing their values with their children) or they can be transmitted unintentionally and indirectly (e.g., through inferences about others' values from their behaviors). Through both routes, individuals create meaning from these shared values, and these values have important implications for interest development. We focus here on some, but not all, of the ways in which the social context can both *directly* and *indirectly* influence interest development through effects on values. Specifically, we explore the role that parents, teachers, and peers play in influencing individual's perception of value and subsequent development of interest. Other chapters in this volume highlight additional routes of social influence on interest (see Master, Butler, & Walton, 2017, Chap. 2; Thoman, Sansone, & Geerling, 2017, Chap. 11).

Direct Sharing of Values to Influence Interest Development Unlike other social roles, the roles of parents and teachers come with expectations of sharing and teaching values. Parents and teachers both want to influence the activities that children and students pursue and the interests they develop. There is likely variability in the extent to which parents and teachers see value sharing as central to their role, but people in these roles seem mostly likely to both directly and indirectly share values in an effort to influence their children's or students' interest development. As Alexander, Johnson, and Leibham (2015) point out in their work with young children, parents and teachers are important socializing agents who co-regulate the development of interests. Parents respond to the interests expressed by their children, but also shape their children's interest development through their actions. For instance, Leibham, Alexander, and Johnson (2005) found that parents' provision of nonfiction books during very early stages of interest development fostered and maintained their children's science interests in the long term.

Eccles and colleagues have described the value transmission between parents and children with respect to achievement values. Their work primarily focuses on differences in how socialization of values translates to gender differences in STEM (science, technology, engineering and mathematics) achievement and choices (Fredricks, Simpkins, & Eccles, 2004; Jacobs, Vernon, & Eccles, 2005), in addition to the transmission of differences in performance expectations for boys and girls (Jacobs & Eccles, 2000). What is clear from these data is that parents' valuing of achievement tasks for their sons and daughters influences their children's subjective values for those achievement domains (Gniewosz, Eccles, & Noack, 2015; Jacobs, Davis-Kean, Bleeker, Eccles, & Malanchuk, 2005).

Based on this research, and the success of the high school utility value intervention (Hulleman & Harackiewicz, 2009), Harackiewicz, Rozek, Hulleman, and Hyde

(2012) conducted a utility-value intervention study with parents which demonstrates the role of parental transmission of values. Parents of 10th and 11th grade students in an ongoing longitudinal study participated; half of the parents were randomly assigned to receive information about how learning math and science was important for their teenagers' lives (i.e., highlighting utility value for their children), and the other half did not. The intervention consisted of two brochures mailed to their homes and access to a web-site that emphasized the importance of math and science for teens, and provided many resources. Results showed that sending utility value information to parents led to increased math and science course-taking by their children in 11th and 12th grade (Harackiewicz et al., 2012), as well as higher ACT scores (Rozek et al., 2017), and that this effect was partially explained by an increase in parental value for math and science, and increase in discussions between parents and teens about math and science. The intervention increased parents' perceptions of the utility value of math and science for their teen, which lead to an increase in their teen's perceptions of the utility value of math and science. Further analyses revealed an interesting pathway for the course-taking effect: parental values, as well as teens' perceptions of parental values, led to teens' increased valuing of math and science, which was then the strongest predictor of course-taking in 12th grade ($\beta = 0.22$, $p < 0.05$; Rozek et al., 2014). Thus, the utility value intervention directed at parents altered both the direct communication of value (through conversations) and indirect communication of value (through teens' perceptions of parental values). We discuss this indirect pathway more in the next section.

Teachers can also influence student value directly by telling students why the material they are learning now is relevant to their personal interests and future goals. Schreier et al. (2014) showed that high school students' values for mathematics was enhanced by teaching that highlighted the relevance of the learning material for the out-of-school context. Student and teachers' perceptions of relevance-oriented teaching not only related to students' current value perceptions, but also positively affected their development over the course of 5 months. Research by Patall, Dent, Oyer, and Winn (2013) shows that when high school students perceive their teachers to provide a reason for their learning activities, it is associated with increased value and interest. Using longitudinal datasets, further research has shown the importance of the perceived meaningfulness of learning material for the development of not only academic values (Roeser, Eccles & Sameroff, 1998), but also interest and choices (Wang, 2012).

In addition to parents and teachers, it seems reasonable that peers can also intentionally shape one another's interests through values (Ryan, 2000, Parker, Rubin, Erath, Wojslawowicz, & Buskirk, 2006). For example, students who perceive little value in biology might try to convince their friends that the class is unimportant and to spend time hanging out rather than studying. Or an adolescent's friends might try to convince her that studying is less cool and interesting than playing video games (suggesting that she should not like or do it). These kinds of examples can be negative or positive to illustrate that peers can try to shape one another's values as a means to influence interest development and continued behavioral engagement with some activity or topic. However, there is little empirical research investigating the effects of such peer pressure on students' academic motivation and values (see Ryan, 2000 for review).

Indirect Sharing of Values and the Influence of the Social Context on Interest Development In addition to making sense of the values that others directly share, people also draw inferences about others' values to decipher their place in their social world. A fundamental principle from social psychology is that people actively create meaning in their social worlds by looking to others and establishing their roles and identities relative to others (Ross, Lepper, & Ward, 2010). That is, people are not simply passive recipients of information; people strive to understand the context we are in, our place in it, and our attitudes and beliefs about it. An important part of self-development is learning, interpreting, and internalizing others' views of us (Cooley, 1902; Meade, 1934; Tice & Wallace, 2003), and identity development involves negotiating our self-concepts and social identities with other people through social interactions (Swann & Bosson, 2008).

Although often neglected in research on development of the self, our interests are an important part of our social identities (see Vallerand, 2017, this volume). The activities we choose to pursue and the kinds of activities that capture our interests are rarely private knowledge. In everyday social interactions people share their daily activities and interests, and the kinds of activities they share become an important part of their social identity (Eccles, 2009; McCaslin, 2009). During such interactions, people draw inferences about one another based on their interests, and just as people become aware of others' views of their talents and capabilities (Bandura, 1986), people also attend to others' judgments and appraisals about their interests (see Thoman, Sansone, & Geerling, 2017, Chap. 2).

Thus, even when others may not intentionally or explicitly communicate their values, an individual's perceptions and active understanding of others' values can shape our interest. In a recent study of high school biology students, Hulleman, Dicke, Kosovich, and Thoman (2016) measured students' perceptions of their peers values for biology (e.g., *"Most of my classmates think biology is important."*), students' personal utility value for biology (e.g., *"How relevant is the course material to your future career plans?"*), and their interest in biology (e.g., *"How much do you enjoy biology?," "Would you be interested in receiving more information about the benefits of biology, and science in general, for your future life? (Yes/No)"*). As presented in Fig. 10.1, the results revealed that perceptions of peers' values in biology predicted students' own values, which then predicted how personally interested students were in biology (Hulleman et al., 2016). This study demonstrates that students are actively generating inferences about their classmates' values, and these perceptions in turn influence the student's own values and interest. This study corroborates previous research findings showing peers' influence on students' academic engagement—especially in teenage years (Fredricks et al., 2004; Juvonen, Espinoza, & Knifsend, 2012; Reschly & Christenson, 2012). More precisely, perceived classmates' valuing of mathematics has been found to be positively associated with students' interest, value beliefs, and positive emotions in math lessons (Frenzel, Goetz, Pekrun, & Watt, 2010; Frenzel, Pekrun, & Goetz, 2007, Schreier et al., 2014).

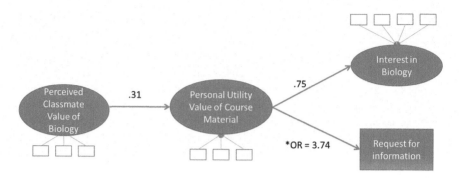

Fig. 10.1 Structural equation path model of the relationship between perceived classmates value, personal value, and interest in biology (*Note:* Unless otherwise specified, values are standardized coefficients from a structural equation model. All values are significant at $p < 0.05$. * Odds ratio from a logistic regression. For details see Hulleman et al., 2016)

Relatedly, studies of friendship groups reveal that values in general develop similarly within peer groups (e.g., Kindermann, 2007; Ryan, 2001).

We can think of this indirect process as a positive influence on value by perceiving that others also value and are interested in the topic. However, the same processes could work to undermine value if other students are disengaged in learning, which could be construed as a lack of value for biology. For example, during a classroom lecture a student could observe his peers seeming to be bored and inattentive. Even though the student is somewhat interested in the topic, he might perceive himself to be the only one who seems to care about biology. This false consensus effect (i.e., overestimating the extent to which our perceptions are typical of others; Ross, Greene, & House, 1977) can facilitate the student changing his attitude about biology in a negative manner in order to align with the perceived group norm (i.e., pluralistic ignorance; Prentice & Miller, 1993). Conversely, a student who lacks value for the topic might perceive the same classroom as validating her attitude, thereby further cementing her lack of value.

Further Questions

Despite the importance of social contexts for interest development, relatively little empirical work has focused on the ways in which other people promote or hinder an individual's interest development. One reason for the slow development in this area of research likely reflects the added methodological and statistical complexity of moving beyond the individual as the unit of analysis. Theory that incorporates specific routes of social influence in psychological models of interest is growing rapidly (as seen in several chapters in this book), and we anticipate an oncoming wave of empirical data in this area. Given our focus here on the role of values in promoting interest, we identify two key unanswered questions that follow from our review.

The Role of Social Influence Change Across Stages of Interest Development Although other people play an important role in shaping each other's values and interests, we expect that effects of social influences are not constant across developmental stages of interest. That is, both direct and indirect sharing of values should have differing effects on interest for someone who is in the early stages of interest development compared to the later stages of having a well-developed interest. This hypothesis is based on two principles. First, in the process of developing a strong interest people likely establish a schema for values related to that topic or activity. For newly sparked interests, a schema for the utility value of the topic or activity may be unknown and never previously considered. Individuals might look to others to fill this knowledge gap (either intentionally or not). For a woman who has a well-developed interest in mountain biking, she has likely already formulated a coherent narrative for why she does it (including what values this activity supports), and would not likely be heavily influenced by her peers. In contrast, it seems far more likely that the woman's interest in mountain biking could be influenced by others at the point when that interest was just starting to develop, such as when she was still learning about the activity and exploring how it related to her other values and goals.

Second, if interests are part of our social identities, we are likely to share that interest with others during the process of interest development, thereby instigating an integration of this interest with our social identity. For Isabel who is just learning to ski and really likes it, that interest will be supported if her parents and peers express excitement for her newfound interest and talk with her about why they like or value skiing, such as the value of being healthy and active or enjoying the mountain scenery. In contrast, if her parents and peers express a strong devaluation of cold-weather activities and point out the many costs of skiing, Isabel may be less likely to maintain that interest given the potential social consequences of persisting. Thus, Isabel's interest is not only a function of her engagement with skiing, but also ongoing social negotiations with others about her identity. In the case of an already well-developed interest, if Marcus has spent years playing and talking about volleyball, he has likely already established this interest in his important relationships. It would be unlikely for Marcus to be influenced by someone who questions the value of volleyball because it would seem inconsistent with his already well-established identity. Thus, his interest in volleyball is likely already seen by others as part of his social identity. New people in his life (e.g., a new neighbor or new friend) who might question this interest would also likely carry less weight compared to all of the people in Marcus' life who already see volleyball as part of his self-definition.

Based on both principles, we would expect that both direct and indirect sharing of values would have a stronger influence on interest development in the early phases. We know of no empirical work investigating this link, but research testing theoretically-grounded predictions about what factors influence interest development differently across stages of development is needed. This work would entail identifying the links between interest development and one's motivations for when and how to actively construct meaning and narratives that position one's interests in a social context.

Are People More Likely to Develop New Interests or Change Interests When They form New Social Groups? People join specific groups on the basis of interest, such as bird-watching groups. Thus, interest in a topic or activity can draw people to others who share that activity, and surrounding oneself with others who share an interest should only serve to strengthen it. However, when people change social groups for reasons other than interest (e.g., moving to a new city or school), we expect that one's interests become more fluid or malleable because of changes in their social context. Educational research suggests that transition periods are often critical to students' academic development and well-being, and that students need additional support during these times (e.g., Anderson, Jacobs, Schramm, & Splittgerber, 2000). If other people influence each other's interest development by sharing values, it follows that life transitions in which one's social group changes should create a context in which interests are particularly malleable. When kids change schools, teenagers start college, or adults begin new jobs, they leave behind many relationships (though some likely persist, especially with greater advances in communication technology). One outcome of this change is that people adapt their social identities in order to fit new friendships and other relationships. Similar to other aspects of one's self-concept, interests, too, should be more malleable in such circumstances. If a boy who loves to play video games moves to a new neighborhood where all of his new peers only want to play outside, the boy is likely to create a new understanding of what it means to be interested in and spend time playing video games. Social influences may push him to spend more time outside than playing video games, talk less about video games with others, and develop a new values-based understanding of what it means to be seen by others as a gamer (i.e., video game enthusiast). Similarly, a girl who has always liked math but never had friends interested in math may find new support (socially) to develop her interest when she moves to a new school where most of the students are math and science focused. Interest researchers have yet to explore how such transitions matter for the development of interest, but as the examples above suggest, we expect that changes in people's social contexts play an important role in why interest should be more malleable during these times.

Conclusion

The fundamental role that value plays in the development and promotion of interest opens up a gateway for the social context to directly and indirectly influence interest development. Although the majority of the extant research literature is focused on direct interventions to influence value, and thereby interest, we outlined several indirect pathways through which the social context can also contribute to individual's perceptions of value. We encourage researchers to explore the direct and indirect influences of the social context on value through both observational and experimental studies so that we can discover additional mechanisms that unlock the interest development process.

References

Ainley, M., Hidi, S., & Berndorff, D. (2002). Interest, learning, and the psychological processes that mediate their relationship. *Journal of Educational Psychology, 94*, 545–561.

Alexander, J. M., Johnson, K. E., & Leibham, M. E. (2015). Emerging individual interests related to science in young children. In K. A. Renninger, M. Nieswandt, & S. Hidi (Eds.), *Interest in mathematics and science learning* (pp. 261–280). Washington, DC: American.

Allen, J., Muragishi, G. A., Smith, J. L., Thoman, D. B., & Brown, E. R. (2015). To grab and to hold: Cultivating communal goals to overcome cultural and structural barriers in first generation college students' science interest. *Translational Issues in Psychological Science, 1*, 331–341.

Anderson, L. W., Jacobs, J., Schramm, S., & Splittgerber, F. (2000). School transitions: Beginning of the end or new beginning? *International Journal of Educational Research, 33*, 325–339.

Atkinson, J. W. (1957). Motivational determinants of risk-taking behavior. *Psychological Review, 64*(6), 359–372.

Bandura, A. (1986). *Social foundations of thought and action: A social cognitive theory.* Englewood Cliffs, NJ: Prentice-Hall.

Bong, M. (2001). Role of self-efficacy and task-value in predicting college students' course performance and future enrollment intentions. *Contemporary Educational Psychology, 26*(4), 553–570.

Brown, E. R., Smith, J. L., Thoman, D. B., Allen, J., & Muragishi, G. (2015). From bench to bedside: A communal utility value intervention to enhance students' science motivation. *Journal of Educational Psychology, 107*, 1116–1135.

Brown, E. R., Thoman, D. B., Smith, J. L., & Diekman, A. B. (2015). Closing the communal goal gap: The importance of communal affordances in science career motivation. *Journal of Applied Social Psychology, 45*, 662–673.

Canning, E. A., & Harackiewicz, J. M. (2015). Teach it, don't preach it: The differential effects of directly-communicated and self-generated utility–value information. *Motivation Science, 1*(1), 47–71.

Cole, J. S., Bergin, D. A., & Whittaker, T. A. (2008). Predicting student achievement for low stakes tests with effort and task value. *Contemporary Educational Psychology, 33*(4), 609–624.

Cook, T. D. (2002). Randomized experiments in educational policy research: A critical examination of the reasons the educational evaluation community has offered for not doing them. *Educational Evaluation and Policy Analysis, 24*(3), 175–199.

Cooley, C. H. (1902). *Human nature and the social order.* New York: Scribner.

Dewey, J. (1913). *Interest and effort in education.* Cambridge, MA: Riverside Press.

Diekman, A. B., Brown, E. R., Johnston, A. M., & Clark, E. K. (2010). Seeking congruity between goals and roles: A new look at why women opt out of science, technology, engineering, and mathematics careers. *Psychological Science, 21*, 1051–1057.

Durik, A. M., & Harackiewicz, J. M. (2007). Different strokes for different folks: How personal interest moderates the effects of situational factors on task interest. *Journal of Educational Psychology, 99*, 597–610.

Durik, A. M., Hulleman, C. S., & Harackiewicz, J. M. (2015). One size fits some: Instructional enhancements to promote interest don't work the same for everyone. In K. A. Renninger, M. Nieswandt, & S. Hidi (Eds.), *Interest in mathematics and science learning* (pp. 49–62). Washington, DC: American Educational Research Association.

Durik, A. M., Shechter, O., Noh, M. S., Rozek, C. R., & Harackiewicz, J. M. (2015). What if I can't? Perceived competence as a moderator of the effects of utility value information on situational interest and performance. *Motivation and Emotion, 39*, 104–118.

Durik, A. M., Vida, M., & Eccles, J. S. (2006). Task values and ability beliefs as predictors of high school literacy choices: A developmental analysis. *Journal of Educational Psychology, 98*, 382–393.

Eccles, J. (2009). Who am I and what am I going to do with my life? Personal and collective identities as motivators of action. *Educational Psychologist, 44*, 78–89.

Eccles, J., Adler, T. F., Futterman, R., Goff, S. B., Kaczala, C. M., Meece, J. L., & Midgley, C. (1983). Expectancies, values, and academic behaviors. In J. T. Spence (Ed.), *Achievement and achievement motives: Psychological and sociological approaches* (pp. 75–146). San Francisco, CA: W. H. Freeman.

Fredricks, J. A., Blumenfeld, P. C., & Paris, A. H. (2004). School engagement: Potential of the concept, state of the evidence. *Review of Educational Research, 74*(1), 59–109.

Frenzel, A. C., Goetz, T., Pekrun, R., & Watt, H. M. G. (2010). Development of mathematics interest in adolescence: Influences of gender, family, and school context. *Journal of Research on Adolescence, 20*(2), 507–537. doi:10.1111/j.1532-7795.2010.00645.x.

Frenzel, A. C., Pekrun, R., & Goetz, T. (2007). Perceived learning environments and students' emotional experiences: A multilevel analysis of mathematics classrooms. *Learning and Instruction, 17*(5), 478–493.

Gaspard, H., Dicke, A.-L., Flunger, B., Brisson, B. M., Häfner, I., Nagengast, B., & Trautwein, U. (2015). Fostering adolescents' value beliefs for mathematics with a relevance intervention in the classroom. *Developmental Psychology, 51*(9), 1226–1240. doi:10.1037/dev0000028.

Gaspard, H., Dicke, A.-L., Flunger, B., Schreier, B., Häfner, I., Trautwein, U., & Nagengast, B. (2015). More value through greater differentiation: Gender differences in value beliefs about math. *Journal of Educational Psychology, 107*, 663–677. doi:10.1037/edu0000003.

Gniewosz, B., Eccles, J. S., & Noack, P. (2015). Early adolescents' development of academic self-concept and intrinsic task value: The role of contextual feedback. *Journal of Research on Adolescence, 25*(3), 459–473.

Harackiewicz, J. M., & Barron, K. E. (2004). Conducting social psychological research in educational settings: "Lessons we learned in school". In A. T. Panter, C. Sansone, & C. C. Morf (Eds.), *The sage handbook of methods in social psychology* (pp. 471–484). Thousand Oaks, CA: SAGE Publications.

Harackiewicz, J. M., Barron, K. E., Carter, S. M., Lehto, A. T., & Elliot, A. J. (1997). Predictors and consequences of achievement goals in the college classroom: Maintaining interest and making the grade. *Journal of Personality and Social Psychology, 73*, 1284–1295.

Harackiewicz, J. M., Barron, K. E., Tauer, J. M., Carter, S. M., & Elliot, A. J. (2000). Short-term and long-term consequences of achievement goals: Predicting interest and performance over time. *Journal of Educational Psychology, 92*, 316–330.

Harackiewicz, J. M., Barron, K. E., Tauer, J. M., & Elliot, A. J. (2002). Predicting success in college: A longitudinal study of achievement goals and ability measures as predictors of interest and performance from freshman year through graduation. *Journal of Educational Psychology, 94*, 562–575.

Harackiewicz, J. M., Canning, E. A., Tibbetts, Y., Priniski, S. J., & Hyde, J. S. (2016). Closing achievement gaps with a utility-value intervention: Disentangling race and social class. *Journal of Personality and Social Psychology, 111*(5), 745–765. doi:10.1037/pspp0000075.

Harackiewicz, J. M., Durik, A. M., Barron, K. E., Linnenbrink, E. A., & Tauer, J. M. (2008). The role of achievement goals in the development of interest: Reciprocal relations between achievement goals, interest and performance. *Journal of Educational Psychology, 100*, 105–122.

Harackiewicz, J. M., & Hulleman, C. S. (2010). The importance of interest: The role of achievement goals and task values in promoting the development of interest. *Social and Personality Psychology Compass, 4*, 42–52. doi:10.1111/j.1751-9004.2009.00207.x.

Harackiewicz, J. M., & Knogler, M. (2017). Interest: Theory and application. In A. J. Elliot, D. Yeager, & C. Dweck (Eds.), *Handbook of competence and motivation (Second Edition): Theory and application*. New York: Guilford.

Harackiewicz, J. M., Rozek, C. S., Hulleman, C. S., & Hyde, J. S. (2012). Helping parents to moti-vate adolescents in mathematics and science: An experimental test of a utility-value interven-tion. *Psychological Science, 43*, 899–906. doi:10.1177/0956797611435530.

Harackiewicz, J. M., Smith, J. L., & Priniski, S. J. (2016). Interest matters: The importance of promoting interest in education. *Policy Insights from the Behavioral and Brain Sciences, 3*, 220–227. doi:10.1177/2372732216655542.

Harackiewicz, J. M., Tibbetts, Y, Canning, E. A., & Hyde, J. S. (2014). Harnessing values to pro-mote motivation in education. In S. Karabenick & T. Urden (Eds.), Motivational interventions, *Advances in motivation and achievement* (Vol. 18, pp 71–105). Emerald Group Publishing.

Hidi, S., & Baird, W. (1988). Strategies for increasing text-based interest and students' recall of expository texts. *Reading Research Quarterly, 23*, 465–483.

Hidi, S., & Renninger, K. A. (2006). The four-phase model of interest development. *Educational Psychologist, 41*, 111–127.

Hulleman, C. S., & Barron, K. E. (2016). Motivation interventions in education: Bridging theory, research, and practice. In L. Corno & E. M. Anderman (Eds.), *Handbook of educational psy-chology* (3rd ed., pp. 160–171). New York: Routledge, Taylor and Francis.

Hulleman, C. S., Dicke, A., Kosovich, J., & Thoman, D. (2016, January). *The role of perceived social norms and parents' value in the development of interest in biology*. Poster presented at the annual meeting of the Society for Personality and Social Psychology. San Diego, CA.

Hulleman, C. S., Durik, A. M., Schweigert, S., & Harackiewicz, J. M. (2008). Task values, achieve-ment goals, and interest: An integrative analysis. *Journal of Educational Psychology, 100*, 398–416.

Hulleman, C. S., Godes, O., Hendricks, B., & Harackiewicz, J. M. (2010). Enhancing interest and performance with a utility value intervention. *Journal of Educational Psychology, 102*(4), 880–895.

Hulleman, C. S., & Harackiewicz, J. M. (2009). Promoting interest and performance in high school science classes. *Science, 326*, 1410–1412.

Hulleman, C. S., Hendricks, B., & Harackiewicz, J. M. (2007, April). *The role of utility value in promoting classroom interest*. Paper presented at the annual meeting of the American Educational Research Association, Chicago.

Hulleman, C. S., Kosovich, J. J., Barron, K. E., & Daniel, D. (2017). Making connections: Replicating and extending the utility value intervention in the classroom. *Journal of Educational Psychology, 109*(3), 387–404.

Jackson, M.C., Galvez, G., Landa, I., Buonora, P., & Thoman, D. B. (2016). Science that matters: The importance of a cultural connection in underrepresented students' science pursuit. *CBE Life Sciences Education, 15*, 1–12.

Jacobs, J. E., & Eccles, J. S. (2000). Parents, task values, and real-life achievement-related choices. In C. Sansone & J. M. Harackiewicz (Eds.), *Intrinsic and extrinsic motivation: The search for optimal motivation and performance* (pp. 405–439). New York: Academic Press.

Jacobs, J. E., Davis-Kean, P., Bleeker, M., Eccles, J. S., & Malanchuk, O. (2005). I can, but I don't want to: The impact of parents, interests, and activities on gender differences in math. In A. Gallagher & J. Kaufman (Eds.), *Gender difference in mathematics* (pp. 246–263). New York: Cambridge University Press.

Jacobs, J. E., Lanza, S., Osgood, D. W., Eccles, J. S., & Wigfield, A. (2002). Changes in children's self-competence and values: Gender and domain differences across grades one through twelve. *Child Development, 73*, 509–527.

Jacobs, J. E., Vernon, M. K., & Eccles, J. S. (2005). Activity choices in middle childhood: The roles of gender, self-beliefs, and parents' influence. In J. L. Mahoney, R. W. Larson, & J. S. Eccles (Eds.), *Organized activities as contexts of development: Extracurricular activities, after-school and community programs* (pp. 235–254). Mahwah, NJ: Lawrence Earlbaum Associates.

Juvonen, J., Espinoza, G., & Knifsend, C. (2012). The role of peer relationships in student aca-demic and extracurricular engagement. In S. L. Christenson, A. L. Reschly, & C. Wylie (Eds.), *Handbook of research on student engagement* (pp. 387–401). New York: Springer.

Kindermann, T. A. (2007). Effects of naturally existing peer groups on changes in academic engagement in a cohort of sixth graders. *Child Development, 78*(4), 1186–1203. doi:10.1111/j.1467-8624.2007.01060.x.

Knogler, M., Harackiewicz, J. M., Gegenfurtner, A., & Lewalter, D. (2015). How situational is situational interest? Investigating the longitudinal structure of situational interest. *Contemporary Educational Psychology, 43*, 39–50.

Leibham, M. B., Alexander, J. M., & Johnson, K. E. (2005). Parenting behaviors associated with the maintenance of preschoolers' interests: A prospective longitudinal study. *Journal of Applied Developmental Psychology, 26*, 397–414.

Lewin, K. (1935). *A dynamic theory of personality*. New York: McGraw-Hill.

Mac Iver, D. J., Stipek, D. J., & Daniels, D. H. (1991). Explaining within-semester changes in student effort in junior high school and senior high school courses. *Journal of Educational Psychology, 83*(2), 201–211.

Master, A., Butler, L. P, & Walton, G. M. (2017). How the subjective relationship between the self, others, and a task drives interest. In P. A. O'Keefe & J. M. Harackiewicz (Eds.), *The science of interest*. Cham: Springer, (this volume).

McCaslin, M. (2009). Co-regulation of student motivation and emergent identity. *Educational Psychologist, 44*, 137–146.

Meade, G. H. (1934). *Mind, self, and society*. Chicago: University of Chicago Press.

Meece, J. L., Wigfield, A., & Eccles, J. S. (1990). Predictors of math anxiety and its influence on young adolescents' course enrollment intentions and performance in mathematics. *Journal of Educational Psychology, 82*, 60–70.

Morgan, C., Isaac, J. D., & Sansone, C. (2001). The role of interest in understanding the career choices of female and male college students. *Sex Roles, 44*(5–6), 295–320.

O'Keefe, P. A., & Linnenbrink-Garcia, L. (2014). The role of interest in optimizing performance and self-regulation. *Journal of Experimental Social Psychology, 53*, 70–78.

Parker, J. G., Rubin, K. H., Erath, S. A., Wojslawowicz, J. C., & Buskirk, A. A. (2006). Peer relationships, child development, and adjustment: A developmental psychopathology perspective. In D. C. D. J. Cohen (Ed.), *Developmental psychopathology, Vol 1: Theory and method* (2nd ed., pp. 419–493). Hoboken, NJ: John Wiley & Sons Inc.

Patall, E. A., Dent, A. L., Oyer, M., & Wynn, S. R. (2013). Student autonomy and course value: The unique and cumulative roles of various teacher practices. *Motivation and Emotion, 37*(1), 14–32.

Prentice, D. A., & Miller, D. T. (1993). Pluralistic ignorance and alcohol use on campus: Some consequences of misperceiving the social norm. *Journal of Personality and Social Psychology, 64*(2), 243–256.

Renninger, K. A. (2000). Individual interest and its implications for understanding intrinsic motivation. In C. Sansone & J. M. Harackiewicz (Eds.), *Intrinsic and extrinsic motivation: The search for optimal motivation and performance* (pp. 373–404). San Diego, CA: Academic Press, Inc.

Renninger, K., & Hidi, S. (2011). Revisiting the conceptualization, measurement, and generation of interest. *Educational Psychologist, 46*, 168–184. doi:10.1080/00461520.2011.587723.

Renninger, K. A., & Hidi, S. (2016). *The power of interest for motivation and engagement*. New York: Routledge.

Renninger, K. A., & Su, S. (2012). Interest and its development. In R. M. Ryan (Ed.), *The Oxford handbook of human motivation* (pp. 167–187). Oxford, UK: Oxford University Press.

Reschly, A. L., & Christenson, S. L. (2012). Jingle, jangle, and conceptual haziness: Evolution and future directions of the engagement construct. In S. L. Christenson, A. L. Reschly, & C. Wylie (Eds.), *Handbook of research on student engagement* (pp. 3–19). New York: Springer.

Roeser, R. W., Eccles, J. S., & Sameroff, A. J. (1998). Academic and emotional functioning in early adolescence: Longitudinal relations, patterns, and prediction by experience in middle school. *Development and Psychopathology, 10*, 321–352.

Ross, L., Greene, D., & House, P. (1977). The "false consensus effect": An egocentric bias in social perception and attribution processes. *Journal of Experimental Social Psychology, 13*(3), 279–301.

Ross, L., Lepper, M., & Ward, A. (2010). Major developments in five decades of social psychology. In S. T. Fiske, D. T. Gilbert, & G. Lindzey (Eds.), *The handbook of social psychology* (Vol. I, 5th ed., pp. 3–50). Hoboken, NJ: John Wiley & Sons, Inc.

Rozek, C. S., Hyde, J. S., Svoboda, R. C., Hulleman, C. S., & Harackiewicz, J. M. (2014). Gender differences in the effects of a utility-value intervention to help parents motivate adolescents in mathematics and science. *Journal of Educational Psychology, 107*(1), 195–206.

Rozek, C. S., Svoboda, R. C., Harackiewicz, J. M., Hulleman, C. S., & Hyde, J. S. (2017). Utility-value intervention with parents increases students' STEM preparation and career pursuit. *Proceedings of the National Academy of Science, 114*, 909–914.

Ryan, A. M. (2000). Peer groups as a context for the socialization of Adolescents' motivation, engagement, and achievement in school. *Educational Psychologist, 35*(2), 101–111. doi:10.1207/S15326985EP3502_4.

Ryan, A. M. (2001). The peer group as a context for the development of young adolescent motivation and achievement. *Child Development, 72*(4), 1135–1150. doi:10.1111/1467-8624.00338.

Shechter, O. G., Durik, A. M., Miyamoto, Y., & Harackiewicz, J. M. (2011). The role of utility value in achievement behavior: The importance of culture. *Personality and Social Psychology Bulletin, 37*(3), 303–317.

Schiefele, U. (1991). Interest, learning, and motivation. *Educational Psychologist, 26*, 299–323.

Schiefele, U., Krapp, A., & Winteler, A. (1992). Interest as a predictor of academic achievement: A meta-analysis of research. In K. A. Renninger, S. Hidi, & A. Krapp (Eds.), *The role of interest in learning and development* (pp. 183–211). Hillsdale, NJ: Erlbaum.

Schreier, B., Dicke, A.-L., Gaspard, H., Häfner, I., Flunger, B., Lüdtke, O., Nagengast, B., & Trautwein, U. (2014). Der Wert von Mathematik im Klassenzimmer: Die Bedeutung relevanzbezogener Unterrichtsmerkmale für die Wertüberzeugungen der Schülerinnen und Schüler [The value of mathematics in the classroom: The importance of a relevanceoriented learning environment for students' value beliefs]. *Zeitschrift für Erziehungswissenschaft, 17*(2), 225–255. doi:10.1007/s11618-014-0537-y.

Simons, J., Dewitte, S., & Lens, W. (2004). The role of different types of instrumentality in motivation, study strategies, and performance: Know why you learn, so you'll know what you learn! *British Journal of Educational Psychology, 74*(3), 343–360.

Smith, J. L., Cech, E., Metz, A., Huntoon, M., & Moyer, C. (2014). Giving back or giving up: Native American student experiences in science and engineering. *Cultural Diversity and Ethnic Minority Psychology, 20*, 413–429.

Swann, W. B., & Bosson, J. K. (2008). Identity negotiation: A theory of self and social interaction. In J. P. Oliver, R. W. Robins, & L. A. Pervin (Eds.), *Handbook of personality: Theory and research* (3rd ed., pp. 448–471). New York: Guilford Press.

Thoman, D. B., Brown, E. R., Mason, A. Z., Harmsen, A. G., & Smith, J. L. (2015). The role of altruistic values in motivating underrepresented minority students for biomedicine. *Bioscience, 65*, 183–188.

Thoman, D. B., Sansone, C., & Geerling, D. (2017). The dynamic nature of interest: Embedding interest within self-regulation. In P. A. O'Keefe & J. M. Harackiewicz (Eds.), *The science of interest*. Cham: Springer, (this volume).

Tice, D. M., & Wallace, H. M. (2003). The reflected self: Creating yourself (as you think) other see you. In M. R. Leary & J. P. Tangney (Eds.), *Handbook of self and identity* (pp. 91–105). New York: Guilford.

Tibbetts, Y., Harackiewicz, J. M., Priniski, S. J., & Canning, E. A. (2016). Broadening participation in the life sciences with social–psychological interventions. *CBE-Life Sciences Education, 15*(3), es4. doi:10.1187/cbe.16-01-0001.

Updegraff, K. A., Eccles, J. S., Barber, B. L., & O'Brien, K. M. (1996). Course enrollment as self-regulatory behavior: Who takes optional high school math courses? *Learning and Individual Differences, 8,* 239–259.

Vallerand, R. J. (2017). On the two faces of passion: The harmonious and the obsessive. In P. A. O'Keefe & J. M. Harackiewicz (Eds.), *The Science of Interest.* Cham: Springer, (this volume).

Wang, M. (2012). Educational and career interests in math: A longitudinal examination of the links between classroom environment, motivational beliefs, and interests. *Developmental Psychology, 48*(6), 1643–1657.

Wigfield, A. (1994). Expectancy-value theory of achievement motivation: A developmental perspective. *Educational Psychology Review, 6,* 49–78.

Xiang, P., Chen, A., & Bruene, A. (2005). Interactive Impact of Intrinsic Motivators and Extrinsic Rewards on Behavior and Motivation Outcomes. *Journal of Teaching in Physical Education, 24,* 179–197.

Chapter 11
How the Subjective Relationship Between the Self, Others, and a Task Drives Interest

Allison Master, Lucas P. Butler, and Gregory M. Walton

Allison Master and Lucas P. Butler contributed equally to this work.

The present chapter explores the hypothesis that an important influence on interest is the perceived or *subjective social context* in which a task is completed.

There is an irony in this focus. When people evaluate their interest in a task, they typically do so with qualities of the task and themselves in mind (Sansone, Thoman, & Smith, 2010): Is this task novel or appealing? Do I feel capable at it? Is it relevant to my identity in some way? This focus on the intersection of a person and a task is also evident in people's experience of being engrossed by a task in the height of interest (Csikszentmihalyi, 1975). We also typically talk about interest in terms of the qualities of people (e.g., "She is interested in biology, but he is interested in history") and of tasks (e.g., "Reading my psychology textbook is more interesting than reading my economics textbook"). Correspondingly, classic theories have emphasized the person-task intersection, such as self-efficacy theory, which emphasizes people's self-assessed ability on a task or in a setting (Bandura, 1997). Current theories of interest have also incorporated situational factors, such as the objective social

Allison Master and Lucas P. Butler contributed equally to this work.

A. Master (✉)
University of Washington, Seattle, WA, USA
e-mail: almaster@uw.edu

L.P. Butler
University of Maryland, College Park, MD, USA
e-mail: lpbutler@umd.edu

G.M. Walton
Department of Psychology, Stanford University, Stanford, CA, USA
e-mail: gwalton@stanford.edu

© Springer International Publishing AG 2017
P.A. O'Keefe, J.M. Harackiewicz (eds.), *The Science of Interest*,
DOI 10.1007/978-3-319-55509-6_11

context in which a person engages with a task, as contributing to interest (Knogler, Harackiewicz, Gegenfurtner, & Lewalter, 2015; Renninger & Hidi, 2016; Sansone & Thoman, 2005).

Extending this approach, we focus on the *subjective* social context in which a task is completed—simply people's perception of the relationship between themselves, a task, and other people engaged in the task. We call this the *triadic relationship* in which a task is completed. In general, we theorize that when people perceive themselves to be connected to others engaged in a task, or working with others on the task rather than separately, this will inspire greater interest and engagement. Consistent with our theorizing, research shows that both children and adults experience greater interest when working with or alongside a partner (Isaac, Sansone, & Smith, 1999). But the social context is also *subjective*—that is, people perceive and draw inferences about their relationships with other people in the setting—and these inferences can be consequential (e.g., Steele, 1997). Imagine going for a hike with another person. Even if the other person walks ahead of you out of sight, your experience is fundamentally different than if you were truly alone because the experience is shared. The subjective social context can also shift in substantive ways even when people engage in a personal task. Consider a student sitting down to work on her math homework. She may be physically alone, yet aware of her friends working through the same problems. She could think of herself and her friends as working on the problems together, for instance if she talked with her friends about the problems earlier in the day or anticipates going through them together the next day in school. Alternately, without such communications, she could think of herself and her friends as working on the same assignment but separately. As this case illustrates, even when people work alone, they may do so on terms defined by their understanding of how the activity is situated in a broader social context.

This chapter focuses primarily on how the triadic relationship between the self, a task, and others engaged in the task gives rise to situational interest, a psychological state influenced by the situation the person is in. This is distinguished from individual interest, an enduring characteristic of the person (Hidi & Renninger, 2006). Interest emerges from a person's affective and cognitive responses to particular content that contribute to a desire to reengage with that content in the future (Hidi & Harackiewicz, 2000; Renninger & Hidi, 2016). While interest is sometimes used interchangeably with intrinsic motivation (Schiefele, 1999), we define the latter as a tendency to engage in activities for their own sake (Sansone & Thoman, 2005). We view interest and intrinsic motivation as having a recursive relationship—increased interest can lead people to increased intrinsic motivation (as measured by greater persistence and goal pursuit, even in the face of challenge), and the experience of being intrinsically motivated can lead to greater interest (Renninger & Hidi, 2016).

The Objective and Subjective Social Context

In focusing on the subjective social context, our argument implies that the social context always plays a part in interest, and a larger part than many existing theories credit. When previous theories have examined the role of the social context, they have tended to emphasize the objective social context. These include the physical presence of others, which can facilitate dominant responses to a task (e.g., Zajonc, 1965); cooperation or competition with others who are physically present (Murayama & Elliot, 2012; Plass, O'Keefe et al., 2013; Tauer & Harackiewicz, 2004); social comparison information, which shows that people often work harder when they compare themselves to someone more capable (Festinger, 1954; Kerr et al., 2007; Taylor & Lobel, 1989); and situations in which people's inputs to a collective task are unmarked, which can elicit social loafing, or in which outcomes are codependent with others who appear incompetent, which can elicit compensatory motivation (Williams & Karau, 1991; Williams, Karau, & Bourgeois, 1993). Alternately, previous theories have emphasized the role of inherently important people, like one's mother, who may be associated with specific motivations (Fitzsimons & Bargh, 2003; Iyengar & Lepper, 1999), or broad threats to one's belonging in general, which can undermine self-regulated goal pursuit (Baumeister, Twenge, & Nuss, 2002).

Complementing these approaches, we argue that the subjective sense that one is connected to others engaged in a task—even to new interaction partners—can transform a person's interest (see Fig. 11.1). This transformation hinges on at least two aspects of an individual's psychological experience of the social context. The first is their perception of the personal connection they have (or do not have) to others engaged with the task. People can automatically take on the goals of others (Aarts,

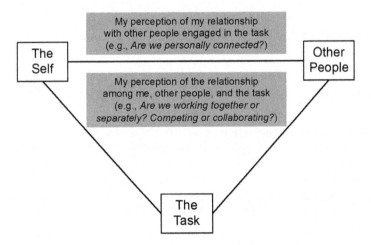

Fig. 11.1 The triadic relationship. Interest is not just a function of the relationship between a person and a task, but also the perceived relationship between a person, a task, and other people

Gollwitzer, & Hassin, 2004); we suggest that when people feel connected to others, they will be more likely to incorporate their interests as their own. The second is a person's perception of the relationship between themselves, others engaged in the task, and the task. When people feel they are working together on a shared task, their interest may increase. This approach emphasizes interest as arising not just from the intersection between a person and a task—such as a person's confidence in their ability—but as a consequence of the triadic relationship among a person, a task, and the other people in the social context.

A primary feature of our approach is that it highlights people's *subjective construal* of the social situation—the situation as understood by the actor. It is this construal that most directly shapes people's behavior (Ross & Nisbett, 1991). In some cases people make sense of their relationships with others in a setting from objective aspects of the social context (e.g., much of the developmental work; Isaac et al., 1999). But we also examine how these perceived relationships can arise from simple symbolic cues. These cues can create a sense of social connection with others engaged in a task or a sense of belonging in a performance domain, holding constant actual interaction and the objective social setting (Carr & Walton, 2014; Murphy, Steele, & Gross, 2007; Walton, Cohen, Cwir, & Spencer, 2012).

In this chapter, we explore how the triadic relationship between the self, a task, and others in the social context shapes situational interest and intrinsic motivation at different stages of development. In infancy, the importance of the social context is clearly illustrated in the overt, visible scaffolding between infants, adults, and learning contexts, as seen in situations involving social referencing and joint attention to an object (Baldwin, 1991; Sorce, Emde, Campos, & Klinnert, 1985) and the use of an adult as a secure base for exploration (Ainsworth, Blehar, Waters, & Wall, 1978). Next, we argue that this triadic relationship remains important for adults, but can also arise in more subtle and complicated forms later in life. Finally, we discuss implications for our understanding of interest, including possible targets for "wise" interventions that could capitalize on triadic relationship processes to boost children's and adults' interest in important academic tasks (see Walton, 2014).

Theoretical Background

Why should the triadic relationship influence interest? An important reason involves the automatic tendency of people to connect to others, the benefits of doing so, and the fact that in doing so people often develop a shared orientation toward important aspects of the world (see Walton & Cohen, 2011b). The need to belong is a basic source of human motivation for adults (Baumeister & Leary, 1995) and children (Over, 2016). One indicator of its importance is in the consequences when it is disrupted. Indeed, when people imagine themselves excluded, they experience emotional and cognitive distress, even in trivial situations (Baumeister et al., 2002; Williams & Nida, 2011). Moreover, from infancy people show a basic orientation toward and coordination with others (Csibra, 2010; Farroni et al., 2005; Morton & Johnson, 1991). Adults unconsciously mimic the behavior of others, and this mimicry both causes social connections and results from social connections (Chartrand & Bargh, 1999). People also overcome barriers to coordinate behavior with others. In one study, people sitting in rocking chairs synchronized their rocking speeds with each other, even when their chairs were designed to rock at different frequencies (Richardson, Marsh, Isenhower, Goodman, & Schmidt, 2007). The pronouns "we" and "us" further have a positive emotional significance that is activated automatically and unconsciously (Perdue, Dovidio, Gurtman, & Tyler, 1990). In close relationships, representations of the self and other can even merge, so that people get the characteristics of the self confused with the characteristics of the relationship partner (Aron et al., 2004).

People also have inclinations to share attention, behavior, and cognitions with others when responding to events in the world or when engaged in tasks. Similar neural mechanisms are involved in monitoring one's own and others' performance, creating parallel responses to events that occur to one person (Sebanz, Bekkering, & Knoblich, 2006). As noted, goals (e.g., to be helpful) can spread from one person to another automatically (Aarts et al., 2004). Suggesting that one function of this sharing is to cement social relationships, these tendencies can be increased by even subtle recognition of the social connections between people. In one study, participants who felt socially connected to a peer (due to shared personal preferences) experienced more similar emotional and physiological states as that peer, and this effect was mediated by their sense of connectedness to that person (Cwir, Carr, Walton, & Spencer, 2011). When people simply believe that they are paying attention to or experiencing something with other people this intensifies responses to that object or event, particularly when people feel connected to these co-observers (see Shteynberg, 2015). In a series of studies, participants made quicker and more accurate judgments about stimuli when they believed similar others were also evaluating the same stimuli, compared to dissimilar others or different stimuli (Shteynberg, 2010). Similarly, sharing goals or emotions with similar others (compared to dissimilar others) intensifies the pursuit of those goals and the experience of those emotions (Shteynberg & Galinsky, 2011; Shteynberg et al., 2014).

This sensitivity to cues that connect a person to others engaged in a task is functional. It brings people closer to others and builds a sense of belonging to a community (Aron, Norman, Aron, McKenna, & Heyman, 2000; Aronson, 2004; Baumeister & Leary, 1995). And it helps people accomplish goals that would be impossible to accomplish alone (Asch, 1952; Vygotsky, 1978). Indeed, theorists suggest that the capacity and desire to share intentions with others confers human many advantages, including the development and transmission of culture and language, and sets us apart from other primates (Tomasello, Carpenter, Call, Behne, & Moll, 2005).

Together, this evidence indicates the importance of social connections to our experiences. The next sections explore empirical evidence for the triadic relationship in more detail.

Evidence from Development

Many theories of development emphasize the way in which adults create social situations that engage infants and young children with tasks that promote exploration and learning (e.g., Ainsworth et al., 1978; Vygotsky, 1978). This tradition suggests that the triadic relationship between an individual, a task, and others in the subjective social context may play a fundamental role in interest from an early age. If so, even young children may be more interested in tasks that are perceived to involve social connection or engagement, and we may see continuity in this effect over the course of development.

Indeed, from the very earliest days of life, infants selectively attend to social stimuli such as eyes and faces, preferentially orienting towards them rather than to non-social stimuli (Csibra, 2010; Farroni et al., 2005; Morton & Johnson, 1991). This early sensitivity sets the stage for the essential role of social relationships and interactions in development. From an early age, infants show a surprisingly sophisticated understanding of the social world. As early as 5 months of age, infants attend to the goals underlying the actions of others (Woodward, 1998). During the second year of life if not earlier they recognize that others are "like them," and that others' actions will be based on their perceptions, just as their own actions are (Meltzoff, 2007). They also draw inferences about others' desires and preferences (Kushnir, Xu, & Wellman, 2010; Repacholi & Gopnik, 1997). Finally, they seek to imitate others in order to affiliate and build social bonds, for example more closely imitating when they have been primed with cues of rejection (Over & Carpenter, 2013). Thus, from early in development, children are attentive to social stimuli and motivated to engage with others to infer others' goals, and to build relationships. From an early age, then, children are equipped to share interests and goals with others.

Moreover, it is clear that this early sociality plays an important role in young children's interest, and that the triadic relationship between the self, a task, and others in the social context is at its core. In the first 2 years of life, as soon as they are capable, children are particularly interested in engaging socially with others on joint tasks. For instance, 12-month-olds point informatively to make others aware of something new (Liszkowski, Carpenter, & Tomasello, 2007) or to locate hidden objects (Liszkowski et al., 2008). Fourteen-month-olds imitate others' goal-directed actions (Meltzoff, 1995) and help others achieve their goals (Over & Carpenter, 2009; Warneken & Tomasello, 2006, 2007). In addition, 2-year-olds are highly interested in collaborative social games (Dunham & Moore, 1995; Ross & Lollis, 1987; Warneken, Chen, & Tomasello, 2006), urging partners to continue participating even when they can accomplish the task alone (Warneken, Gräfenhain, & Tomasello, 2012). They also spontaneously help adults achieve their instrumental (Warneken & Tomasello, 2006) and social goals (Beier, Over, & Carpenter, 2014).

Children are also interested not only in engaging with others or helping others with their goals, but in collaborating on a shared task. They show some basic cooperative skills at 14 months, coordinating their actions with an adult partner in order to achieve a goal such as retrieving a toy (Warneken & Tomasello, 2007). Between ages 2 and 3 they begin to collaboratively solve simple physical problems (Ashley & Tomasello, 1998; Brownell & Carriger, 1990). By 3 they prefer to work cooperatively rather than work alone (Rekers, Haun, & Tomasello, 2011). This preference may confer benefits. In one study, 4- and 5-year-olds who worked on a task in pairs showed more positive affect, performed better on the task, and remembered it better than children who worked alone, especially the 5-year-olds (Perlmutter, Behrend, Kuo, & Muller, 1989). And children who made music together (i.e., had a shared goal in their music playing, by drumming together rather than independently) were more likely to spontaneously engage in prosocial behavior later, suggesting a link between social connection around a task and later social motivations (Kirschner & Tomasello, 2010). Finally, it appears that children are sensitive to cues in interpersonal interactions that help to define their relationships with others. In one study, preschoolers showed significantly more helping behavior when the person needing help had first engaged them in reciprocal, rather than parallel play (Barragan & Dweck, 2014). By middle school, the relationship may be more complex. In one study, middle-school students showed higher situational interest when they engaged socially in a math game, either competitively or cooperatively, than when they played individually (Plass, O'Keefe et al., 2013). When taken together, these streams of research show that children have a drive not only to engage socially with others from birth but to do so in a collaborative, cooperative manner centered around the triadic relationship between the self, a task, and other people in the social context.

These past studies have focused on the objective social context; however, recent research also finds that young children are also responsive to subtle cues that shape the subjective social context in which they complete a task and, moreover, these cues inspire motivation and interest. One set of studies focused on the connection a child may feel with peers engaged in a task (Master & Walton, 2013). Preschoolers were given the opportunity to work on a challenging puzzle for as long as they liked. Before beginning, children in one condition were told they were part of "the puzzles group," thus giving them a group identity associated with the task; children in the other condition were told that they were "the puzzles child," giving them a personal identity associated with the task. All children then worked on the puzzle on their own. Those in the group condition persisted nearly 30% longer than children in the non-social identity condition. A second study found that merely being assigned to a group but one not associated with puzzles did not produce the same increase in motivation. Only when the group identity was associated with puzzles, creating a triadic relationship between the self, the task, and other children, did motivation increase. A third study extended the findings to word learning: children assigned to a group associated with a task *learned* more from the task than children assigned a personal identity associated with a task. Follow-up studies find that children also report greater enjoyment for and are more likely to prefer tasks completed as part of a task-oriented group (Master, Cheryan, & Meltzoff, 2017). These studies illustrate how the triadic relationship between the self, a task, and others in the social context can boost persistence, learning, and interest early in development.

A second set of studies examined whether cues that merely represent one as working together on a task, even absent a group identity, might have similar effects (Butler & Walton, 2013). As in the studies just described, preschool-aged children were given the opportunity to work for as long as they liked on a challenging puzzle and did so on their own. In one condition, however, children first viewed a video of a child in another room starting to work on the puzzle, were told the video was live and were told that they and the other child were "doing the puzzle together." In the other condition, children saw the same video but were told that this was a recording from a different day when the other child had also done the puzzle. Thus, as in the studies on belonging to a group, the objective situation was identical across conditions—children worked alone on a puzzle task—but the *construal* of the situation varied. Children led to see the situation as one in which they were collaborating with another child worked more than 40% longer on the puzzle than children led to think of themselves as simply working on the same task another child had also worked on; they also reported enjoying the task more. A second study found that the working-together condition also increased persistence and enjoyment relative to a second control condition, one in which another child worked on the same puzzle at the same time but without creating the same triadic relationship—one where children were told they were taking turns with the other child.

These studies provide promising evidence that perceived triadic relationships may play an important role in even young children's situational interest.

Evidence from Adulthood

The previous section showed that the triadic relationship between the self, a task, and others in the social context is present and psychologically meaningful early in childhood. Cues that encourage young children simply to construe a situation as one in which they are connected to others associated with a task or jointly engaged on a task boosts children's motivation and situational interest.

We now turn to relevant evidence in adulthood. It is certainly possible that the triadic relationship between the self, a task, and others in the social context wanes in importance as adults become more independent and autonomous. Indeed, as we grow older, we are less likely to need overt scaffolding from others. However, we argue that the social context and real and perceived relationships with others remain important, and do so even when they operate in the background as people focus on a task (Csikszentmihalyi, 1975). This may be most likely when people are considering a new, unfamiliar domain or task. First, we discuss evidence that people value objects and experiences more if they are connected to others. We then examine whether people show greater interest and motivation for tasks that are social, even as a consequence of subtle cues.

Do We Value Social Objects and Experiences More?

Pablo Neruda's *Ode to Things* describes a love for all things because they "bear the trace of someone's finger" (Neruda, 1994). Of course, we do not assign more value to used objects, which might be less useful, or objects like t-shirts that have been physically touched by others, which might be off-putting (Argo, Dahl, & Morales, 2006). But we perceive more value in objects that belonged to someone admirable, such as Albert Einstein, and less value in those that belonged to someone evil like Hitler (Newman, Diesendruck, & Bloom, 2011), an effect shown even by young children (Gelman, Frazier, Noles, Manczak, & Stilwell, 2015). And obviously objects that are handmade and thus less common can be more valuable than objects from a factory. But holding all of those things constant, the mere idea that an object has a social history, that a person, even a generic stranger, contributed to its creation, makes it more appealing. In one study participants learned that a product was "made by people using machines in a small factory in Nebraska," prioritizing the role of people. This "social trace" caused people to value those objects more than objects "made by machines run by people in a small factory in Nebraska" (Job, Nikitin, Zhang, Carr, & Walton, 2017). Simply prioritizing the social history of the object increased its value.

We also value activities more when they are social. One study gave adults a choice between completing a "dull" activity (e.g., listening to audio-tones) or a parallel "appealing" activity (e.g., listening to music). When both activities would be done alone, unsurprisingly participants strongly preferred the appealing activity. When the dull activity could be done with others, however, participants' preference for that activity relative to the appealing activity rose by 40% and they reported a smaller difference in how enjoyable they anticipated the activities being (described in Walton & Cohen, 2011b). When a task is social, it affords opportunities for social connections, exchanging emotions, and collaborating, placing it in a different light. Thus, both objects and activities take on additional value and become more interesting when connected to others.

Does Social Connection Increase Our Interest and Motivation?

Objective features of the social context in which people complete a task that facilitate connections with others can increase interest and intrinsic motivation. As mentioned previously, simply working with another person increases interest in an activity (Isaac et al., 1999). The experience of talking with others about an activity or class can also increase people's current and future interest in that activity or class (Thoman, Sansone, Fraughton, & Pasupathi, 2012; Thoman, Sansone, & Pasupathi, 2007). Other research has found that membership in academic groups in real-world classrooms can promote learning and achievement (Aronson & Osherow, 1980; Johnson & Johnson, 2009), while feeling socially connected to peers and teachers in school in general predicts greater intrinsic motivation for academic tasks (e.g., Furrer & Skinner, 2003; Goodenow, 1992; Hamre & Pianta, 2005).

These studies examined real social interactions. However, echoing the recent developmental research presented earlier (Butler & Walton, 2013; Master & Walton, 2013), subjective social cues can also define a triadic relationship between a person, a task, and others in the social context and thereby increase interest. As in the developmental work, research with adults has examined cues that convey two important representations of this triadic relationship: a sense of connection to others associated with a domain and a sense of working together with another person.

How Social Belonging Boosts Interest and Motivation Even minimal cues that establish a sense of social connection with others can facilitate the social sharing of interest and motivation. We call these cues "mere belonging."

One series of studies tested this hypothesis in the context of students' motivation for math (Walton et al., 2012). In one study, participants read an article about a math major who either shared their birthday or did not. Those for whom the math major shared their birthday persisted longer on a math puzzle and reported greater interest in math, an effect mediated by a greater sense of connection to math. In another study, participants told they were part of a minimal "numbers group" persisted longer on an insoluble math puzzle than participants told they were the "numbers person." In a third study, participants who read that the math department offered opportunities for collaboration and positive social interactions likewise showed greater motivation in math.

These findings and follow-up studies on goal activation (Walton et al., 2012) suggest an active process in which a social connection with others increases the activation of others' goals and interest in pursuing them (see also Brannon & Walton, 2013; Cwir et al., 2011; Master & Walton, 2013). This effect can be observed even when people's behavior is freely chosen and in private, suggesting that people have internalized the interests and motivations of others for themselves.

How Working Together Boosts Interest and Motivation Another important representation of the triadic relationship is whether people think of themselves as working with others or separately from others. Although working together can be created by the objective social context (Isaac et al., 1999), subtle cues can also signal a state of working together and facilitate interest and intrinsic motivation (e.g., Butler & Walton, 2013). For example, as noted earlier students may study on their own for a class but, having exchanged tips and encouragement on the material with peers, may thereby experience a feeling of working together as they study. Absent such communications, even students working on a group project may construe their personal labor as separate from even if coordinated with other students' labor. We argue adults as well as young children respond to cues that evoke the feeling of working together with increased interest and motivation, and do so over and above simply working at the same time on the same task as others.

Testing this hypothesis, in one series of studies, participants worked alone on an insoluble puzzle. However, some participants were treated as partners working with others on the task, while others were treated as working in parallel with others—at the same time, in the same environment, and on the same task, but not as together (Carr & Walton, 2014). Participants came to the laboratory in small groups, met, and then went to individual rooms where they were assigned to a condition. In the working-together condition, the experimenter told participants that the study concerned tips and puzzles and that they were "working together" with the other participants. The experimenter then explained that a coin flip (ostensibly determined by chance) would determine whether the participant would write a tip to another participant or receive a tip from one. All participants in this condition were then told that they had been assigned to receive a tip. The control condition was identical except that participants were not told that they were "working together" and believed they would write a tip for or receive a tip from the experimenter rather than another participant. In this condition participants thus learned that they would be working at the same time and on the same task as others in the same environment but without cues that signaled a state of working together.

This procedure held constant an array of other factors. The recipient of the tip was ostensibly random, and thus not a signal of the perceived ability of the recipient. The tip participants received in both conditions was provided quickly and recounted an unsuccessful strategy for the puzzle; it thus provided minimal information about the other person's performance. In both conditions, participants also worked alone, in separate rooms, on their own task.

Across five experiments, participants in the working-together condition persisted 48–64% longer on the puzzle, rated the task as more enjoyable, were more likely to say that they had worked hard on it because it was interesting, were more engaged in the task (as shown by better memory for it later), and performed better on it.

Why did the feeling of working together increase interest, intrinsic motivation, and performance? It was not because of external pressures—there was no difference in participants' feelings of obligation to others or sense of competition with others. It was also not because of negative emotions—there was no evidence that working together increased worries about being evaluated or judged based on their performance. Instead, cues of working together created a feeling of working together with others on a challenging task. When we engage in a task jointly with others, the task takes on social meaning that can help turn work into play (see also Shteynberg & Galinsky, 2011).

Applications and Intervention

We have argued that the triadic relationship between the self, a task or domain, and other people in the subjective social context can have a powerful effect on interest and motivation from our earliest days through adulthood. In incorporating the subjective social context, this perspective complements previous research on interest and motivation that focuses on the relationship between a person and a task, such as how choice (Cordova & Lepper, 1996) and beliefs about individual autonomy and competence (e.g., Bandura, 1997; Carver & Scheier, 2001) drive interest, as well as recent work emphasizing the importance of the objective social context (Knogler et al., 2015; Renninger & Hidi, 2016; Sansone & Thoman, 2005). The crux of our proposal is that individuals' construal of a task as one in which they feel connected with others and jointly engaged with others can have major impacts on interest, even from the earliest years of development.

Taken together, this research suggests promising potential targets for interventions to raise interest and motivation in important school, work, and other contexts. Such interventions would harness the power of this triadic relationship. Although not narrowly targeted at the triadic relationship we have discussed here, research demonstrates that interventions to promote students' sense of belonging in school can have powerful and lasting effects on motivation and achievement (Walton & Cohen, 2007, 2011a; Walton, Logel, Peach, Spencer, & Zanna, 2015; Yeager et al., 2016).

These interventions are predicated on research indicating that students who face social stigma, negative stereotypes, or the underrepresentation of their group in school can, as a consequence, harbor persistent doubts about whether they belong (Walton & Cohen, 2007). This question of social belonging can lead students to infer from even commonplace negative events like feeling lonely or receiving critical academic feedback that they do not belong in general in school. This prevents students from engaging with others in school and developing interest in coursework (Cheryan, Master, & Meltzoff, 2015; Mendoza-Denton, Downey, Purdie, Davis, & Pietrzak, 2002). To address this worry, the social-belonging intervention offers students a more hopeful narrative for making sense of daily adversities. Through stories from older students, first-year students learn that worries about belonging are normal in an academic transition and improve with time, not proof of a lack of belonging. Students then have the opportunity to reflect on these ideas and write about how this process of change has been true for them. In one trial, this exercise completed in an hour-long session in the first year of college raised African American students' achievement through graduation, halving the racial achievement gap over this 3-year period (Walton & Cohen, 2011a). Although interest was not measured, it is likely that feeling a secure sense of belonging allowed students to relax and pursue their academic interests. Such benefits have been observed in a variety of groups that are marginalized in academic settings, including among women in male-dominated engineering fields (Walton et al., 2015) and among diverse disadvantaged ethnic-minority groups and first-generation college students (Stephens, Hamedani, & Destin, 2014; Yeager et al. 2016). This research illustrates the importance of how students make sense of their social relationships in school. What might an intervention that targeted the triadic relationship precisely look like? Such an intervention would help people see themselves as connected to others engaged in a setting or a task, or as working with others in or on it. Importantly, this may be done through subjective cues that signal the relationships among the self, a task, and others—it may not require a change in the objective social context (Wing & Jeffery, 1999). This area of research is growing rapidly; here are some promising early examples.

Extending the research we presented earlier on "mere belonging" (Walton et al., 2012), one intervention provided 9th grade teachers information about personal similarities they shared with a random subset of their students (Gehlbach et al., 2016), which presumably led teachers to interact with these students in ways that facilitated stronger relationships. This raised course grades for Black and Latino students, for whom personal relationships in school may otherwise be weakest, reducing the achievement gap between those students and White and Asian students by 60%.

Or consider social-norm interventions. People are often thought to conform to social norms merely because what others do is taken as a sign of what is effective and what is sanctioned (Cialdini & Trost, 1998). However, normative appeals can also often represent a collective effort toward a common goal and invite people to work together toward this goal. For instance, Goldstein, Cialdini, and Griskevicius (2008) induced more hotel guests to reuse towels with a normative appeal that explicitly invited people to work together ("JOIN YOUR FELLOW GUESTS IN HELPING TO SAVE THE ENVIRONMENT. Almost 75% of guests…[reuse] their towels more than once," capitalized in the original) as compared to an appeal that focused only on the environmental benefits ("HELP SAVE THE ENVIRONMENT"). Did the aspect of the appeal that invited people to "join" with others to accomplish a goal evoke a feeling of working together and contribute to its effectiveness?

Testing this hypothesis, Howe, Carr, and Walton (under review) manipulated whether appeals in three contexts merely provided normative information ("Most people do X") or also invited people to "join in" and "do it together." As predicted, as compared to both a no-norm control condition and mere normative information, participants expressed greater interest in giving to a charity and greater motivation to reduce personal carbon emissions when exposed to working-together normative appeals; these effects were further mediated by greater feelings of working together with others toward a goal. Finally, in a field experiment, restrooms on a college campus randomly assigned stickers that combined normative information with an appeal to work together to reduce paper towel use showed significantly greater reductions in paper towel use over 2 weeks than restrooms where the stickers provided only identical normative information.

These results suggest the power of the perceived triadic relationship to motivate behavior in prosocial and environmental contexts. They raise intriguing questions about past research, such as whether classic interventions commonly understood as demonstrating the power of normative influence also evoked a sense of working with others toward a goal (e.g., Lewin's [1947] "cheap meat" intervention). Finally, although these studies have not examined interest and motivation in school or work settings, in combination with laboratory research (Carr & Walton, 2014) they suggest the potential promise of working-together interventions in these settings and the importance of research that pursues this question.

Conclusion

From early in life the subjective social context shapes children's approach to learning and sets the stage for the development of interest into adolescence and adulthood. Clearly more research is needed both to deepen our theoretical understanding of these processes and to translate these lessons into interventions that can promote students' development. However, it is clear that creating a sense of personal connection can help students develop interest and thrive in academic contexts.

References

Aarts, H., Gollwitzer, P. M., & Hassin, R. R. (2004). Goal contagion: Perceiving is for pursuing. *Journal of Personality and Social Psychology, 87*, 23–37.

Ainsworth, M. D. S., Blehar, M. C., Waters, E., & Wall, S. (1978). *Patterns of attachment: A psychological study of the strange situation.* Hillsdale, NJ: Erlbaum.

Argo, J. J., Dahl, D. W., & Morales, A. C. (2006). Consumer contamination: How consumers react to products touched by others. *Journal of Marketing, 70*, 81–94.

Aron, A., McLaughlin-Volpe, T., Mashek, D., Lewandowski, G., Wright, S. C., & Aron, E. N. (2004). Including others in the self. *European Review of Social Psychology, 15*, 101–132.

Aron, A., Norman, C. C., Aron, E. N., McKenna, C., & Heyman, R. (2000). Couples' shared participation in novel and arousing activities and experienced relationship quality. *Journal of Personality and Social Psychology, 78*, 273–284.

Aronson, E. (2004). Reducing hostility and building compassion: Lessons from the jigsaw classroom. In A. G. Miller (Ed.), *The social psychology of good and evil* (pp. 469–488). New York: Guilford Press.

Aronson, E., & Osherow, N. (1980). Cooperation, prosocial behavior, and academic performance: Experiments in the desegregated classroom. In L. Bickerman (Ed.), *Applied social psychology annual* (pp. 163–196). Beverley Hills, CA: Sage.

Asch, S. E. (1952). *Social psychology.* New York: Prentice-Hall, Inc.

Ashley, J., & Tomasello, M. (1998). Cooperative problem-solving and teaching in preschoolers. *Social Development, 7*, 143–163.

Baldwin, D. A. (1991). Infants' contribution to the achievement of joint reference. *Child Development, 62*, 874–890.

Bandura, A. (1997). *Self-efficacy: The exercise of control.* New York: W. H. Freeman.

Barragan, R. C., & Dweck, C. S. (2014). Rethinking natural altruism: Simple reciprocal interactions trigger children's benevolence. *Proceedings of the National Academy of Sciences, 111*, 17071–17074.

Baumeister, R. F., & Leary, M. R. (1995). The need to belong: Desire for interpersonal attachments as a fundamental human motivation. *Psychological Bulletin, 117*, 497–529.

Baumeister, R. F., Twenge, J. M., & Nuss, C. K. (2002). Effects of social exclusion on cognitive processes: Anticipated aloneness reduces intelligent thought. *Journal of Personality and Social Psychology, 83*, 817–827.

Beier, J. S., Over, H., & Carpenter, M. (2014). Young children help others to achieve their social goals. *Developmental Psychology, 50*, 934–940.

Brannon, T. N., & Walton, G. M. (2013). Enacting cultural interests: How intergroup contact reduces prejudice by sparking interest in an out-group's culture. *Psychological Science, 24*, 1947–1957.

Brownell, C. A., & Carriger, M. S. (1990). Changes in cooperation and self-other differentiation during the second year. *Child Development, 61*, 1164–1174.

Butler, L. P., & Walton, G. M. (2013). The opportunity to collaborate increases preschoolers' motivation for challenging tasks. *Journal of Experimental Child Psychology, 116*, 953–961.

Carr, P. B., & Walton, G. M. (2014). Cues of working together fuel intrinsic motivation. *Journal of Experimental Social Psychology, 53*, 169–184.

Carver, C. S., & Scheier, M. F. (2001). *On the self-regulation of behavior.* Cambridge, England: Cambridge University Press.

Chartrand, T. L., & Bargh, J. A. (1999). The chameleon effect: The perception–behavior link and social interaction. *Journal of Personality and Social Psychology, 76*, 893–910.

Cheryan, S., Master, A., & Meltzoff, A. N. (2015). Cultural stereotypes as gatekeepers: Increasing girls' interest in computer science and engineering by diversifying stereotypes. *Frontiers in Psychology, 6*, 49.

Cialdini, R. B., & Trost, M. R. (1998). Social influence: Social norms, conformity and compliance. In D. T. Gilbert, S. T. Fiske, & G. Lindzey (Eds.), *The handbook of social psychology, Vols. 1 and 2* (4th ed., pp. 151–192). New York: McGraw-Hill.

Cordova, D. I., & Lepper, M. R. (1996). Intrinsic motivation and the process of learning: Beneficial effects of contextualization, personalization, and choice. *Journal of Educational Psychology, 88*, 715–730.

Csibra, G. (2010). Recognizing communicative intentions in infancy. *Mind & Language, 25*, 141–168.

Csikszentmihalyi, M. (1975). *Beyond boredom and anxiety.* San Francisco, CA: Jossey-Bass.

Cwir, D., Carr, P. B., Walton, G. M., & Spencer, S. J. (2011). Your heart makes my heart move: Cues of social connectedness cause shared emotions and physiological states among strangers. *Journal of Experimental Social Psychology, 47*, 661–664.

Dunham, P. J., & Moore, C. (1995). Current themes in research on joint attention. In C. Moore & P. J. Dunham (Eds.), *Joint attention: Its origins and role in development* (pp. 15–28). Hillsdale, NJ: Erlbaum.

Farroni, T., Johnson, M. H., Menon, E., Zulian, L., Faraguna, D., & Csibra, G. (2005). Newborns' preference for face-relevant stimuli: Effects of contrast polarity. *Proceedings of the National Academy of Sciences of the United States of America, 102*, 17245–17250.

Festinger, L. (1954). A theory of social comparison processes. *Human Relations, 7*, 117–140.

Fitzsimons, G. M., & Bargh, J. A. (2003). Thinking of you: Nonconscious pursuit of interpersonal goals associated with relationship partners. *Journal of Personality and Social Psychology, 84*, 148–164.

Furrer, C., & Skinner, E. (2003). Sense of relatedness as a factor in children's academic engagement and performance. *Journal of Educational Psychology, 95*, 148–162.

Gehlbach, H., Brinkworth, M. E., King, A. M., Hsu, L. M., McIntyre, J., & Rogers, T. (2016). Creating birds of similar feathers: Leveraging similarity to improve teacher-student relationships and academic achievement. *Journal of Educational Psychology, 108*, 342–352.

Gelman, S. A., Frazier, B. N., Noles, N. S., Manczak, E. M., & Stilwell, S. M. (2015). How much are Harry Potter's glasses worth? Children's monetary evaluation of authentic objects. *Journal of Cognition and Development, 16*, 97–117.

Goldstein, N. J., Cialdini, R. B., & Griskevicius, V. (2008). A room with a viewpoint: Using social norms to motivate environmental conservation in hotels. *Journal of Consumer Research, Special Issue: Consumer Welfare, 35*, 472–482.

Goodenow, C. (1992). Strengthening the links between educational psychology and the study of social contexts. *Educational Psychologist, 27*, 177–196.

Hamre, B. K., & Pianta, R. C. (2005). Can instructional and emotional support in the first-grade classroom make a difference for children at risk of school failure? *Child Development, 76*, 949–967.

Hidi, S., & Harackiewicz, J. M. (2000). Motivating the academically unmotivated: A critical issue for the 21st century. *Review of Educational Research, 70*, 151–179.

Hidi, S., & Renninger, K. A. (2006). The four-phase model of interest development. *Educational Psychologist, 41*, 111–127.

Howe, L. C., Carr, P. B., & Walton, G. M. (Under review). Normative appeals that invite people to work together toward a common cause are more effective.

Isaac, J. D., Sansone, C., & Smith, J. L. (1999). Other people as a source of interest in an activity. *Journal of Experimental Social Psychology, 35*, 239–265.

Iyengar, S. S., & Lepper, M. R. (1999). Rethinking the role of choice: A cultural perspective on intrinsic motivation. *Journal of Personality and Social Psychology, 76*, 349–366.

Job, V., Nikitin, J., Zhang, S. X., Carr, P. B., & Walton, G. M. (2017). Social Traces of Generic Humans Increase the Value of Everyday Objects. Personality and Social Psychology Bulletin, 43(6), 785–792.

Johnson, D. W., & Johnson, R. T. (2009). An educational psychology success story: Social interdependence theory and cooperative learning. *Educational Researcher, 38*, 365–379.

Kerr, N. L., Messé, L. A., Seok, D., Sambolec, E. J., Lount, R. B., & Park, E. S. (2007). Psychological mechanisms underlying the Köhler motivation gain. *Personality and Social Psychology Bulletin, 33*, 828–841.

Kirschner, S., & Tomasello, M. (2010). Joint music making promotes prosocial behavior in 4-year-old children. *Evolution and Human Behavior, 31*, 354–364.

Knogler, M., Harackiewicz, J. M., Gegenfurtner, A., & Lewalter, D. (2015). How situational is situational interest? Investigating the longitudinal structure of situational interest. *Contemporary Educational Psychology, 43*, 39–50.

Kushnir, T., Xu, F., & Wellman, H. M. (2010). Young children use statistical sampling to infer the preferences of other people. *Psychological Science, 21*, 1134–1140.

Lewin, K. (1947). Group decision and social change. *Readings in Social Psychology, 3*, 197–211.

Liszkowski, U., Carpenter, M., & Tomasello, M. (2007). Pointing out new news, old news, and absent referents at 12 months of age. *Developmental Science, 10*, F1–F7.

Liszkowski, U., Carpenter, M., & Tomasello, M. (2008). Twelve-month-olds communicate helpfully and appropriately for knowledgeable and ignorant partners. *Cognition, 108*, 732–739.

Master, A., Cheryan, S., & Meltzoff, A. N. (2017). Social group membership increases STEM engagement among preschoolers. *Developmental Psychology, 53*, 201–209.

Master, A., & Walton, G. M. (2013). Minimal groups increase young children's motivation and learning on group-relevant tasks. *Child Development, 84*, 737–751.

Meltzoff, A. N. (1995). Understanding the intentions of others: Re-enactment of intended acts by 18-month-old children. *Developmental Psychology, 31*, 838–850.

Meltzoff, A. N. (2007). 'Like me': A foundation for social cognition. *Developmental Science, 10*, 126–134.

Mendoza-Denton, R., Downey, G., Purdie, V. J., Davis, A., & Pietrzak, J. (2002). Sensitivity to status-based rejection: Implications for African American students' college experience. *Journal of Personality and Social Psychology, 83*, 896–918.

Morton, J., & Johnson, M. H. (1991). CONSPEC and CONLERN: A two-process theory of infant face recognition. *Psychological Review, 98*, 164–181.

Murayama, K., & Elliot, A. J. (2012). The competition–performance relation: A meta-analytic review and test of the opposing processes model of competition and performance. *Psychological Bulletin, 138*, 1035–1070.

Murphy, M. C., Steele, C. M., & Gross, J. J. (2007). Signaling threat: How situational cues affect women in math, science, and engineering settings. *Psychological Science, 18*, 879–885.

Neruda, P. (1994). *Odes to common things*. Boston: Little, Brown, and Company.

Newman, G. E., Diesendruck, G., & Bloom, P. (2011). Celebrity contagion and the value of objects. *Journal of Consumer Research, 38*, 215–228.

Over, H. (2016). The origins of belonging: Social motivation in infants and young children. *Philosophical Transactions of the Royal Society B, 371*, 20150072.

Over, H., & Carpenter, M. (2009). Eighteen-month-old infants show increased helping following priming with affiliation. *Psychological Science, 20*, 1189–1193.

Over, H., & Carpenter, M. (2013). The social side of imitation. *Child Development Perspectives, 7*, 6–11.

Perdue, C. W., Dovidio, J. F., Gurtman, M. B., & Tyler, R. B. (1990). Us and them: Social categorization and the process of intergroup bias. *Journal of Personality and Social Psychology, 59*, 475.

Perlmutter, M., Behrend, S. D., Kuo, F., & Muller, A. (1989). Social influences on children's problem solving. *Developmental Psychology, 25*, 744–754.

Plass, J., O'Keefe, P. A., Homer, B. D., Case, J., Hayward, E., Stein, M., & Perlin, K. (2013). The impact of individual, competitive, and collaborative mathematics game play on learning, performance, and motivation. *Journal of Educational Psychology, 105*, 1050–1066.

Rekers, Y., Haun, D. B., & Tomasello, M. (2011). Children, but not chimpanzees, prefer to collaborate. *Current Biology, 21*, 1756–1758.

Renninger, K. A., & Hidi, S. (2016). *The power of interest for motivation and learning.* New York: Routledge.

Repacholi, B. M., & Gopnik, A. (1997). Early reasoning about desires: Evidence from 14-and 18-month-olds. *Developmental Psychology, 33*, 12–21.

Richardson, M. J., Marsh, K. L., Isenhower, R. W., Goodman, J. R., & Schmidt, R. C. (2007). Rocking together: Dynamics of intentional and unintentional interpersonal coordination. *Human Movement Science, 26*, 867–891.

Ross, H. S., & Lollis, S. P. (1987). Communication within infant social games. *Developmental Psychology, 23*, 241–248.

Ross, L., & Nisbett, R. E. (1991). *The person and the situation: Perspectives of social psychology.* New York: McGraw-Hill.

Sansone, C., & Thoman, D. B. (2005). Interest as the missing motivator in self-regulation. *European Psychologist, 10*, 175–186.

Sansone, C., Thoman, D. B., & Smith, J. L. (2010). Interest and self-regulation: Understanding individual variability in choices, efforts and persistence over time. In R. Hoyle (Ed.), *Handbook of personality and self-regulation* (pp. 192–217). Malden, MA: Blackwell.

Schiefele, U. (1999). Interest and learning from text. *Scientific Studies of Reading, 3*, 257–280.

Sebanz, N., Bekkering, H., & Knoblich, G. (2006). Joint action: Bodies and minds moving together. *Trends in Cognitive Science, 10*, 70–76.

Shteynberg, G. (2010). A silent emergence of culture: The social tuning effect. *Journal of Personality and Social Psychology, 99*, 683–689.

Shteynberg, G. (2015). Shared attention. *Perspectives on Psychological Science, 10*, 579–590.

Shteynberg, G., & Galinksy, A. D. (2011). Implicit coordination: Sharing goals with similar others intensifies goal pursuit. *Journal of Experimental Social Psychology, 47*, 1291–1294.

Shteynberg, G., Hirsh, J. B., Apfelbaum, E. P., Larsen, J. T., Galinsky, A. D., & Roese, N. J. (2014). Feeling more together: Group attention intensifies emotion. *Emotion, 14*, 1102–1114.

Sorce, J. F., Emde, R. N., Campos, J. J., & Klinnert, M. D. (1985). Maternal emotional signaling: Its effect on the visual cliff behavior of 1-year-olds. *Developmental Psychology, 21*, 195–200.

Steele, C. M. (1997). A threat in the air: How stereotypes shape intellectual identity and performance. *American Psychologist, 52*, 613–629.

Stephens, N. M., Hamedani, M. G., & Destin, M. (2014). Closing the social class achievement gap: A difference-education intervention improves first-generation students' academic performance and all students' college transition. *Psychological Science, 25*, 943–953.

Tauer, J. M., & Harackiewicz, J. M. (2004). The effects of cooperation and competition on intrinsic motivation and performance. *Journal of Personality and Social Psychology, 86*, 849–861.

Taylor, S. E., & Lobel, M. (1989). Social comparison activity under threat: Downward evaluation and upward contacts. *Psychological Review, 96*, 569–575.

Thoman, D. B., Sansone, C., Fraughton, T., & Pasupathi, M. (2012). How students socially evaluate interest: Peer responsiveness influences evaluation and maintenance of interest. *Contemporary Educational Psychology, 37*, 254–265.

Thoman, D. B., Sansone, C., & Pasupathi, M. (2007). Talking about interest: Exploring the role of social interaction for regulating motivation and the interest experience. *Journal of Happiness Studies, 8*, 335–370.

Tomasello, M., Carpenter, M., Call, J., Behne, T., & Moll, H. (2005). Understanding and sharing intentions: The origins of cultural cognition. *Behavioral and Brain Sciences, 28*, 675–735.

Vygotsky, L. S. (1978). *Mind in society: The development of higher mental processes*. Cambridge, MA: Harvard University Press.

Walton, G. M. (2014). The new science of wise psychological interventions. *Current Directions in Psychological Science, 23*, 73–82.

Walton, G. M., & Cohen, G. L. (2007). A question of belonging: Race, social fit, and achievement. *Journal of Personality and Social Psychology, 92*, 82–96.

Walton, G. M., & Cohen, G. L. (2011a). A brief social-belonging intervention improves academic and health outcomes of minority students. *Science, 331*, 1447–1451.

Walton, G. M., & Cohen, G. L. (2011b). Sharing motivation. In D. Dunning (Ed.), *Social motivation* (pp. 79–101). New York: Psychology Press.

Walton, G. M., Cohen, G. L., Cwir, D., & Spencer, S. J. (2012). Mere belonging: The power of social connections. *Journal of Personality and Social Psychology, 102*, 513–532.

Walton, G. M., Logel, C., Peach, J. M., Spencer, S. J., & Zanna, M. P. (2015). Two brief interventions to mitigate a "chilly climate" transform women's experience, relationships, and achievement in engineering. *Journal of Educational Psychology, 107*, 468–485.

Warneken, F., Chen, F., & Tomasello, M. (2006). Cooperative activities in young children and chimpanzees. *Child Development, 77*, 640–663.

Warneken, F., Gräfenhain, M., & Tomasello, M. (2012). Collaborative partner or social tool? New evidence for young children's understanding of joint intentions in collaborative activities. *Developmental Science, 15*, 54–61.

Warneken, F., & Tomasello, M. (2006). Altruistic helping in human infants and young chimpanzees. *Science, 311*, 1301–1303.

Warneken, F., & Tomasello, M. (2007). Helping and cooperation at 14 months of age. *Infancy, 11*, 271–294.

Williams, K. D., & Karau, S. J. (1991). Social loafing and social compensation: The effects of expectations of co-worker performance. *Journal of Personality and Social Psychology, 61*, 570–581.

Williams, K. D., Karau, S. J., & Bourgeois, M. J. (1993). Working on collective tasks: Social loafing and social compensation. In M. A. Hogg & D. Abrams (Eds.), *Group motivation: Social psychological perspectives* (pp. 130–148). Hertfordshire, England: Harvester Wheatsheaf.

Williams, K. D., & Nida, S. A. (2011). Ostracism consequences and coping. *Current Directions in Psychological Science, 20*, 71–75.

Wing, R. R., & Jeffery, R. W. (1999). Benefits of recruiting participants with friends and increasing social support for weight loss and maintenance. *Journal of Consulting and Clinical Psychology, 67*, 132–138.

Woodward, A. L. (1998). Infants selectively encode the goal object of an actor's reach. *Cognition, 69*, 1–34.

Yeager, D. S., Walton, G. M., Brady, S. T., Akcinar, E. N., Paunesku, D., Keane, L., Kamentz, D., Ritter, G., Duckworth, A. L., Urstein, R., Gomez, E., Markus, H. R., Cohen, G. L., & Dweck, C. S. (2016). Teaching a lay theory before college narrows achievement gaps at scale. *Proceedings of the National Academy of Sciences of the United States of America, 113*, E3341–E3348.

Zajonc, R. B. (1965). Social facilitation. *Science, 149*, 269–274.

Index

© Springer International Publishing AG 2017
P.A. O'Keefe, J.M. Harackiewicz (eds.), *The Science of Interest*,
DOI 10.1007/978-3-319-55509-6

Printed by Printforce, the Netherlands